W9-BLO-857

The Mark Inside

The Mark Inside

A Perfect Swindle,
a Cunning Revenge,
and a Small History of the Big Con

AMY READING

ALFRED A. KNOPF   NEW YORK   2012

THIS IS A BORZOI BOOK
PUBLISHED BY ALFRED A. KNOPF

Copyright © 2012 by Amy Reading

All rights reserved.
Published in the United States by Alfred A. Knopf,
a division of Random House, Inc., New York, and in
Canada by Random House of Canada Limited, Toronto.
www.aaknopf.com

Knopf, Borzoi Books, and the colophon are registered
trademarks of Random House, Inc.

Excerpts from *Fighting the Underworld* by Philip S. Van Cise.
Copyright 1936 by Houghton Mifflin Harcourt Publishing Company.
Copyright © Renewed 1964 by Philip S. Van Cise. Used by permission of
Houghton Mifflin Harcourt Publishing Company. All rights reserved.

Library of Congress Cataloging-in-Publication Data
Reading, Amy.
The mark inside : a perfect swindle, a cunning revenge, and a small history of the
big con / by Amy Reading.
p. cm.
Includes bibliographical references and index.
ISBN 978-0-307-27248-5 (hardcover)
1. Swindlers and swindling—United States—History. I. Title.
HV6695.R43 2012
364.16'3—dc23   2011024919

Jacket image: © Tetra Images/Getty Images
Jacket design by Chip Kidd

Manufactured in the United States of America
First Edition

Contents

The Mark Inside

Prologue

The train screeches into Union Station with a whistle and a chuff of steam. A man disembarks, breathes in the dry mountain air, and steps unnoticed into the slipstream of the new city, guarding his anonymity with silence and caution. Before anything else, before even showing his face in a hotel lobby, he must change his appearance. A barber will not be sufficient for what he has in mind. He heads down Seventeenth Street in search of a beautician.

Under the ministrations of a young woman whose curiosity about him must go unsatisfied, the man's gray hair is dyed dark brown, and so are his shaggy eyebrows and long mustache. The eyebrows are left to form a hood over his glittering blue eyes, but the mustache is trimmed and curled at the ends in a clumsy attempt at style. His thick hair is shaped into a supremely unflattering bowl cut, long enough in the back to form a roll of hair over his collar. The man begins to arrange his features to match his new appearance.

Later, in his hotel room, he opens his valise and selects a straw-colored linen suit. It is light enough for the August weather, and it has a strap across the back that pulls the fabric into a little gather. He decides this unfashionable feature will aid his disguise, which is rapidly evolving to be that of a Texas cotton grower. He will hunch himself over, he thinks, like a man who has picked cotton his whole life. The suit's only liability is that its thin fabric cannot conceal a gun holster. He tucks a gun in at his hip and conceals it with his hand, as if his bones ache. A cane in the other hand, a small Panama hat perched on his new cut, and his disguise is complete.

He spends some time before his bathroom mirror, practicing his new, slow gait. He pitches his voice up an octave and draws it out in a country twang. His features have settled into a pleasant, open countenance.

And all the while, he runs through his story in his mind. He knows that his costume is important but his story is crucial. Everything will depend on how convincingly he plays his role. He mentally rehearses the sequence of scenes, tries out a few improvisations. The man is confident the story will work. He has told countless versions of it, and he knows it well. And he knows the mark's responses almost better than his own lines. The mark has no idea how long the man has been studying his movements, actions, and habits.

Only one task remains. The man sits down at his hotel desk and begins to write. In short order, he produces a small sheaf of letters, some of them in his own large, looping handwriting, and others in a smaller, feminine style. One letter in particular requires his utmost attention, a letter to himself from his wife back home in—he thinks for a moment—Ferris, Texas. He keeps it short and legible at a glance. Several phrases seem to leap off the page: "the hundred acre oil lease" and "drillers have struck oil." Smiling to himself, he ends the letter with a truly heartbreaking expression of love and devotion, then proceeds to fold, crease, and stain his little collection of letters until they look as if they've been read and reread. He places them in a pocket, picks up his hat and cane, and sets forth on the downtown streets.

It is time to announce his presence in the city. He slowly makes his way up and down Seventeenth Street, his back bent, surveying the passersby from underneath his hat and his eyebrows. It doesn't take long to spot his mark. He knew it wouldn't, and a small electric charge runs down his back. They are in front of the post office, and together, with invisible choreography, the man and his mark enter the lobby. With deliberateness, the man hobbles to the general delivery window and asks loudly, "Any mail for L. A. Mulligan?" And the con has begun.

CHAPTER ONE

Confidence

J. Frank Norfleet was feeling confident as he strode into the St. George Hotel in Dallas. He'd just arrived from Dublin, Texas, where he'd sold a carload of mules at an admirable profit. He was a prosperous fifty-four-year-old rancher from the Texas Panhandle, a third-generation pioneer who had worked his whole life to turn the prairie, now swept clean of Indians and buffalo, into a profitable ground for agriculture and livestock. Since he was a teenager, he'd herded sheep and hogs, driven cattle across the open range, and fenced thousands of acres of pastureland. He'd made foreman on the Spade Ranch in Hale County at a young age and saved his modest wages until, when he was forty-nine, he was finally able to afford his own land. He purchased about 8,000 acres near the Spade Ranch and continued to raise livestock in small numbers, investing the profits in adjacent land until his ranch had grown to 20,000 acres. On this November day in 1919, he was in Dallas for his biggest deal yet: he planned to sell 2,050 acres of improved land and use the proceeds to buy a choice 10,000-acre parcel from the nearby ranch of Captain Dick Slaughter, the heir of a renowned cattle baron.

Norfleet was as straight as they come. He had banned gambling from the Spade Ranch. "I don't drink, chew tobacco, smoke, cuss, or tell lies," he would say, his light blue eyes glinting. "The last is the most important. I never tell a damn lie." His fierce work ethic and his ability to turn manual labor into a small fortune rightly gave him confidence—hard-earned, time-tested confidence in his own discernment—which in turn allowed him to bestow his trust on others. He prized honesty and square dealing above all else. His word was his bond, and he planned to seal the Slaughter deal with a handshake, because a man wore his integrity as visibly as he wore his mustache.

But to anyone watching, J. Frank Norfleet looked exactly like a sucker. At five feet five in his cowboy boots, he towered above exactly no one, and with his legs bowed from years in the saddle and his suit pants shoved into his boots, he was conspicuous as someone out of his league in the big city. And there were in fact two people watching him make his entrance, two members of the cast who were already at their stations, in costume and with their lines at the ready. Reno Hamlin sat in the hotel lobby, while one of his colleagues hovered just outside the building, peering inside for Hamlin's signal. Hamlin had dressed to match Norfleet, and with his square head, thick neck, and stocky build he made a convincing Texas countryman.

Hamlin could see from yards away the palpable relief in the cowboy's eyes when he spotted one of his own kind among the urbanites, and the two men soon fell to talking. Hamlin introduced himself as Miller, a mule buyer from Hill County, Texas. He had also just arrived in Dallas, but his mind was on where he'd come from. "I saw the best carload of mules unloaded at Dublin the other day I ever saw in this country," he told Norfleet. "I want to buy a carload just like them." Norfleet's eyes lit up. Sure enough, Hamlin had unknowingly been admiring Norfleet's mules, and within minutes they had given each other their word that Hamlin would buy a shipment of them, as well as two freight cars of kafir corn and maize.

After the initial onrush of good feeling, Norfleet explained to his new friend that he couldn't deliver his goods right away because he was stuck in the city, searching for a buyer for his farm and waiting for Captain Slaughter to return to Dallas so they could close the land deal. "Norfleet, I may help you out," said Hamlin. He had a friend who was a purchasing agent with the Green Immigration Land Company in Minneapolis—a businessman scouting land in Texas. Perhaps he might be interested in Norfleet's land? Hamlin gave the secret signal to his confederate out on the sidewalk.

Into the hotel lobby strode W. B. Spencer, and amid exclamations of surprise over the coincidence Hamlin introduced him to Norfleet as Charles Harris. Spencer's costume contrasted starkly with Hamlin's. He was a young man with finely etched features, his curly hair swept back off his brow as if he were facing the wind of the future. He wore a crisp suit, the embodiment of the successful businessman. Hamlin began excitedly talking up Norfleet's farm, its smooth, level land, the particulars of its cultivation, the schoolhouse and church on its grounds. Spencer smiled noncommittally at Hamlin's overeager monologue. He patiently explained that he was currently negotiating land in Williamson County and wasn't free to embark on a new deal. He wouldn't want Norfleet to get his hopes up.

But when the three men met the next day, Spencer was far more effusive. He told Norfleet that the owners of the Williamson County land had decided not to sell because of the recent oil boom and, though he had never purchased land as far west as Hale County, he was now rather desperate and therefore willing to consider Norfleet's property. He took down the description from Norfleet and telegrammed it to his superiors. In the meantime, he invited Norfleet to check out of the St. George and share his double room at the Jefferson Hotel. He tumbled over himself with eagerness in his invitation, explaining that he wanted to show Norfleet his credentials, which were back at the room, and anyway he could save Norfleet a bundle in hotel bills. Norfleet accepted, charmed by the man's youthful friendliness. Spencer's boss, Garrett Thompson, soon telegrammed to say he was passing through Dallas and would love the opportunity to meet Norfleet. Would Norfleet agree to meet him at the Adolphus Hotel the next day?

Courted by three successful businessmen, wined and dined at the city's best hotels, his down payment on the Slaughter land growing plumper by the hour, Norfleet must have felt as if something great were just beginning. In fact, something great was already well under way. Just twenty-four hours had elapsed and already he was deep into the big con.

When Norfleet stepped into the St. George Hotel, he entered a tightly scripted drama with nine acts, each with its own distinct function in conveying the mark toward the climax when his money will be whisked away. Even the mark has his lines, and just because he doesn't know them does not mean he won't say them at exactly the right moment. He will, because the dialogue is designed so that his responses are the most predictable things he *would* say in such a situation. The play hinges on three psychological moments, when the mark must make a decision that will propel him further inside. Any objections he might muster have already been taken into account and rejoinders to them devised. Norfleet's role called for him to play himself, a part at which he excelled, but in a context designed so that his own earnest words would betray him. Confidence men took inordinate pride in the structured nature of their profession. Instead of the violence and mayhem of other kinds of theft, they relied solely on a perfectly constructed piece of theater.

Con artistry may seem, at times, like the art of controlling a mark's mind, but Norfleet made the decisions he did only because his swindlers so completely engineered his interpretation of events. He perceived his initial encounters with the two men as organic happenstances. In fact the swindlers had framed his experiences so that even the backdrop of urban life—the hotel lobbies, the streets, the office buildings—became props in their drama; the strangers around them became unwitting extras. The big con works because it makes use of a time-honored technique from stage magic, the one-ahead, in which the trick begins before the performer formally introduces it to the audience; it is the most elaborate form of misdirection because it leads the mark to misperceive the nature of the entire situation. In the face of the one-ahead, Norfleet's defenselessness was absolute—who, in his boots, would possibly guess that such an elaborate performance has been devised just for him?

The first of the nine acts began before Norfleet even walked into the St. George, when Reno Hamlin had *put the mark up* for fleecing. Hamlin had trawled the lines at the train station and the hotels, eavesdropping on conversations and peering over counters at registers and receipts, until he had identified someone promising. Norfleet was no redneck blusterer, no wide-eyed naïf, no freewheeling gambler, no shyster on the make. What about him interested Hamlin? Hamlin had sifted the crowd with a particular set of criteria. His next mark would have to be, first and foremost, an out-of-towner so that he wouldn't be able to turn to his local banker for advice during the swindle or encounter the con men after his money vanished. He would be from a second- or third-tier American city, traveling alone in a large city for business purposes. It goes without saying that his mark would be male, for women rarely had the fortune, autonomy, and wherewithal to make investment decisions with the decisiveness that the con required. He would be a prosperous, substantial citizen in his community. More than that, he would be a self-made man, accustomed to both hard work and seizing the main chance. He must be able to raise $20,000, $30,000, $40,000, even $50,000 in a day or two, but he must not have so much money that he would refer a deal to his bankers and accountants. He wouldn't be overly familiar with the financial industry. Norfleet fit that role in almost every particular.

The second act was to *play the con* for him: gain his confidence and bait him with thoughts of lucrative business deals. Hamlin and Spencer, the steerers, calibrated their offers to seem eminently plausible, not wanting to arouse Norfleet's suspicion. By the second day, they had succeeded in imaginatively increasing his wealth. At first glance, their two-step approach—first Hamlin's mules and then Spencer's land—might seem unnecessarily elaborate. Why not hook Norfleet simply by providing him with what he sought in Dallas, a buyer for his land? Norfleet and Hamlin would never again discuss that carload of mules. In fact, Hamlin exited the stage of Norfleet's drama after the second day, his work complete. He had effectively recast the frame of meaning around Norfleet's activities in Dallas, and the nested business deals had drawn Norfleet deep into the heart of the con.

Norfleet was now firmly under Spencer's sway. In the third act, *roping the mark,* the steerer transfers the mark's loyalties to the insideman, also called the spieler. It was time for the wallet drop. The next day, Spencer and Norfleet went to the Adolphus Hotel, and Spencer asked Norfleet to wait in the lobby while he inquired at the front desk after his boss at Green Immigration Land, Garrett Thompson. Spencer let him sit for a few minutes, contemplating the Flemish tapestries, the Circassian walnut, and the gold leaf of Dallas's finest hotel. Then he stepped up behind him to say that Thompson hadn't yet checked in. One of his hands invisibly slipped into the seat cushion.

Just then, Norfleet felt something pressing into his thigh from the back of the chair. He reached down and discovered a bulging billfold. Flipping through it to uncover its owner's identity, he found $240 in cash, a Masonic card, a copy of a bond payable to McLean & Company for $100,000, a cipher code card, a United Brokers' member card, and various other documents, all made out to J. B. Stetson. "What shall we do with it?" Spencer prompted. Norfleet gave the correct answer: they should immediately return the wallet to its rightful owner. At the front desk, they learned that Stetson was staying at the hotel, then they went upstairs and knocked on his door.

The door opened a crack. Norfleet asked if he was speaking to Mr. Stetson. The face behind the door said that was he. Norfleet asked if he had lost anything. The man answered no and slammed the door in Norfleet's face.

Norfleet had just met Big Joe Furey, whom the newspapers called "the cleverest bunco man in the country."

The two men gave each other baffled looks, but they could do nothing more than return to the elevator. Seconds later, the hotel room door opened again, and Furey came bursting through, shouting, "Gentlemen! Gentlemen! I have just discovered that I have lost a very, very valuable pocketbook." He ushered the two men into his room and stood before them, a tall man with intense greenish blue eyes. One of the many reasons that Joe Furey was so good at his job was his imposing presence, but he was nonplussed to find that he did not have the desired effect upon Norfleet, who made Furey describe the wallet in painstaking detail before he would hand it over. Furey melted into gratitude and pressed $100 on both men, telling them it would be a favor for him if they accepted. Spencer pocketed his reward, then watched with bemusement as Norfleet huffily waved his money away. Clearly the cowboy did not think of himself as a man on the lookout for easy money.

It was Furey's job to introduce act four, in which he would *tell the mark the tale* of how he could earn a fabulous sum. Furey began by apologizing for his initial rudeness. "I thought you were newspaper reporters," he confided. Lately he'd been hounded by journalists wanting interviews, and the more he refused, the harder they tried to obtain an audience. But the very last thing he could afford was publicity. Spencer and Norfleet leaned in. Furey answered their questioning gazes by reaching into his wallet and pulling out a letter from his employer, United Brokers, which warned him against talking with reporters. He explained that his company preferred to keep out of the limelight because it did not serve the average investor. It operated on behalf of a group of Wall Street firms that had formed a clandestine syndicate to control the market. His job was to play the stock exchange according to encrypted telegrams sent to him by his boss.

"Gentlemen, without this wallet I would be helpless to do my company's business today." He pointed to his desk. "Here are six messages and without my code card in that book I could not do my company's business." He explained that he was due on the exchange in a few minutes, and with that he excused himself to decipher his instructions. He furrowed his brow, he flushed red, he perspired. He was the very picture of an important man under a great mental strain. At last he finished, and handing a sheaf of newspaper articles and documents to the two men to keep them busy, he dashed out of the hotel room.

Spencer and Norfleet were as mystified as if Furey had himself spoken in cipher. In the opulent suite, surrounded by two trunks overflowing with the finest men's attire that the cowpuncher had ever seen, Norfleet read through the businessman's papers just as fast as Spencer fed them to him. The documents were so clouded with opaque references they did little to enlighten him. He gathered, though, that United Brokers wanted to consolidate financial power in New York and extinguish the smaller regional exchanges. They controlled large enough blocks of stock that they could swing the entire market with their buy and sell orders, and since Furey always knew their manipulations in advance, he could place opportunistic orders to extract money from the regional brokerage houses. Spencer amplified the suggestive power of Furey's documents by murmuring at repeated intervals, "We are very fortunate in making the acquaintance of such a big man."

At length, Furey strode back into the room, electrified with the success of having taken $20,000 from the exchange. He turned to Norfleet. "I will have to go back to the Exchange to finish the day's work. My brother, you refused to accept the $100.00 reward which I offered you for finding my pocketbook. Would you mind my placing that money on the market and would you accept what money it might earn?" Well, Norfleet could hardly say no to that. Spencer also put his reward money up for speculation, and Furey left. Twenty minutes later, he returned and proudly flourished $800 for each man. "This is what your $100.00 made for you!" he crowed.

Who could resist *the convincer*? Furey was standing before Norfleet, holding out money with absolutely no strings attached, money that Norfleet had no reason to refuse because in no way did it violate his code of honor. The mark had reached the fifth act and the first psychological moment. Would he reach out and take the money? He did, and as soon as he accepted it, he also accepted the logic of the game. The convincer works even on marks who are not fundamentally motivated by greed, because it exploits empiricism, the most basic tool for perceiving reality. We have been evolutionarily programmed to believe only what we can experience with our five senses, and so all the swindler must do is embed a rigged proof in his script. It is a con man's truism that no mark in history has ever walked away from the big con once the convincer has had its effect.

As the three men said their good-byes that afternoon, Furey pulled Norfleet aside and asked if he might meet the Texan the next day in order to make him a proposition. Norfleet readily agreed. In the meantime, riding high on the exhilaration of his new acquaintances and conquests, he finalized the deal for the Slaughter land, known locally as the Sandhill Pasture, paying $5,000 in cash from the sale of his mules and signing a promissory note for the remaining $90,000, due in forty-five days. The next day, *The Dallas Morning News* admiringly reported the latest acquisition of Mr. Norfleet, who "started in as a $30-a-month 'cowpuncher' and has amassed large holdings."

The following day, both Spencer and Norfleet met Furey in his hotel room, but the broker immediately sent Spencer downstairs to get a newspaper. Spencer had held the upper hand in their friendship until now, despite being twenty years Norfleet's junior, by virtue of his business success and relative sophistication. Furey's maneuver to separate the two suddenly elevated Norfleet over the excitable land dealer. Furey was now handing Norfleet responsibility for his own decisions.

Furey confided that all the outward trappings of his success had become sources of worry rather than pleasure. He described the mortgage he held on the $300,000 apartment in Manhattan where he lived with his wife and three children. "I can wake up at night with a start of fear when I think of that heavy debt that is on the roof that shelters my wife and babies. If anything happens, I have only $12,500 to pay that $100,000 indebtedness." With one stroke, Furey rendered Norfleet equal with him: virtually the same amount of savings and the same amount of debt. Across the cultural gap between a Manhattan apartment and a Texas ranch, their interests were aligned.

Furey explained what he had in mind. He expected that today's tips from United Brokers would net a significant profit, one that a private investor might reap as well as the company itself. He was not permitted to place his own money on United Brokers' stock picks, but another man could. Only once before had he drawn money out of the market for a private individual, when he made $200,000 for his old friend

Chief Justice Hughes of the New York Supreme Court (in the big con, the swindlers are forever invoking the unimpeachable authority of a judge, wise, wealthy, yet wholly outside the market). Would Norfleet consent to place Furey's money on the exchange but sign his own name on the stock orders, then split the profits that would tumble out from United Brokers' inside tips?

Norfleet stood poised at the second psychological moment of the big con, the moment that has received the greatest amount of attention in the literature of confidence artistry: the moment when the mark is invited into a shady deal. To the swindlers themselves, the analysis of this moment couldn't be simpler. You may not be able to cheat an honest man, but a dishonest man has it coming. The big con works because so many legitimate businessmen will so readily discard legality and morality if the money is easy enough. Over and over, con men have testified to their own sense of moral superiority over their marks. One insideman said that, like himself, "the men I swindled were also motivated by a desire to acquire money, and they didn't care at whose expense they got it. I was particular. I took money only from those who could afford it and were willing to go in with me in schemes they fancied would fleece others." Another swindler made allowances for his marks' greed but detested their hypocrisy. "I have often wondered at the moral and ethical point of view of so many respectable men I have duped. These men were nearly all persons of substance and standing. They had the reputation of being absolutely upright; no breath of scandal ever touched them, and yet whenever and however I have encountered them they have invariably been ready to go in for sharp practices of this sort."

Norfleet later recalled that Furey "stated he was confident that I was an honest, straight-forward man in whom he could place confidence and trust, and asked if I would be willing to go into the proposition. I told him I would be willing, provided it was perfectly legitimate. He assured me it was strictly business and being done every day." Confidence, trust, honesty, legitimacy, strictly business. Perhaps these words were a mere smoke screen for the wink that the two men exchanged as they uttered them. Or perhaps Norfleet truly did believe in Furey's integrity, and therefore plunged into business with him on the strength of a few totemic words intoned with authority. Norfleet's later recollections played it straight: Furey invited him into the deal, Norfleet asked if it was aboveboard, and then he acquiesced. No questions about where United Brokers got its intelligence, no qualms about sharing this intelligence as an outside party, no hesitation about exposing himself to criminal charges in a potentially unethical transaction. And so this most loaded of scenes, when Norfleet turned over his confidence to a trickster, remains obscured.

Note that at this stage Furey asked Norfleet only for his confidence, not his money. Shady or not, the threshold for Norfleet's acquiescence was low because it cost him so little. An effective swindling script will never, ever appear to offer the mark something for nothing. Everyone is on guard against swindles, fraud, and even overly strident advertising pitches. The con man must circumvent this suspicion by seeming to be—and appealing to the mark as—*homo economicus,* that quintessentially capitalist creature whose every action is dictated by rational, perfectly informed economic self-interest.

And so the swindler claims to possess a fabulous moneymaking secret, but it is crucial that the money not seem *too* free, or else it will strike the mark as miraculous, and he will wonder why the con man has approached him rather than keeping the profit to himself. The key is to structure the secret so that it is worthless unless the grifter can share it with someone trustworthy. The con man alone cannot realize the profit just beyond his reach, but he will let the mark in on the deal and split the pot if the mark contributes his own particular value. And so the con man extends generosity to the mark, but not in the way that you might expect. He grants the mark the opportunity to give the con man something he needs. The swindler has created a gratifying paradox, a situation in which the mark can act in the highest fulfillment of his own self-interest only by helping someone else.

Norfleet was being reeled in gradually yet inexorably, but first Furey added a little flourish: Could Norfleet vouch for Spencer's trustworthiness? At this question, Norfleet balked, momentarily upsetting the script that he didn't know he was following. He said that he had known Spencer only for a few days and could not take responsibility for his participation. Furey smoothly ad-libbed, saying Spencer struck him as an "honest, hard working young business man"—those key words again—and with Norfleet's consent they'd invite him into the scheme. Norfleet agreed, and the game was back on track. When Spencer returned to the room, he jumped at Furey's idea, eagerly explaining that his father's mill business had acquainted him with brokerages and he was, unlike Norfleet, comfortable with the financial details of the transactions.

Furey took the men down to the exchange early the next morning and gave them a tour of the busy offices. Norfleet had every reason to be impressed with the bustle and gravity of the business being conducted in the suite of rooms. A man chalked prices on a blackboard as fast as they came scrolling out of the ticker. Every telephone was in use as clerks received and transmitted orders. Messengers weaved through men lined up to speak with brokers. The set that Norfleet's swindlers had provided for his fleecing was jaw-dropping in its authenticity. It was, in fact, real. Furey was passing off the Dallas Cotton Exchange, which dealt strictly in futures contracts for cotton, as a stock exchange for shares in national and international corporations. The clerks and brokers were unwitting extras in Furey's drama, and they acted their hearts out, until gradually one figure emerged from the background with his hand extended. Furey introduced him as Edward McDorney, the secretary of the exchange, a stolid, well-to-do man with a square face and an engaging professional manner whose real name was E. J. Ward. He greeted Norfleet and Spencer cordially but asked them if they were members of the exchange. When they answered in the negative, Ward said, "I am very sorry to do so, but I shall be forced to invite you outside as members only are allowed here." Norfleet and Spencer instantly accepted the invitation and returned to the Adolphus to await Furey.

Furey's script here departs from the standard one. Furey and Spencer were, it seems, running a shoestring operation, playing the big con on Norfleet without the benefit of "a store," or a rented suite of rooms that they could furnish as a brokerage house and to which they could steer victims in quick succession. Instead, they were running a variant known as "playing to the wall." They ran the con out of Furey's hotel room, with a script that permitted Norfleet to see the exchange but that included a plausible reason, the line about membership, to explain why he could only interact with it through an intermediary. Hereafter, only Furey and Spencer would enter the exchange, though Norfleet continued to be implicated in their dealings. Conceptually, the tale remained straightforward: Norfleet would play the stock market as if it were a fixed lottery.

Back at the hotel, Furey studiously filled out the paperwork for the day's trading. He filed two separate sheaves of orders, one with his name on behalf of United Brokers and a mirror set on joint behalf of Norfleet and Spencer. With their consent he added their $800 windfall to the investment pool. Once again, Norfleet's memories of this moment are imprecise, but the annals of con literature contain many examples of the standard swindling script. Furey would most likely have claimed to be trading options contracts on margin. Let's say the victim puts up $2,000—money he'd earned solely from the convincer—as a minimum margin against $20,000 borrowed from the broker. He'd then take out a call option on twenty thousand shares of, say, Mexican Petroleum on a two-point margin, opening at a share price of $174 and closing at $176⅛. If the stock acts as expected—as it always does—the price goes up, and the mark can call in his options at the strike price, then turn around and sell them at the market rate for a $2 profit per share (after broker's fees). Once he repays the loan, he has cleared $40,000, a lavish return on his initial $2,000 investment.

Don't peer too hard at these details. Furey's account of what he was doing on the exchange was not meant to withstand the level of scrutiny that a skeptical outsider would bring. His story only needed to cohere for a short time, to be roughly plausible. Norfleet certainly didn't muster any objections. He had no reason to be in a skeptical frame of mind, having risked nothing of his own. Furthermore, he would not even have been able to find the right vocabulary to interrogate this logic, so foreign was he to the realm of high finance.

While Furey pretended to execute his arcane investment rites in the members-only exchange, he let Norfleet pace the floor of his luxurious cage. At last, upon the close of the markets, Furey sauntered into the hotel room with his arms full of bundled cash. He opened his arms over the bed, and the money tumbled out—$68,000 in all. Norfleet's share of the profits, between the earnings from his $800 and his cut of Furey's money, came to an unbelievable $28,000, or what would be $350,000 today. Of course, there was probably only about $5,000 in real currency on that bed. Furey would have made up a boodle of newsprint sandwiched between real $100 bills. He might have dramatically counted out a few thousand dollars in real currency into Norfleet's hands. But did Norfleet take the time to unwrap the bundles and inspect each bill? No, he did not, and no sucker before him ever discovered the deception either. As fast as he could, Norfleet wrapped his cash into newspaper and rolled it under his arm. He was just heading toward the door of Furey's room, when it opened on its own. In rushed E. J. Ward, the secretary of the exchange, waving his hands to stop Norfleet from leaving. Their bets had been improperly placed, he explained, because neither man was a member of the exchange. "I have to ask," Ward continued, "if you are in a position to confirm the bids in case you had lost?" Spencer and Norfleet looked at each other, their fat fortunes suddenly vulnerable in their arms. Of course they could not back their bids. As quickly as they had won it, their money threatened to vanish.

Furey, Spencer, and Ward had pulled off the third psychological moment. Once threatened, the mark's profit grows even more valuable, and he will do virtually anything to protect it. He has held the money in his hands, felt its heft and solidity. It is at once magical—because he has done so little to acquire it—and material. His friends have consistently framed it as "winnings," as if he'd been harmlessly gambling, but in fact he hasn't spent or speculated his own money. Nor does he need to do so now.

Furey stepped in with a solution, pointing out that the rules of the exchange stipulate that so-called settlement days are the first and fifteenth of each month. As the fifteenth of that month fell on a Saturday, Spencer and Norfleet technically had until Monday the seventeenth to guarantee their bids. Ward conceded Furey's point. He insisted on reclaiming the cash, but he agreed to hold it in the exchange's safe and issue the men a due bill, which would itself be good for credit on the exchange, until they could retroactively back their initial bid with cash. Norfleet would not need to spend his own money, merely flourish it to prove his creditworthiness, in order to get his treasure out of hock. He had no trouble agreeing to the arrangement.

This was simultaneously the most important and the weakest scene in the con men's script. Aside from the obvious fiction of United Brokers' infallible predictions of the market, the tale that Furey and Ward told does not make sound financial sense. For one thing, even in the bull market of the postwar era, the swindlers riotously exaggerated how far they could leverage the mark's small pool of cash. Second, it is difficult to envision a scenario in which the mark would need to match the full amount of the investment he'd just made. Con men, though, were entirely untroubled by these holes. Everything Furey said needed only to nudge Norfleet to the next line in the play.

After Ward left with the boodle, Furey turned to Spencer and Norfleet and gravely promised to get their money back. It was his fault they were in this mess, since he had assumed his introduction would be as good as a membership card, and as a gentleman he intended to do right by them. Of course, the matter was quite delicate because of his fear of publicity. If his bondman at McLean & Company caught scent of their transactions, he'd be ruined. Fortunately, he knew just the man to trust, Judge Hughes, the man for whom he'd made $200,000. Furey immediately wired Hughes and almost immediately received a telegram stating that the judge was on a bear hunt and would be out of contact for days.

Thus began act six as the three men commenced an intricate, tightly spiraled dance around the topic of personal finance. Spencer and Furey proceeded to *give the mark the breakdown,* gently sussing Norfleet out to determine how much money they could squeeze from him. Norfleet, to his credit, led by staunchly informing the others that he had no money. Gradually, though, the image of those cash bundles waiting patiently in their vault worked on his mind, until finally he guessed that maybe he could raise, oh, about $20,000 from his bank. Spencer thought he could scare up $35,000 from his home in Salina, Kansas, and Furey promised to cover the rest.

Furey and Spencer's work in Dallas was nearly done, and Furey would soon be able to relinquish his costly hotel room. The seventh act of the play was to *put the mark on the send* to collect the money from his bank. This is always a fragile juncture in the big con's script. When a mark goes back home, he is potentially vulnerable to the sounder wisdom of his loved ones. Yet the underworld is rife with stories of marks whose bankers flatly informed them that they were in the midst of a con, yet who withdrew their money anyway and returned to their new friends.

Norfleet's crew took no chances. Spencer's initial approach to Norfleet gave him the perfect excuse to accompany the Texan back to Hale County: he would inspect Norfleet's ranch and make his final decision about acquiring it for the Green Immigration Land Company. Under the guise of sifting the soil through his fingers, assessing the rental properties, and walking the ranch's fence line, Spencer kept Norfleet under constant surveillance for the next three days. As he sat at the kitchen table and ate Eliza Norfleet's meals, he diligently questioned the couple about the ranch's operation, stoking Norfleet's cupidity with his steady interest. At last, he announced that he was quite impressed with Norfleet's farming and would purchase the land for $102,600—more than enough to cover Norfleet's debt on the Slaughter ranch. Their business concluded most satisfactorily, Norfleet and Spencer headed back to Dallas, stopping at Norfleet's bank in Plainview to borrow the cash.

The mark had successfully passed under his wife's discerning eye. He'd said all the right things to his banker, and he held the actual cash under his arm. Norfleet was primed and ready for the eighth act, *taking off the touch,* when the money under his arm would vanish before he'd quite realized that he'd handed it over. Yet Spencer witnessed something at Norfleet's ranch that convinced him the cowboy was good for another go-round. Was it the ease with which Norfleet conjured up the money, was it the sanguinity of his wife, was it the untouched savings account that was the land itself? Spencer toted up the evidence before his eyes and concluded that Norfleet's gullibility was nowhere near exhausted. Once in Dallas, the two men received a telegram from Furey informing them that business had taken him to Fort Worth and instructing them to meet him there at the Terminal Hotel, where they'd be able to post their money and communicate long-distance with the Dallas exchange. And in Fort Worth, they played the con for Norfleet all over again.

Wind the reel back to the day that Furey took Norfleet to the Dallas Cotton Exchange, then replay those same scenes in Fort Worth: the brief glimpse of the exchange, the return to the hotel room for the intense mental effort of code deciphering, the identification of a sure bet. Furey suggested that prior to posting their pool of money on the exchange to free up the money in the Dallas vault, they place the $68,000 pool on United Brokers' current stock pick. "This is our last day on the anxious seat," he reassured them. He wrote out the option order and gave it to Spencer to deliver. Spencer returned just minutes later and brandished his receipt triumphantly, but when Furey examined it, he cried, "Spencer, you have ruined us! You have lost every dollar we have and that we had coming to us." Spencer had exactly reversed Furey's instructions and had purchased instead of sold the shares. As suddenly as they had grown rich, the three men were now in deep debt.

Spencer began to weep with grief. He confessed that the $35,000 he'd just lost was all the money he'd inherited from his dead mother and that his father would probably disown him when he found out. "I could knock your head off, you poor miserable wretch!" Furey said in disgust. But then he sighed and explained that they just might salvage their money. Like an older brother perpetually righting the disasters of his young charges, Furey set off for the exchange to try to hedge the loss before the market closed for the day. He managed to place one order, selling $80,000 worth of stock at a two-point margin for a profit of $160,000, of which one-third was Norfleet's. His vaulted treasure had just swelled from $28,000 to $45,000. That evening, Charles Gerber, the secretary of the Fort Worth exchange, visited them in their hotel room. In contrast to the easy professionalism of Furey, Spencer, and Ward, Gerber's manner was distinctly menacing, his eyes and mouth mere slashes cut into his doughy face. Gerber made the now-familiar objection that as nonmembers Norfleet and Spencer were technically unable to bid on the Fort Worth exchange, and to claim their earnings, they were required to guarantee their bid by posting the amount of their profit.

Without an instant's hesitation, Norfleet again traveled to Hale County to raise the funds. His wife chided him for indulging in speculation but otherwise let him off easy and encouraged him to see the deal through to the end. Norfleet borrowed $25,000 from his brother-in-law and returned with the cash to Fort Worth. It was an identical replay of the previous sequence of events, but with one minor deviation that the swindlers would soon discover. This time, when Norfleet collected the money, he also stuck a .32-caliber automatic in his coat pocket.

The three men reconvened at the Westbrook Hotel in Fort Worth and pooled their money. They had raised a total of $70,000, still $10,000 shy of their target. Spencer proposed to cover the deficit by traveling to Austin to cash in some hitherto-unmentioned Liberty Bonds, after which he would wire the money directly to Norfleet. The men agreed that Furey would take the cash they had raised so far to Dallas the next morning, where his company was transferring him for additional trading, and there he would apply it toward the due bill, and then deposit the final installment when it arrived from Austin.

Why that bothersome $10,000 shortfall? Furey and Spencer had pretended to raise $45,000 to complement Norfleet's $25,000; why not pretend to have raised the full amount, to stave off the mark's suspicion and hurry the play along to its denouement? Once again, what looks like an unnecessary and distracting detail conceals an elegant function.

Furey and Spencer were paving the way for the final scene of the big con in which they *blow off* or *cool out the mark*. The swindlers design the endgame so that the mark willingly returns to his regular life without complaint. The expulsion from the con might be violent, as when the swindlers fake a bloody shoot-out and convince the mark to flee before the police arrive. More commonly, though, this stage is peaceful, bureaucratic, and frustratingly elongated so that the mark never quite knows when the con has ended. The error that defers the big pay-out is merely procedural—Spencer's $10,000, say, never arrives from Austin—and the mark must meet one of his swindlers in yet another city to resolve the mix-up. The mark travels out of state for the rendez-vous, only to be redirected to another city, then another, and so on until he finally gives up and returns home, crestfallen, poorer, but wiser.

Sometimes the mark is so thoroughly cooled he doesn't even realize he's been conned. Some have invested so much of their hopes in the promise of a fast buck that even their swifter losses barely dent their ardor. They remain convinced of the viability of the con man's scheme, believing only that they've suffered the kind of unlucky break inevitable in business—and in gambling. Some victims actually seek out their swindlers a second time, begging for a chance to up the ante and throw more money at the big treasure just beyond their reach. In swindling argot, they're addicts.

That night in the Westbrook, Spencer and Furey took the precaution of searching Norfleet's belongings, and they discovered the gun in his overcoat. Was Norfleet smart to the con? He had come this far and hadn't kicked to the police, so they couldn't be sure. They knew the next day would require a light touch, and above all else they mustn't appear to be manipulating their mark's actions. When Norfleet searched for his coat the next morning and couldn't find it or the gun, they said nothing. When he casually stated that he was going out on a small errand, again they said nothing; they played out his invisible rope and let him out of the hotel room alone. Furey swiftly packed for his trip to Dallas and was nearly finished when Norfleet returned to the West-brook. The two swindlers waited, poised, for Norfleet to confront them, and he did, but it was merely to pose a change of plans. Norfleet said that he was unwilling to let Furey take off with the money; he wanted to hold on to his portion of the cash until the full amount had been raised and the partners could make the final settlement at the exchange together. Furey imperceptibly exhaled. Norfleet's words did not live up to their fears, and they were not enough to deter Furey from his script. He imperiously brushed aside Norfleet's objections, then rolled up the money in some newspaper, stuck the bundle under his arm, and went into the hall to ring for the elevator.

But Norfleet wasn't done with his confrontation. He followed Furey into the hall and jammed a double-action Smith and Wesson between the newspaper bundle and Furey's ribs. "You are going back to the room to settle the matter, or this will be as good a place to settle it as any," Norfleet growled.

"Don't do anything rash, for God's sake! I will go back to the room," Furey cried.

As he reentered the hotel room, Norfleet swung the gun at Spencer, who stayed perfectly in character and grew instantly histrionic. He grabbed a chair and raised it over his head, then thought better and seized a Bible, which he placed over his heart. As Norfleet began shouting that his friends were "partners" and "first-class crooks," Spencer blubbered, "Before my Angel Mother, on my bended knees, with this Bible uplifted to my God in Heaven, I swear to you that I never did, nor never will prove false to you, and that I never did see this man before I met you." It was an ad-libbed speech. If a mark gets wise, the standard script calls for roughing him up and knocking him out long enough to make an escape.

Curiously, Norfleet would later tell two different versions of what happened next. In one, Furey gave in, contemptuously throwing the bundle on the bed and saying, "Take the money and go to blazes with it if you can't stand by the agreement we made." If this is the way it went down, it would have been a classic move, keeping the mark on the defensive. Furey would not have been above deliberately inviting Norfleet's skepticism, part of a ploy to demonstrate that he did not have as much at stake as the mark did. Norfleet did not relish considering himself someone who had welshed on a deal, and it took him only a few seconds to realize that without Furey's cooperation, he'd still be $20,000 in debt and unable to ransom his profit.

In the second version, Furey broke the tension with a truly brilliant bit of improvisation. As Norfleet waved the gun around and Spencer shouted and cried, Furey grew quiet. Catching Norfleet's eye, Furey made a Master Mason's grand hailing sign of distress: he extended both his arms out from his shoulders and raised his forearms up at the elbows like a goalpost and then lowered them to his sides three times in swift succession. The gambit worked, and Norfleet pocketed the gun, wholly unwilling to threaten a brother lodge member. Furey walked toward him and said, "You came very near having a brain storm, didn't you, Brother? Don't that satisfy you? You know I have trusted you with sixty and seventy thousand dollars at a time in your room overnight, and not once did I question your honesty, then when I started away with this money I only thought I was doing what had been agreed on."

In both versions of the story, Furey designed a compromise. Spencer had just received a wire from Garrett Thompson confirming the Green Immigration Land Company's desire to purchase Norfleet's ranch. Norfleet would accompany Spencer to the express office and collect $30,000, the first installment of the purchase price. Of course, that money would have to be held in a safety-deposit box until Thompson's attorneys had certified Norfleet's title to the land, but it would act as earnest money to confirm Thompson's intentions and would put his mind at ease. Then Spencer would head to Austin for his Liberty Bonds. Norfleet would meet Furey at the Cadillac Hotel in Dallas at ten o'clock the next morning, and together they would redeem the majority of the due bill with the $70,000 cash. This plan mollified the rancher. He and Spencer left for the express office, and Furey left to catch his train with the money.

The very instant they parted from Norfleet, the swindlers knocked down their sets and wiped off their stage makeup. They fled the theater on the first outbound train while Norfleet was still treading the boards. It wasn't until the next day, when he arrived at the Cadillac Hotel a half hour early and discovered that Furey had never registered, that he began to wise up. Even then, he waited in the lobby for an hour. He told the clerk to keep a lookout for Furey, then he dashed around to the St. George, the Jefferson, and the Adolphus. He returned to the Cadillac and waited some more, but by then he knew the truth. He'd been had. His last-minute departure from the script meant that the con men had no opportunity to cool him out, so his awakening came fast and hard. He had handed over $45,000 in borrowed money, the equivalent of $560,000 in today's currency. He owed $90,000 on the Slaughter land, or $1.1 million in contemporary valuation. The game was up, and he was worse than broke.

CHAPTER TWO

Benjamin Franklin's Disciples

Confidence artistry began one day in May 1849 when a well-dressed young man named Samuel Williams—or was it Samuel Thomas? or William Thompson?—walked up to a stranger on the streets of lower Manhattan and engaged him in a few minutes of intimate small talk. The stranger felt that he knew but couldn't place this friendly fellow; certainly he seemed like an old friend who was delighted to see him. Williams (as we'll call him) then asked the stranger, in a disarmingly direct manner, whether or not he had confidence in him. When the man answered yes, the only possible answer in polite conversation, Williams said jovially, "Have you confidence in me to trust me with your watch until to-morrow?" In high humor, his mark handed over his gold watch. And Williams sauntered off into the city, laughing and promising over his shoulder that he'd return the watch the next day. In the span of just a few days in May, he swindled John Deraismes out of a watch valued at $114, John Sturges out of a watch worth $80, and Hugh C. McDonald out of a watch valued at $100.

A few weeks later, Hugh McDonald was walking down Liberty Street when he spotted a familiar figure. He alerted a nearby police officer, and Williams found himself caught by his own mark. He was taken into police custody—though not before he tried to bribe McDonald into dropping the charges. He went before the magistrate, and when it was found that he was "a graduate of the college at Sing Sing," he was committed to prison to await a trial. *The New York Herald* broke the story in its Police Intelligence column the next day, and the newspaper immediately recognized that it was witnessing an entirely new genre of criminal enterprise. It was a reporter at the *Herald* who coined the name "Confidence Man" and who urged New Yorkers to stop by the Tombs for a look at him; then the *New-York Tribune* and *National Police Gazette* also picked up the story. Two days later, the *Herald* reported, "Yesterday, in consequence of the publicity given in the daily journals respecting the arrest of Samuel Williams, the 'confidence man,' quite a numerous attendance was brought to the police office, who were all anxious to witness a man who could so far humbug any sensible man." He was peered at like an animal in a zoo. One visitor from Philadelphia identified him as Edward Stevens, a petty criminal whose first arrest was for stealing a "firkin of lard" and who was known in the underworld as a spotter, a stool pigeon, or a betrayer of confidences. The *Herald* noted Williams's reactions to his visitors: "The prisoner, yesterday, at being shown to so many persons, asked if he was a wild beast, and appeared to be much vexed and alarmed at the identifications." After all, he was far subtler than a pickpocket or safecracker. He himself described his effect on his marks as "putting them to sleep."

Nonetheless, he met the fate of a common criminal. After sending a lady friend to attempt to bribe Hugh McDonald a second time, and after being duped by his own bondsman and left to rot in jail, the Confidence Man went before a jury, who handed him a guilty verdict without even leaving their seats. He headed back to his alma mater to serve a two-and-a-half-year sentence. By then, though, a second confidence man by the name of Julius Alexander—or was it Byron Alexander?—was on the prowl.

Williams's was a remarkably distilled act of trickery, and it seized the public's imagination. The *National Police Gazette* crowed loudly at the conviction of "Confidence" but ended its coverage of Williams on a worried note: "We trust this word in time will not be thrown away." In fact, the very opposite happened, and the term "confidence man" almost instantly entered popular discourse. Two weeks after Williams's arrest, Burton's Theatre on Chambers Street in New York presented a farce titled *The Confidence Man*. Eight years later, in 1857, Williams's fame was still strong enough that he would have been recognizable as the model for Herman Melville's protagonist in *The Confidence-Man*, about an unnamed swindler who roams the decks of a Mississippi steamboat on April Fools' Day, cheating passengers out of money by disparaging their willingness to trust him. Melville's confidence man taunts a potential dupe, "What are you? What am I? Nobody knows who anybody is. The data which life furnishes, towards forming a true estimate of any being, are as insufficient to that end as in geometry one side given would be to determine the triangle." The *National Police Gazette* formalized the new criminal pastime by defining "confidence man" in its 1859 *Rogue's Lexicon:*

> CONFIDENCE MAN. A fellow that by means of extraordinary powers of persuasion gains the confidence of his victims to the extent of drawing upon their treasury, almost to an unlimited extent. To every knave born into the world it has been said that there is a due proportion of fools. Of all the rogue tribe, the Confidence man is, perhaps, the most liberally supplied with subjects; for every man has his soft spot, and nine times out of ten the soft spot is softened by an idiotic desire to overreach the man that is about to overreach us. This is just the spot on which the Confidence man works.

As early as 1860, police captains in New York estimated that close to one in ten professional criminals in their city was a confidence man. With just that one sentence—"Have you confidence in me to trust me with your watch until to-morrow?"—Williams had conceived an entire industry.

The Confidence Man did not, of course, invent confidence artistry; he merely perfected a particularly efficient and viral adaptation of it. Williams's thievery had such an instantaneous impact because it crystallized a set of anxieties that had plagued Americans since before they were Americans. In the seventeenth and eighteenth centuries, as the colonists argued and fought their way to nationhood, a central question that threaded through their debates was: What is the right and proper investment of confidence? Virtually all colonial enterprises—education, judicial courts, taxation, self-defense, currency, churches—required an element of trust, because the colonists had rejected the tradition, class structure, and institutional memory to bolster them. Just as merchants extended credit to grease the engine of trade, so did citizens extend confidence to the strangers who visited their distant towns and the authority figures who ruled them from afar.

And so genuine confidence men, those who betrayed the trust

placed in them, captured the public imagination as symbols of the nation-building project. The colonists understood them not as outlaws, or as exceptions to the rules that governed democratic society, but as the logical extension of those rules. Con men differ from later American frontier heroes such as cowboys and private eyes, men who placed themselves beyond the edge of civilization and exercised their freedom by fighting lawlessness. Con men work firmly within the structures of American democratic capitalism, exploiting uncharted territory inside the system itself. They are the innovators and entrepreneurs of such a society, no less than was Benjamin Franklin, their closest forebear. Even in their day, the stories of early American swindlers laid bare a terrible truth. Their country needed them. The new nation would never have prospered without imposture, speculation, and counterfeiting, because America was, from its inception, a confidence trick.

In 1739, Benjamin Franklin, then a printer, invited into his home a schoolmaster named William Lloyd, who impressed him with his excellent manners and learning. Lloyd knew Latin and Greek, which Franklin found humbling because he was struggling to teach himself Latin on the side. After the schoolmaster had departed, Franklin saw with dismay that he'd helped himself to a "fine . . . ruffled" shirt and a handkerchief "mark'd with an F in red silk." His guest was no schoolmaster, and his name was not Lloyd. Franklin had been duped, almost certainly by Tom Bell, the most notorious impostor of the American colonies.

Like Franklin, Bell was the son of an upwardly mobile family in Boston. Like Franklin, he had attended the Boston Latin School and obtained an excellent education, advancing even further than Franklin, who was forced to leave at age ten when his father could no longer afford the tuition. Bell's diploma gained him entry to Harvard, but in 1729, the year before he matriculated, his sea captain father unexpectedly died, throwing the rest of the family on hard times. His mother sold off some property, and Bell entered college as planned, but it was an uneasy fit. He lacked the resources to consort with his prominent classmates, and he lacked the discipline to apply himself to his studies. A few weeks into his first year, he earned a reprimand from the faculty for "Saucy behavior," and the next two years were peppered with punishments for stealing letters, wine, and, most egregiously, a chocolate cake. The latter finally got him expelled in his junior year.

Like Franklin, he began adulthood without money, reputation, a trade, or a patron. And so he faked it. He ordered a silk jacket and hose on credit (and later lost the lawsuit the tailor brought against him for failing to pay), then steadily acquired the rest of a wardrobe in lieu of a résumé. By adopting the dress of a minister, a schoolteacher, or a gentleman, he talked his way into households like Franklin's and passed himself off as a man of worth, earning free room and board while the deception lasted and often upgrading to a new suit of clothes or a new mount on his way out the door. He forged letters of introduction to ingratiate himself with wealthy families and to obtain business loans from them. His travels took him from Massachusetts to Barbados, with stops at the penitentiary in between. The farther he traveled and the more frequently his deceptions were unmasked, the wider grew his notoriety as a mumper—someone who cheats as well as begs. It was hard to attain celebrity in the mid-eighteenth century when it took weeks for news to travel by horseback. Yet before long, articles about Bell referred to him as "a famous impostor" or "the famous, or rather infamous Tom Bell," and the mumper's artistry became increasingly difficult to practice as he began to be recognized. He was almost as renowned in his time as Franklin himself.

Even beyond the striking similarities of their early lives, the two men could be described in nearly identical terms. Both were self-made men who found opportunity in the undefined crevices between social classes. Both exhibited the self-reliant individualism by which colonists characterized themselves in opposition to the Crown. Perhaps most crucially, both manipulated appearances to cultivate impressions among their peers. In perhaps the most frequently quoted passage of his auto-biography, Franklin says, "In order to secure my Credit and Character as a Tradesman, I took care not only to be in *Reality* Industrious & frugal, but to avoid all *Appearances* of the Contrary. . . . [T]o show that I was not above my Business, I sometimes brought home the Paper I purchas'd at the Stores, thro' the Streets on a Wheelbarrow." Franklin performed his hard work as a printer for his neighbors. It is passages like this that have led some historians to place Franklin somewhere on the slippery continuum between huckster and con man. Franklin was, in John Updike's estimation, "an inveterate impersonator." His personality was constructed of sheathed layers, "one emerging from another like those brightly painted Russian dolls which, ever smaller, disclose yet one more, until a last wooden homunculus, a little smooth nugget like a soul, is reached."

The trouble was, Bell's pretenses revealed as hollow that which he imitated. Bell's education not only gave him rudimentary Greek and Latin; it also schooled him in the manners of the elite, so that when he passed himself off as a refined gentleman, he gave a letter-perfect performance. He knew how to tie a cravat, knew the family trees of New England's dynasties, knew how to pronounce the names of distant places, knew how to conduct a fluent conversation ranging amusingly on literature, philosophy, and current events. His travels only added to this storehouse of competencies, because in the mid-eighteenth century only ministers and peddlers were as well traveled as swindlers, and people looked to such men for news from faraway colonies. Bell knew, in other words, how to manipulate the social markers by which the elite identified themselves. Bell's exploits revealed gentility as a covertly political project. Politeness was supposed to be synonymous with moral authority, granting its bearer a natural power over lower, coarser citizens. Colonial elites used the conventions of gentility to retain hierarchies in a democratizing society, a way to define who should naturally rule over the masses. Bell implicitly demonstrated how easily these conventions could be counterfeited, thus reopening the question of how a purportedly classless society should be organized.

In January 1792, a letter reached William Duer at his stone and brick mansion in the Hudson River valley. Duer was the master of Philipse Manor Hall, the former county seat of Frederick Philipse, a wealthy Dutch trader and the founder of the town of Yonkers. Philipse had been an unrepentant Loyalist, and when war broke out, he was arrested and his fine house confiscated by the State of New York. Not only did Duer purchase it at auction for a sliver of its value; he also paid for it with money earned from veterans' pay notes that he'd bought at a discount from desperate soldiers and then redeemed at face value from the government. He lived like a baron as he presided over the estate, attended by liveried footmen under the rococo ceiling. So the letter that reached him from a stranger in a debtor's prison in Baltimore that January had little impact on him. "From ill-placed Confidence I have been steeped in Poverty to the very lips," the letter began, "I have borne the proud Man's Contumely, and the oppressor's wrong; I have felt scorn, and Contempt; and even Insult with Impunity. In this State Poverty is one of the Greatest of Crimes, and of that offense I have been convicted Seven long years." The letter writer had heard of Duer's financial success and wrote about his own experiences with debt in order to caution Duer against continuing in his present course. "I sincerely wish, that you would set limits to your Desires. If you had drank deep, as I have done, of the bitter Cup of adversity, you would never Risk Independence again. May the voice of friendship take the liberty to intreat you to stop in time; and sit down, with so ample an Independance [*sic*], in peace of Mind, and Body!"

Duer did not stop in time. Two months later, he moved from Philipse Manor Hall to the third floor of the New Gaol in lower Manhattan to begin his own seven-year term for insolvency—not, like his Baltimore correspondent, because he'd misplaced his confidence, but because he'd stolen confidence from so many others. He would spend the next seven years mustering all of his resources to obtain an early release, to no avail. He died there at the end of his term in 1799, the scourge of the thousands who had invested with him and who became paupers and debtors themselves when his insolvency triggered the first financial crash in the nation's young history.

William Duer was born in England, educated at Eton, and schooled in market relations at his father's prosperous West Indies plantations. He left Antigua for New York in 1768 with a "handsome pecuniary legacy," which he eventually supplemented with his marriage to the wealthy Catherine Alexander, daughter of Major General William Alexander, Lord Stirling. Duer came to the thirteen colonies to fulfill a contract to supply the British navy with masts and spars formed of New World wood, but as the war approached and the British let his contract expire, he smoothly shifted to provisioning New York's Fort Miller with wood for barracks and frigates, eventually expanding to alcohol, horses, ammunition, and cattle. By October 1776 he was profiting more than $1,000 a month at a time when other citizens were being asked to weather hardships on behalf of the war effort.

Even had he played by the rules, Duer's position as a middleman between farmers and army provisioners would have opened him to patriotic wrath, because it was in his interest to underpay civilian merchants and overcharge the government. But Duer played dirty. He manipulated the price differences by hoarding goods, which led to shortages and higher prices; he paid himself before he paid his suppliers; he paid his suppliers in depreciated Continental currency while hoarding the more valuable specie; he obtained commodities from the enemy and paid for them with American agricultural products, for which he faked customs clearances and bribed officials at foreign ports; and he used public money to speculate in bills of exchange, keeping the profits for himself.

William Duer was America's first high-flying speculator at a time when speculation was a sin and bankruptcy a crime. When the British colonists moved in, they had no capital other than their own future productivity, but they disdained speculation as antithetical both to the Puritan values of thrift and industry and to the Whig values of self-reliance and civic participation. To eighteenth-century clergymen, artisans, and yeomen farmers, the merchant capitalism that the Dutch brought with them from Flanders and Antwerp was far more treacherous than the simple, steady accumulation of wealth that in Protestant theology bespoke God's will for the chosen. The speculator made money by exchanging paper, and he built fortunes out of airy nothings. Colonists feared that profit untethered from labor, whether speculation or gambling, would encourage dissolute lifestyles untethered from morality. Cotton Mather warned that "gains of money or estate, by games, be the games what they will, are a sinful violation of the law of *honesty* and *industry*, which God has given us."

In pre-Revolutionary days, the rhetoric invoked a more secular hell, the threat of enslavement. Benjamin Franklin, in *Poor Richard's Almanack*, warned against allowing one's paper wealth to outstrip one's resources, in such now-familiar maxims as "He that goes a borrowing goes a sorrowing," "When you run in Debt, You give to another Power over your Liberty," "The Borrower is a Slave to the Lender, and the Debtor to the Creditor," and "Rather go to Bed supperless than rise in Debt." Thomas Jefferson was deeply suspicious of the effects of capital derived from sources other than direct labor and trading. As secretary of state, he led the opposition to a federal bank and the government-backed financial instruments that would entice and enable speculators. He thrust on President Washington his belief "that all the capital employed in paper speculation is barren and useless, producing, like that on a gaming table, no accession to itself, and is withdrawn from commerce and agriculture, where it would have produced addition to the common mass: that it nourishes in our citizens habits of vice and idleness, instead of industry and morality." Government, in Jefferson's opinion, had as little business in the fiscal arena as it did in the religious, and citizens should be free to create their own local networks of trade without the seduction of government-backed bonds and securities.

But the republican ideology of public virtue and self-restraint was insufficient to the demands of the times. The Revolutionary War hammered on the moral opposition to speculation until it began to give way in the exigencies of the fight. Many of the private merchants who supplied the troops speculated with the bills of exchange that they received as payment, as did Duer.

Duer went much further. His privileged social position enabled him to help shape the government's fiscal policies in his own interests. He was elected to the Continental Congress in 1777, appointed secretary of the Treasury Board in 1786, and appointed assistant secretary of the Treasury in 1789 under Alexander Hamilton (whose wife was a cousin of Duer's wife).

In the 1780s, Americans found themselves in a changed economic landscape, and the plentiful opportunities for money made purely from money led to a "spirit of speculation." In 1780, Congress depreciated its national currency, giving investors the opportunity to exploit the difference between face value and trading value. When soldiers were discharged, they were paid with settlement certificates that themselves became a kind of currency, traded at ten or fifteen cents on the dollar. Indeed, each new form of government issue, from land warrants to debt certificates, turned ordinary citizens into speculators. Duer's friend Hamilton conceived a bold plan to fund the war retroactively while stimulating the new nation's economic growth: he proposed that the federal government purchase the Continental Congress's securities at face value in return for interest-bearing bonds in the new national government. True, Hamilton's plan would create a moneyed elite among the merchants and bankers who held the government securities, but it would also free capital to water the parched nation, and Hamilton defined capital broadly. "Every thing that has value is capital—an acre of ground, a horse, or a cow, or a public or private obligation, which may, with different degrees of convenience, be applied to industrious enterprise," he wrote in answer to his critics, namely Jefferson and James Madison, who thought that speculation deadened industrious enterprise. Hamilton wanted to make debt productive for the new nation.

Duer, of course, was one of those elites in a position to gain from Hamilton's plan, and he endorsed it in his official capacity as assistant secretary, but he also benefited from insider knowledge of it. It was strictly illegal for him to profit from his foreknowledge of Hamilton's national funding scheme, but the lure was too great, and he began "talking outdoors" to speculator friends, who invested his money in government securities using their names.

Even this most advantageous government position proved too constraining for Duer's speculative lust, and he voluntarily left his post at the Treasury after only six months to return to the financial industry. He then launched the project that would send him plummeting into debtor's prison. Together with Alexander Macomb, a fellow wealthy New Yorker and former war supplier, he spread rumors that he was about to charter a new bank, called the Million Bank. Hamilton reacted exactly as Duer expected: he opposed the new bank on the grounds that speculators would withdraw capital from the recently formed Bank of New York and the soon-to-be-established New York branch of the Bank of the United States, weakening both with the loss of specie and reputation. The next stage of the script called for Bank of New York stock prices to fall, at which point Duer and Macomb would corner the market and gain a controlling interest in the bank. The final, astonishingly audacious stage called for leveraging their capital to do the same to shares of the Bank of the United States—at which point a single investor would be in charge of one of the federal government's most powerful financial institutions. But news of Duer's intentions on the Bank of New York leaked, and he had to act faster than he'd planned to raise enough capital. He sold one of his estates and "borrowed" money from his other concerns, and then he frantically started to borrow money from everyone who trusted him, promising them fantastic returns.

The unraveling came quickly. Other wealthy investors thwarted Duer's designs on the Bank of New York, in part by withdrawing gold and silver from their accounts, which forced banks to call in loans, drove up interest rates, and made it ruinously expensive for Duer to borrow money. At the same time, Duer was suddenly summoned to Philadelphia to answer nettlesome questions about a $240,000 gap in the Treasury books from the time of his tenure there. And then his debts fell due. Duer was arrested for insolvency the very day after the Bank of the United States, the bank he hoped to control, opened for business. He owed an astonishing $475,000 to his associate Walter Livingston, or about $11 million in today's currency. And he owed far smaller amounts to dozens and dozens of New Yorkers. One contemporary calculated his total indebtedness at $3 million, or $70 million in today's currency. The losses rippled out from there. Livingston, of course, declared bankruptcy, as did Macomb and about twenty-three other speculators. Soon the effects of Duer's overreach spread beyond New York's financial elite to the rest of the market. Real estate prices dropped, credit seized up, and about $5 million in shareholder value simply evaporated. Thomas Jefferson, for one, felt delicious vindication that the speculators had finally gotten their just due. He was confident that now people would return to "plain unsophisticated common sense." Madison, too, believed the crash to be gratifyingly fatal: "The gambling system . . . is beginning to exhibit its explosions."

Jefferson's vindication, though, was a deceptive one. Like Bell, Duer was not an exception to the rule of post-Revolutionary market relations. His career utterly exemplified early capitalism. In fact, Duer's leveraged trading and subsequent bankruptcy, which represented the worst in eighteenth-century financial transgressions, would simply be considered ordinary business today, when bankruptcy is no longer a crime and business failure has lost much of its stigma. The panic Duer incited was sensational but shallow, and it prompted speculators not to reform their gambling impulses but to normalize them by founding the New York Stock Exchange.

One way to describe the evolution of American capitalism in the nineteenth century is the steady domestication of gambling. By the end of the century, gaming had been outlawed, but speculation had been entirely institutionalized, codified, and tamed. It began just a few decades after Duer's calamity, when New York State was hugely successful at raising capital to dig the Erie Canal from Albany to Buffalo, beginning with the Canal Act of 1817. The state paid for the construction through bonds sold not to the merchant elite, who scorned the project, but to ordinary savings bank clients in New York City, who

realized fabulous returns when the canal opened in 1825, two years ahead
of schedule. Wall Street princes took note, and when western land and
railroad companies adopted the Erie Canal strategy, the money poured
in. There was no turning back the stock ticker. America in the nineteenth century was speculating its way westward.

In Melville's *Confidence-Man,* an old man sits at a marble table as white
as his own snowy hair. By the light of the single lamp in the gentleman's
cabin on the Mississippi steamboat, with the confidence man bending
over his shoulder, the old man takes out two bills from his vest pocket
and proceeds to compare them against the *Counterfeit Detector,* a guide
to each of the denominations of currency printed by each of the hundreds of banks in existence by the mid-nineteenth century. The old man
learns from the *Detector* that if his $3 bill from the Vicksburg Trust and
Insurance Banking Company is legitimate, "it must have, thickened
here and there into the substance of the paper, little wavy spots of red;
and it says that they must have a kind of silky feel, being made by the
lint of a red silk handkerchief stirred up in the paper-maker's vat." The
confidence man asks him if his bill passes muster. "Stay," says the old
man, as he continues to read and scrutinize, "that sign is not always to
be relied on; for some good bills get so worn, the red marks get rubbed
out. And that's the case with my bill here—see how old it is—or else
it's a counterfeit, or else—I don't see right—or else—dear, dear me—I
don't know what else to think." And so he tries again. "It says that, if
the bill is good, it must have in one corner, mixed in with the vignette,
the figure of a goose, very small, indeed, all but microscopic; and, for
added precaution, like the figure of Napoleon outlined by the tree, not
observable, even if magnified, unless the attention is directed to it." The
old man cries despairingly, "Now, pore over it as I will, I can't see this
goose." The confidence man urges him to give up "a wild-goose-chase,"
throw the *Detector* away, and simply spend the money as if it were good.

   "As if": in those two small words lies much of the basis for market
relations in the late eighteenth and early nineteenth centuries. Speculators like Duer frightened more conservative investors because their
heedless stock manipulations laid bare the groundless nature of the
growing economy that rose from nothing more than borrowing and
leveraging. But the even more alarming truth was that it wasn't only the

"stock-jobbers," "plungers," and "jackals" who risked everything in the chase for future profits. Every last person who participated in the market was a speculator, simply by his use of paper currency. It wasn't until surprisingly late in American history, with the passage of the National Bank Acts of 1863 and 1864, that the country had a national system of banking and a standardized national currency backed by U.S. Treasury securities. Before then, state-chartered banks purportedly guaranteed their notes with specie—metal money in the form of gold and silver resting undisturbed in their vaults—but most banks issued far more notes than they could back if every one of them were redeemed. Banknotes were thus speculative bills of exchange. One commentator in 1839 called them "*credit*-money, or *confidence*-money," deriving their value solely from the "*promise to pay*, which, by universal understanding, is meant to signify a promise to pay *on condition of not being required to do so*." And so it was up to the bearer or receiver to decide whether or not to extend confidence to the bank behind it. If, as frequently happened, the bank's reputation softened or collapsed, all of its bills in wallets and cash registers would instantly depreciate. Most of the bills in circulation did not trade at their face value, and so newspapers published rates of exchange between different local and regional currencies. Buying goods required the discernment of an art historian and the numerical nimbleness of a mathematician. Sometimes it was easier—and more profitable—to turn off one's doubts and simply pass money *as if* it were real.

Paper money, for all its glaring flaws, was an absolute economic necessity. Before the discovery of native silver and gold mines, North America consistently found itself on the short end of a trade imbalance in specie with other nations, as the metal money flowed overseas to pay for the finished goods that could not yet be made in America. Colonists experimented with various mediums of exchange, such as wampum in New England, tobacco in the South, and playing cards in Canada. But as networks of trade expanded and thickened, especially at the ports, merchants needed something fungible across local regions to clear the path for their commodities. By the mid-nineteenth century, each of the colonies had issued its own paper currency. Pennsylvania, for instance, had issued about 45,000 pounds' worth of currency in 1723 and 1724, backed not by specie but by the land assets of those who borrowed the currency from the government and by the future taxes that could be paid with the currency. But, like most such issuances, Pennsylvania's currency was set to expire and be withdrawn from circulation in 1731. One of the most ardent supporters of continuing the paper money project was Benjamin Franklin.

Though *Poor Richard's Almanack* relentlessly warned against the enslavement of personal debt, Franklin also fervently believed that a tradesman's good credit was essential to building his strong reputation, and that dependence was a necessary first step to independence. When he looked around at the stagnant state economy, dousing it with an influx of paper money seemed to him solid fiscal policy. In 1729, just twenty-three years old, he published an anonymous pamphlet titled *A Modest Enquiry into the Nature and Necessity of a Paper Currency*. He argued that a greater amount of currency in circulation would drive down interest rates and encourage spending and building. He admitted that this policy would not be popular with moneylenders, land speculators, and the lawyers who profited from debt disputes, but surely all of the "Lovers of Trade" could see the benefits of inexpensive debt. Franklin's view prevailed. In his *Autobiography*, he recalled that though the pamphlet did not bear his name, "My Friends there [at the Pennsylvania statehouse], who conceiv'd I had been of some Service, thought fit to reward me, by employing me in printing the Money, a very profitable Job, and a great Help to me." Franklin would continue printing millions of dollars' worth of currency for Pennsylvania, Delaware, and New Jersey until 1764. He implored his fellow citizens to have confidence in the state, then profited mightily from their investment.

Franklin designed as well printed currency, inventing his own method of "nature printing" to transfer the imprint of a sage leaf to the paper bill via a copperplate press in order to guarantee the bill's authenticity. Each of the banks that issued currency devised its own markers of validity, but the result was a disorienting array of denominations and designs—a situation practically calculated to encourage counterfeiting. It was up to the bearer to decipher the signs and ascertain the legitimacy of the notes in his or her wallet, or up to the shopkeeper to determine whether he or she would accept the note proffered across the counter. Purchases in dry goods stores and taverns often began with the same matchup between bill and *Counterfeit Detector* that engrossed Melville's old man.

Yet there were precisely as many ways to pass fake currency as there were ways to detect it, for each method devised to identify a counterfeit bill spawned a twin method for ensuring its smooth passage. For instance, pamphlets like the *Counterfeit Detector* reproduced the signatures of bank presidents and cashiers so that storekeepers could verify the signatures on banknotes. But those same pamphlets acted as primers for counterfeiters to practice their handwriting. Or counterfeiters would game the pamphlets: they would issue false notes with a noticeable flaw; then, after the next pamphlet had been published which mentioned the flaw, they'd correct that single detail for a new issue of notes, which would then pass scrutiny because that detail would be the only aspect that bearers would check. Best of all, counterfeiters could simply counterfeit counterfeit detectors, and substitute them in shops with sleight of hand. As Melville's confidence man points out to the disquieted old man, the tools for increasing confidence in the money supply have exactly the opposite effect: "Proves what I've always thought, that much of the want of confidence, in these days, is owing to these Counterfeit Detectors you see on every desk and counter. Puts people up to suspecting good bills. Throw it away, I beg, if only because of the trouble it breeds you."

One counterfeiter in the late eighteenth century used the confusion around paper currency to justify his art. "Money, of itself," he argued, "is of no consequence, only as we, by mutual agreement, annex it to a nominal value, as the representation of property. Anything else might answer the same purpose, equally with silver and gold, should mankind only agree to consider it as such, and carry that agreement into execution in their dealings with each other." Value is not inherent in money because of the intrinsic worth of its materials. It is the product of a contract between bearer and receiver. In the hustle and bustle of the marketplace, it mattered little how full a given bank's coffers were; what mattered was the interaction at the moment of exchange: Could the bill pass? The counterfeiter urbanely concluded that this rendered a false bill no less valuable than a real one. "Therefore, we find the only thing necessary to make a matter valuable, is to induce the world to deem it so."

The counterfeiter was Stephen Burroughs, a man who knew much about confidence and how to manipulate it, for he was an impostor cut from the same die as Tom Bell. He too was born to a respectable family in 1765—his father was a clergyman in Hanover, New Hampshire—

and he too had a classical education at Dartmouth that ended in an early departure for youthful high jinks like stealing a watermelon and attending class without shoes. With boyish romanticism, he conceived the idea of setting off to sea, so he pretended to have medical training and set sail on a privateer as the ship's physician. On the journey home, the captain locked him in irons for stealing wine, and he once again found himself in New England, thrust back upon his own resources. Stealing a page from Bell's playbook, Burroughs boosted ten of his father's sermons, acquired some ministerial garb from another clergyman, and descended upon Pelham, Massachusetts, in 1784 to give the weekly sermon, which was so successful the townspeople hired him as their preacher. Upon discovering his deception, the Pelhamites ran him out of town, but hardly had he gotten out of earshot of their invectives than he was caught passing counterfeit coin and sentenced to three years in "the Castle," a jail on Castle Island in Boston Harbor. After his release, Burroughs tried his hand at respectable living, starting a family and a business, but he discovered his true genius only after moving to lower Canada, where he began forging American coins and bills with such skill that his reputation seeped back over the border and he became a kind of mythic outlaw hero. In the early nineteenth century, every instance of counterfeit immediately invoked Burroughs as its putative source.

For Burroughs, the turn from imposture to counterfeiting was entirely natural. In fact, he might have said that the two practices are different sides of the same coin: both entail passing into circulation untrue representations whose authenticity is explicitly in question. For both, the success of the endeavor is determined at the moment of exchange. Unlike magicians and swindlers working the big con, Burroughs could not make use of the one-ahead by preparing his deception in advance. Any moment of commerce in the late eighteenth and early nineteenth centuries was already framed as an occasion for suspicion and enhanced scrutiny.

And yet this structural parallel between imposture and counterfeit did not prevent early Americans from equating the face value of paper money with the public reputation of the men printing it. At the very close of his *Autobiography*, Franklin describes an instance when the Pennsylvania legislature came close to repealing 100,000 pounds of currency. Franklin was able to stop the repeal and buoy the value of all the currency in circulation by signing his name to a document promising the bearers that the new issuance would not detrimentally affect their investment. Franklin converted confidence in himself into confidence in the state, yet his signature was no less abstract than the state's promise to redeem the note for specie.

Magically, incredibly, the paper money handed from money belt to till to pocketbook around the colonies and states did what it was supposed to do. America between the Revolution and the Civil War experienced dramatic economic development as the frontier moved westward and the eastern cities commercialized. This development happened not *despite* but *because of* counterfeit. At a time when the appetite for development outstripped the available credit, the fake bills that inflated the money supply performed a public service, especially in the West. A Michigan citizen testified that "counterfeiting and issuing worthless 'bank notes' . . . was not looked upon as a felony, as it would be today. Of course it was taken for granted that it was a 'little crooked,' but the scarcity of real money, together with the necessity for a medium of exchange, made almost anything that looked like money answer the purpose."

The historian Stephen Mihm in *A Nation of Counterfeiters* argues that this dimension of nineteenth-century history should rewrite economic theory. When the story of American capitalism is told from the perspective of imposture, speculation, and counterfeiting—from just below the surface of a vast deception—it looks not like Max Weber's theory of the "plodding, methodical, gradual pursuit of wealth" described in *The Protestant Ethic and the Spirit of Capitalism*. Rather, it is "the get-rich-quick scheme, the confidence game, and the mania for speculation" that drove our nation into the modern age. Against a litany of reasons why it was foolish to do so, Americans simply decided to have confidence.

CHAPTER THREE

Cowboy Justice

The sucker never squeals. The con is so cleverly designed, the theory goes, and the mark's complicity so tightly secured that he will never report the crime. Even if the mark realizes the game was rigged, he cannot risk exposing himself to the contempt of his business colleagues or even prosecution, and so he merely sighs at his own expensive gullibility. Every swindler finds a way to mention this in every interview, article, and memoir, a boast disguised as a sociological principle. And like most things that swindlers say, it isn't true. Suckers squeal all the time. One of Reno Hamlin's marks, who'd been taken for $1,500, kicked just days after Hamlin posed as a mule buyer for Norfleet. While Spencer and Furey put Norfleet on the send and took off the touch, Hamlin found himself in jail for conspiracy to commit a felony.

For Norfleet, the stakes were considerably higher than $1,500. In his autobiography, he described his mental anguish when he realized that all of his and his brother-in-law's savings had vanished and he was deeply in debt for the ranch he'd just purchased: "Forty-five thousand dollars gone! Ninety thousand dollars in debt! Fifty-four years old! The three facts crashed on my brain. To all else I thought or spoke, these piercing realities were an overtone. Forty-five thousand dollars gone! Ninety thousand dollars in debt! Fifty-four years old! The knowledge paralyzed, then shook me like an earthquake, crumbling my castles into ashes about my feet." The crowds in the hotel lobby twirled around him. He felt dizzy and disoriented. "My God! My God!" he cried out. When he noticed people staring at him and parents drawing their children to their sides, he hurried to his hotel room to wrest control of his mind.

Something happened to Norfleet in his hotel room that day, something difficult to explain. Swindlers and sociologists tend to describe the big con in mechanistic terms, as if the script were a well-wrought assembly line that takes up a man, deftly works on him, and spits him out the other end as a dupe with empty pockets. In their understanding, the big con works so well because confidence is so easy to generate. Confidence is more than blind faith, but less than perfect knowledge. It is, according to the dictionary, "a mental attitude of trust"—the *feeling* of trust—rather than trust itself. Push the right psychological buttons and the swindler can create a hologram of trustworthiness in a mark's mind. This, of course, contradicts everything Norfleet would have liked to believe about himself. He was fond of considering himself a man of experience, knowledge, and charm. But Furey and his gang operated with a different understanding of human nature. They knew that this very belief was one of the buttons they could push to produce confidence and flip open Norfleet's wallet.

Yet if the average person underestimates his own gullibility, the average swindler overestimates the predictability of human nature. Perhaps we do have psychological buttons that make it easier to access our confidence than we'd like to think, but no one can control precisely what happens when those buttons are pushed. Norfleet's fleecing shows us that the experience is more alchemical than mechanical. When Furey and his men filled Norfleet's mind with their seductions, then sent him reeling into the realization of his suckerdom, their words mixed with everything else in his mind—his family's proud history on the Texas plains, his cowboy notion of justice, the decades he'd spent on the prairie in solitude tending to cattle and his own soul—to form a volatile mixture. Norfleet emerged from the big con as a changed man, stone-broke but wealthy in outrage.

In his hotel room, Norfleet draped a damp towel on his perspiring forehead and lay down on the bed. He closed his eyes and thought of the five men whom he'd considered his friends. It seemed truly unbelievable to him that they were not who they said they were, and he found that he could not quite "see" them anymore, their visages suddenly as changeable as their characters. And so, like a sick man wrenching himself back to health, Norfleet mustered all his mental discipline to counteract this drift. Lying on the bed with his eyes closed, he made himself retrieve every last detail of the five men, calling them up one by one and preserving them in his mind with the fixative of his rage. Furey was first, with his "round, smooth face that radiated health and vigor; his greenish blue eyes and their magnetic pull." Only in retrospect did Furey seem like "a serpent coiled." Next was Spencer, who impressed him with "his splendid military carriage," his "keenness, alertness, a wide-awakeness and up-to-dateness" that allowed him to wear his fine clothes with flair. Only a slightly crooked nose marred his polished exterior. Like Furey, though, Spencer had a tell that hinted at the subterfuge behind his mask. When he smiled, "his lips parted and their edges, like thin rose petals rolled back into his mouth leav-

The Furey gang in the mug shots that Norfleet used to track them down

ing a noncommittal expression upon his handsome face." Hamlin's disguise as a mule buyer was convincing because he was even "built like a burro," with glossy black hair and weather-beaten features. Ward, the Dallas exchange secretary, was the quintessential businessman who appeared to Norfleet the most well-bred member of the gang. Gerber, the Fort Worth exchange secretary, was pure menace, with "two bullet eyes of black" and a sneering mouth. "If I were to be killed," Norfleet thought, "this man would be my murderer. He was the death-dealer of the organization."

Sitting up and shaking himself from his trance, Norfleet wondered what time it was. He called the reception desk, and the operator informed him that it was 10:30 a.m. That couldn't be right, he told himself, since he'd returned to his room after 10:00 a.m. He cupped his chin in his hand, and with a start he felt bristles on his face. He rushed to the mirror, then rushed back to the phone to call the operator again and ask her what *day* it was. It was 10:30 in the morning on the day *after* Furey had stood him up. He'd spent twenty-four hours on the bed, zeroing his mind on his targets. The extraordinary energy powering his anger convinced Norfleet that he was right to line the five men up in his sights. "I knew they were mine for all time," he wrote. "From that moment I began the chase, the world my hunting ground."

He went to Pinkerton's Detective Agency in Fort Worth. One of its agents accompanied him to visit the chief of police and the county sheriff. Then he took the next train to Dallas, where he called upon the captain of the police force. The officials he met at all four agencies were friendly enough but entirely noncommittal in their promises to help him. Norfleet swiftly realized that the only person with the motivation to hunt for his swindlers in whatever corner of the nation they were hiding was he, and that his search would require the very broadest net and the most creative approach possible. So he swallowed his shame and met with reporters from several newspapers, as well as the Associated Press, and told them the entire tale of his swindling, concluding with a direct appeal to readers for their help in locating the men.

Then, finally, he returned to his ranch. This was the hard part. With no small amount of trepidation, he confessed to his wife the enormity of their loss, and then he broached the subject of retribution. He knew he had shrunk in her eyes; he'd just compromised her faith in him by charging so bullishly into the stock swindle. But he also knew that his home life would never be the same until he could right the wrong. "Wife," he declared, "I want to go after those crooks myself. I want to go get them with my own wits and gun." Eliza Norfleet understood precisely the nature of the man she had married, and instantly she granted him her confidence. "Of course you do," she replied. "I'll take care of the ranch. You just go and get those good-for-nothing crooks. And remember, Frank, bring them in alive. Any fool can kill a man."

With those words Eliza entirely altered the nature of Norfleet's story, changing it from a Western to something new. In his worldview, Furey's gang had "forfeited their lives to me by betraying my trust." Their infraction was so offensive that Norfleet never questioned his right to exact cowboy justice with the muzzle of his gun, and he was renowned in the Panhandle for his quick draw and lethal accuracy. Eliza made him rethink his strategy. When he set forth from Hale Center in December 1919, he did pack a gun, but he resolved to catch the swindlers with guile rather than violence—to entrap the con men within their own code of nonviolent trickery.

Joe Furey didn't know whom he was dealing with when he fingered J. Frank Norfleet. Eliza knew. Norfleet's bankers knew, too, because when he stopped in Plainview, the good men at the Guaranty State Bank assured him that they were unconcerned by his temporary financial embarrassment and could wait for him to settle his debts. His promise was good credit; his morals grew out of the land just as sturdily as his crops and livestock. He was the third generation of Norfleets to ranch in Texas, and he and Eliza had claimed, fenced, and farmed the land just as the region became integrated into the national economy. In part, the story of how he grew wealthy enough to be worthy of swindling is also the story of how industrialism manufactured the perfect conditions for the big con.

In later years, Norfleet was an unapologetic storyteller, and he would always start by telling the story of his last name. In the seventeenth century, he would say, two Scottish brothers joined a ship sailing for America by the northern route. The ship was dashed to pieces on the high seas, and the only survivors were the brothers, who washed ashore in Virginia. According to family lore, the colonists took in the two men from the North Fleet and rechristened them "The Nor'fleet Boys," their original surname swept off in the ocean. Both brothers grew into respected planters, and their dynasties would forever bear the sign of their almost unbelievable resilience.

The Norfleet families farmed in Virginia until the mid-nineteenth century. Jasper Holmes Benton Norfleet, Frank's father, moved with his family to Texas in 1854, when he was twelve, settling in Gonzales, just east of San Antonio. Jasper came of age along with the state of Texas. As a seventeen-year-old in November 1859, he volunteered as a private of the Texas Rangers and spent the next six months fighting in the bloody Texas-Indian wars. A year after he married Mary Ann Shaw, a reckless tomboy two years his junior, Jasper joined the Confederate army, where he served until he was struck by rheumatism sometime in 1864. Jasper and Mary Ann's first child, James Franklin, was born on February 23, 1865. Jasper's cattle ranch prospered after the war, and he built his family a fine stone house. One day when the Norfleets were away from home, a band of about three hundred Apaches destroyed the house and stole seventeen hundred head of cattle. Jasper was forced to start all over again, and as he grew older, Frank joined in the family livelihood.

Frank would often tell a revealing story about his father—a story that would also prove prophetic for his own great adventures. When Frank and his siblings were young, they learned to read at something less than a one-room schoolhouse, a modest outdoor school under a brush arbor. A Yankee teacher named Mr. Denny ran the school, and he boarded for a time with the Norfleets, amusing them all with "the peculiar quirking of his mouth" when he spoke. And then the school term came to an end. Frank would say, "I remember that he stalked off down the road with his flowered carpetbag, refusing to pay my mother the amount he owed her for board." This Jasper could not stand. He set his shoulders, caught himself a fresh horse, and took off after the schoolteacher, catching up with him outside the general store in San Saba, where he could hear Mr. Denny's booming voice bragging about how he had walked off the Norfleets' ranch without paying. "Th' bed and board was not worth a cent! Why, man, there was even no tea! Think of it! No tea! Th' same old thing day after day. I'd never pay a copper cent for such and be domned to ye." Jasper stepped inside. He was much smaller than Mr. Denny, but in a quiet, steady voice he asked the schoolteacher if he truly meant to steal those months of labor from

Mary Ann Norfleet. Mr. Denny roared out that he did. Jasper's eyes flashed and he reached for his holster, then checked himself and reached for a wooden stick instead. Mr. Denny also lunged for it but too late, and Jasper's blow landed between his eyes. Mr. Denny was knocked unconscious, and when he came around, he grudgingly instructed the postmaster, who also happened to be treasurer of the school board, to pay Jasper in full. If Frank knew this story of avenged injustice so well, it was because he was the seven-year-old secretly following his father on his own horse—named Old Denny—with his pockets full of stones to throw at the schoolteacher should his father require assistance.

In 1879, when Frank was fourteen, he made his first foray into the Panhandle to join a buffalo hunt. While the Native Americans on the Texas plains had been defeated, killed, or herded into reservations by the close of the Red River War in 1875, the buffalo hung on a bit longer. Uncountable millions of American bison used to roam the plains, eating the short, curly buffalo grass. Hunters used to tell of climbing a bluff, looking down, and seeing half a million animals at one glance. The Plains Indians hunted them to eat and trade, but it wasn't until the white men created a market for their fur that their numbers began to precipitously diminish. Once steamboats ascended the Missouri River and railroads forged across the plains, it became economically efficient to transport the hides to cities, where a robe that traded for less than $5 on the range would fetch between $15 and $40 at select furriers. When tanners learned to turn buffalo hides into strong leather for use as industrial belting in steam engines in the 1870s, the fate of the buffalo was sealed: the Industrial Revolution literally as well as metaphorically drove the buffalo to extinction. In just three years, 1872 to 1874, over three million buffalo were slaughtered, and by 1875 only about ten thousand buffalo survived in the Texas Panhandle, their very last refuge in the West. For the next few decades, settlers found the plains colored white with buffalo bones. Homesteaders making the arduous journey to town for supplies would bring no money, instead collecting the bones along the way to sell in the cities for $21 per ton, later to be crushed and converted into phosphate for fertilizer.

While Norfleet was on the buffalo hunt, a man rode up with his wife and three children and asked to join their poker game. He ran a blazer on them, which is a cowboy's way of saying he swindled them, and the hunters did the only thing possible. They dug a hole and rolled him into it, burying him with his boots on. His grave marker was a hackberry tree from which they'd hanged another man. Norfleet said, "The woman and her babies were better off without the father." One of the babies was near death with a bowel complaint, probably the result of alkaline water, and while the father would have let her die, the buffalo hunters treated her "with utmost respect and care." Norfleet himself went out to kill a fat calf and fry up its tallow. He browned some flour in the fat, mixed in an alarming amount of salt and pepper, and thinned the paste in more grease. "I took the baby in my arms and began feeding it the thick gravy from the end of my finger. It went to sucking that finger like a starving cub." He proudly reported that the baby grew up into a fine woman.

Frank never really returned home after the buffalo hunt, and he spent the next ten years as an itinerant cowhand on the plains. In 1886, when he was just twenty-one years old, the brothers Dudley H. and John W. Snyder hired him and nineteen other cowboys to drive two herds of cattle numbering in the thousands from central Texas to the free range of the Panhandle. The cattle ate their way across the plains, while the herders existed on what they could fit onto the wagon. When they arrived in the Panhandle and claimed a range, only Norfleet would agree to stay and look after the cattle, so the Snyders selected a mount of about a dozen horses and left him alone. Norfleet would always remember that date, June 22, 1886, because it was the longest day of the year—and that year it was the loneliest. But he impressed the Snyder brothers with his work, and in 1889, when the Snyders sold the Spade Ranch to Isaac L. Ellwood, Norfleet "went along with the deal almost like a chattel." Not that he minded. Norfleet was an independent man, and though he worked for Ellwood for seventeen years and even named his firstborn son after him, he did not once lay eyes on his employer in those first fifteen years. Ellwood made him foreman, bestowed on him his confidence and some stationery with "J. F. Norfleet, Foreman" at the top, and went back home to Illinois.

Norfleet may have been in the middle of nowhere, but he was on the cutting edge of progress. Isaac Ellwood was part of a new breed of Texas rancher—the speculating kind. After the Panhandle was divided into twenty-six counties in 1876, land-speculating syndicates, formed from eastern and foreign capital, moved in to color the map. They bought up the smaller, independent ranches like the Spade, joined them with adjacent properties, and created vast holdings owned by corporations and managed from afar. Many of these corporate ranches failed, despite the state's subsidization of the industry through open range, free water, and free grass. But the stream of capital watered a handful of inventions that themselves proved explosively profitable.

Seasonal roundups of free-range cattle worked well enough, and they were a much-needed excuse for some rather rambunctious cowboy socializing, but ranch managers figured they could make more money if they could control where the cattle roamed. It was costly to find them and separate them each spring and summer, and when winters were bad, hordes of invading cattle from the Dakotas, Kansas, Nebraska, and Colorado would move in and steal their grass. The problem that cattle ranchers faced was how to build barriers on the limitless horizon. Norfleet's boss, Isaac Ellwood, was the co-inventor and manufacturer of barbed-wire fencing, which revolutionized the cattle industry. At first, ranchers tried bare wire fencing, but the implacable cows just slipped right through it. Next they tried twisting barbs around the smooth wire, but the cows figured out how to slide the barbs into bunches and then slither through the gaps. Finally, Ellwood and his partner, Joseph Glidden, invented a way to twist two smooth wires together to hold the barbs in place. The cows were finally contained. Norfleet's main task on the Spade, then, was to install Ellwood's wire, and by the time he was done, he had fenced 246,000 acres of Texas plains. In the meantime, Ellwood's company expanded and reorganized as the Superior Barbed Wire Company in 1881, which later became part of United States Steel, the world's first billion-dollar corporation.

It might look easy to twist some wire around itself and convert that into a paper fortune on the New York Stock Exchange. But Norfleet's job as a Texas cattle rancher was to convert grass into meat into money, season after season. Norfleet's letters to D. N. Arnett, Ellwood's manager, from these early years tell of near-constant hardships. The unspoken question that his letters address is whether there is enough grass to "make feed" or sustain the herd, between droughts in the summer and thick pelts of snow in the winter. In June 1892, Norfleet wrote, "The drouth is at last broken we have just had the heaviest rain I ever saw it come up with a terrible storm and hail that did a great deal of damage." Not only did the storm pound into mud the few shards of grass that remained from the drought, but it also destroyed two of the windmills on which the ranch relied for irrigation. Several summers later, Norfleet reported that his cattle were "eating loco," a poisonous weed that is the first green thing to sprout on the prairie in the spring. Norfleet, though, was optimistic that one rain would produce enough grass to save the herd in time for the September roundup. He ended his letter to Arnett, who lived in Colorado City, on a characteristic note: "Am sorry to hear the Grasshoppers are causing such a loss to the good people of that country."

These years are marked by what Norfleet did without. For one thing, he did without money entirely. In his first year at the Spade Ranch, he spent a grand total of fifty cents of his year's wages for stamps and stationery to write to his mother. With his gun and a horse, he was replete within himself. He drank alcohol only medicinally, adding whiskey to his tallow-flour-pepper-and-salt recipe when his digestion required it. And he was equally demanding of those in his employ. As foreman of the Spade, he had many young boys under his care, impressionable boys who had hurtled themselves into cowboy life with no experience of the wider world. "I took a notion that I was not going to let the boys gamble in my camp," Norfleet later wrote, "because I had seen serious difficulties arise over a game of cards"—if you call seeing a man buried alive for running a blazer a *difficulty*—"and to keep things from going that way, I refused to allow any gambling." Instead, he would read them a sermon by the Reverend DeWitt Talmage that he'd cut out of the newspaper called "A Wayward Son Is the Heaviness of His Mother." He says he never once got to the end of that sermon. He'd get partway through, and one of the ranch hands would suddenly stand up and announce that it was time to let the horses out. "And when they got outside the door I could see them get out their old big red bandana handkerchiefs and wipe their eyes."

Norfleet told at least three different stories of how he met Mattie Eliza Hudgins, the future Mrs. Norfleet. There's the version steeped in the romance of the western frontier: he rode into Palo Pinto County to scout for fence posts, and there he watched, enchanted, as a young girl rode by on a quarter horse, handling her mount with expert grace. "It seemed after that," he would say, "that the only good posts in Texas grew on Keechi Creek in Palo Pinto county." There's the melodramatic version: a young girl stood on the banks of a shallow creek in Texas, about to be baptized. Just as she stepped into the waters, she heard the pounding of hooves, and from within the crowd of onlookers emerged a cowpuncher, who dismounted and waded into the stream next to her. "I'd like to be baptized, too, parson, if you're willin'," he drawled. After the brief ceremony, the man waved at the girl and rode off as abruptly as he'd arrived. And then there is the likely version: as manager of the Spade Ranch, Norfleet had been away from civilization for two solid years. He traveled to Epworth to pick up his mail at the Hesperian Hotel, run by Eliza's sister and brother-in-law. Eliza recalled that when he walked in, he was the "ugliest thing I ever saw until he bathed and duded up a bit." She turned him down when he asked her for the first dance at a ball in Epworth. In all three versions, though, Norfleet was an unrelenting suitor, and the couple were married at her family's home by the Reverend Horatio Graves, the first permanent settler of Hale County, on June 13, 1894.

Norfleet swore to his wife that she was the prettiest woman in four counties. "I was the *only* woman in four counties," she later recollected (meaning, presumably, the only *white* woman). Norfleet was proud of his accomplishment: "I got her cut off from brush country . . . and never let her get back to the cedar post breaks. It was the most important event in my life, getting Eliza for my wife."

Eliza could ride as well as any ranch hand, and she joined Norfleet on his rounds at the Spade until their daughter Mary was born in 1894. In March 1895, Norfleet filed a claim as a homesteader under the same act by which his grandfather had become a landowner in 1854, which entitled him to 160 acres after a three-year residency. Frank and Eliza saved enough to buy another sixteen sections of adjoining land, over 10,000 acres, which the Pre-emption Act priced at a mere $1.25 an acre. Over 4.8 million Texas acres were converted from public land into private homesteads under these acts.

Eliza and Frank got right to work making a home: they dug a big hole, covered it with poles, and then piled on layers of hay, tow sacks, and dirt, leaving a gap at the back end for a chimney. This was a dugout, the Texan prairie version of a proud and ancient architectural form, and though it might not have looked like much, it was near impervious to weather. The occasional herd of cattle might run over the roof and crash through, but after they had finished laughing, they'd simply build a new dugout and resume their business. The Norfleets' second child, Frank Elwood, known as Pete, was born in the dugout in 1899. By the time Robert Lee came along in 1905, the Norfleets had upgraded to a frame house, and Ruth was born in 1908 in a dwelling that anyone would recognize as a home, with several full rooms. Upward progress continued outside with the construction of a windmill to pump water from deep under the prairie. Then they began amassing a herd of cattle, until finally Frank left the Spade Ranch and struck out on his own, and he would never again work for an employer. The Norfleets' lives were twice riven by tragedy, when Mary died of diphtheria at age seven and when Robert Lee drowned at age two, but Frank and Eliza never dwelled on these sadnesses when recounting their early years. Their narrative was always one of steady material improvement. "From this time on, it seemed that everything to which we placed our hands prospered and multiplied," Frank would recall.

Their home was always open to visitors. One time Eliza woke up to find every bed in her house taken and sixteen pallets spread out on her yard. Another time she gave up her own bed and slept on the dining room table. One day, the family had just finished eating the noon meal when a man knocked on their door and asked for something to eat. Eliza made him up a plate, and when he was finished, he took off his wide belt, which had a pouch that hung down almost to his knees. He opened the pouch and spilled out gold dollars onto the table. He urged Eliza to take some, but she steadfastly refused. The man packed up his gold, went out back to the pasture, and spent the night under the mesquites. He was gone the next morning.

Yet by the time Norfleet was in his forties, he'd become a businessman with a keen eye for the main chance, someone not typically given to passing up gold dollars. In 1907, the Panhandle Short Line Railroad surveyed a proposed track between Vega and Big Spring that would run right through his property. That July, Norfleet and nine other men formed a corporation and platted a town ten miles west of the town of Hale Center, and they named it Norfleet. They hauled in a post office and a schoolhouse from nearby hamlets, and the postmaster built a general store. Norfleet began building a new house so that his children could attend the school. Pete, who was then seven years old, knew how to read every cow brand in the West but didn't know the alphabet. Norfleet had just gotten the framework up when he heard that the railroad had lost its financial backing and wouldn't be laying any more track. As quickly as they had arrived, the buildings were carted off. Norfleet

J. Frank Norfleet as a
young man

loaded the frame of his house onto a wagon and moved it to a draw
south of Cotton Center, where he finished it in time for the family
to move in on Christmas Eve. Norfleet officially became a ghost town
in 1913.

Norfleet continued adding horses, mules, and cattle to his ranch
and breeding them with a discerning eye, so that in addition to selling
them in the city by the carload each fall, he supplied breeding stock to
nearby ranchers. And he continued to amass ranch land. By 1919, the
year of his swindling, Norfleet was wealthy, the West Texas equivalent
of landed gentry.

Looking back on how he had accumulated and then lost his fortune,
J. Frank Norfleet considered his swindling to be entirely commensurate
with his other business dealings. "Quite frank"—as he put it—"I was
gullible." But he argued that his gullibility was only business instinct by
a different name. "With us of the Plains country, a man's word was his

bond. Our cattle deals, our land sales—transactions running into many thousands, frequently—were often completed 'sight unseen,' the whole agreements being based on verbal representations and verbal understandings. We never doubted each other; in fact, no graver insult could have been passed upon a neighbor than to demand legal formalities in dealing with him. If I was gullible, I was simply following the reasoning habits I had acquired in my lifetime of experience." It was a cowboy code of honor, and it persisted because it worked—not to mention that if it didn't work, if you ran a blazer on someone, you'd get shot, buried, or hanged.

But in their descriptions of this code, Texans dwelled less on the ever-present threat of violence and more on the generosity and largeness of heart that enabled all those handshakes. One Panhandle lawman in the late nineteenth century, a man named Jim Gober, the first sheriff of Potter County, a man tough enough to fatally wound the crooked town constable in a saloon fight, wrote down his version of the code in his autobiography, *Cowboy Justice*. "It's the degree of confidence and trust one places in me that measures my interest in them. If anyone comes to me in trouble and confides their grievances to my keeping, I immediately reciprocate with sympathy to the value of their spirit of confidence." Gober's words are practically an instruction manual for how to swindle him, and that is exactly the source of his pride in his ethics. He would rather be wrong than be distrustful.

Of course, we shouldn't be entirely taken in by the chest-pounding rhetoric in the cowboy code of justice. Mrs. Cicero Russell, the daughter of a Texas pioneer and cattle rancher, remembers that the code was only selectively in effect. "I tell you every[one] in this country stole cattle. Even my father has stolen nice heifer calves and nobody, even the big cattle men, ate their own cattle. When they wanted beef, they found a fat beef animal belonging to somebody else." Or take the testimony of Matthew "Bones" Hooks, a Panhandle horse wrangler. He was called before a judge who was also a prominent cattleman to testify in a dispute. "Bones, do you know anyone who has stolen cattle—" the judge started to ask, but just as Bones opened his mouth to answer, the judge caught the glint in his eye and hastily added, "—now?" He knew Bones was about to tell the courtroom the story of how he and the judge got their start in the ranching business by stealing a calf together.

Cattle rustling was as easy as one snip to the barbed-wire fence that Isaac Ellwood had worked so hard to develop and Norfleet to install.

If we take Norfleet at his word, his code of justice was so thorough-going it prevented him from returning to life as usual after it was violated, just as his father could not rest until the schoolteacher had made restitution to him. Everything he and his father had built in their combined sixty-five years as western pioneers vanished on that November day in 1919, except the conviction that dishonesty and deception could not be tolerated. The fabric of Norfleet's worldview was so thoroughly rent that he would put his entire life on hold to repair it.

Yet in his quest to patch the hole in his world, Norfleet ripped many new holes in it. He told his tale many, many times over the course of his long life: to the Texas legislature in 1921 to ask for reimbursement for his vigilante quests, to a subcommittee of the Sixty-eighth U.S. Congress in March 1924, to Max Bentley for a magazine serial in *McClure's* later that summer, to Gordon Hines for a newspaper serial that ran throughout Texas in 1927 and was republished as a book, to audiences around the nation in a lecture tour that retraced the steps of his hunt. His tale was worked up into a radio drama. Norfleet Productions began but never finished a silent film, starring J. Frank Norfleet as himself and supposedly directed by a relative of D. W. Griffith's, but what film existed has been lost since the 1920s.

The foundational text of Norfleet's story is his autobiography, *Norfleet: The Actual Experiences of a Texas Rancher's 30,000-Mile Transcontinental Chase After Five Confidence Men.* He wrote it in conjunction with an uncredited ghostwriter said to be the mother of Leif Erickson, who would later portray Big John Cannon in the Western television series *The High Chaparral,* and he published it with a regional press in 1924. Norfleet's gruff, no-nonsense voice comes through loudly, but other voices can be faintly heard behind his. In many ways, Norfleet's true-life story follows the literary conventions of the dime novels that he and his ghostwriter might have been reading at the time. Cowboy stories from Bret Harte to Zane Grey had already carved out a template for the adventures of a principled outsider who takes justice into his own hands to defend a preindustrial social order. Detective stories such as the Deadwood Dick tales portray operatives who infiltrate criminal gangs by passing as one of their members. Both kinds of popular novels were written specifically in opposition to urban capitalism, with their heroes as scrappy entrepreneurs of the lawless frontier. Norfleet's memoir prompts the question: Was his book shaped to fit these successful literary formulas, or did dime novels shape Norfleet's choices for how to live his life?

At the barest minimum, we can say that Norfleet did not alter the outline or details of his story as he repeated it. In almost every particular, Norfleet's autobiography precisely tallies with the many other versions of his story circulating through the media in the 1920s. Discrepancies, such as the dueling accounts of what happened in that Fort Worth hotel room when he pulled a gun on Spencer and Furey, are few. Perhaps this consistency is what makes Norfleet trustworthy.

Or perhaps it makes us his marks, because his story of what happened just after he realized he'd been conned snags on improbable coincidences, split-second timing, and clues that surface a bit too conveniently. In fact, the first two inductive leaps he made when beginning his hunt for Furey are so eyebrow raising that we never even have a chance to suspend our disbelief. Norfleet does not take the time in his autobiography to gain our confidence and soothe our ruffled suspicion. He plunges into the narrative as heedlessly as if, well, as if he were a hotheaded cowboy charging with an outstretched pistol into a den of thieves. His adventures are just too spellbinding. He must be putting us on.

CHAPTER FOUR

Humbug

When Norfleet asked himself where in the whole blessed country to begin looking for five men skilled in the arts of subterfuge, the image of a little red notebook floated up before his mind's eye. He hadn't consciously noted it before, but now that he thought about it, he remembered it as Furey's address book. He turned it around in his head, put it back down on the imagined hotel bed where he first saw it, and then on impulse picked it back up and opened it. The mental trick worked. Inside, he "saw" a long list of names written in different hands, and one in particular stuck out to him, a Mr. S. N. Cathey from Corpus Christi. Norfleet knew Cathey well, had hired one of his relatives on the Spade Ranch thirty years earlier, and though the name hadn't stirred anything in him when he first encountered it, he suddenly realized its potential significance. Cathey was now a landowner like himself, and his name was surely in the little red book because he was on Furey's sucker list. A flood had recently devastated Corpus Christi, and Norfleet could easily imagine Furey persuading Cathey to liquidate his already sodden real estate in pursuit of more durable coinage. Norfleet's first trip was to Corpus Christi to see if his old friend had encountered the gang of five, but he was told that Cathey was away in California on a prospecting trip.

While he was at it, Norfleet spent a night in San Antonio. He figured that since it was a sporting town, Furey's crew might have stopped over to spend some of the money they'd just lifted from him. He knew that detectives always start with hotel registers, so he headed to the St. Anthony Hotel and asked the clerk for the "tattle-tale." He saw that a certain "J. Harrison" had checked in a few days ago, and the *J* was written with the same flourish by which J. B. Stetson, a.k.a. Joseph Furey, had signed his bid sheets in the Dallas and Fort Worth stock exchanges. The clerk described Harrison as "about two hundred, great big fellow, good dresser, usually wore a black derby, good mixer and never drank." Norfleet thought, "There was no doubt now about him being Stetson," but J. Harrison had checked out and left no clues on his future destination.

Norfleet returned home to brainstorm the matter further, but it was Eliza who gave him his next lead. As they sat together one day, talking over the case while Norfleet cleaned his rifle, she mused that when Spencer had visited their ranch to survey it for the Green Immigration Land Company, he had spoken learnedly and amusingly of his travels all around the country—everywhere except the state of California, all mention of which was conspicuously absent in Spencer's conversation. Could it be, she wondered, because that is where the gang hides out? "You've hit it! You've hit it! That's it! That's the very reason they never yipped a word about the Golden State," Norfleet shouted, leaping up from his chair. His mind instantly made all of the connections. "It all comes to me now. See! they made a getaway from here the minute they got my money," he conjectured. "Sure as shooting, they gathered up Cathey at Corpus Christi and the whole outfit hit it straight for sunny Cal." The story felt so right to him that he wasted no time. Eliza helped him pack, and within two hours he was on his way to California.

This very thinnest of leads shot him all the way across the plains and deserts to San Bernardino. Why San Bernardino? Simply because he had to get off the train somewhere, and he decided to work the state from the bottom up. Norfleet later offered no other explanation for charging forth, as if this explanation sufficed. It was dusk when he arrived, and the decorations strung around the town reminded him that it was Christmas Eve; the holiday had utterly fled his mind when he'd had his revelation. As he walked around the neighborhoods, imagining the families inside and wondering what his own family was doing back at the ranch, he experienced the first—and really the only—moment of doubt in his quest. He longed to get right back on the train and return home before he exposed himself as a fool. But as he walked, the sights before his eyes began to meld with the thoughts constantly looping through his mind. He caught himself imagining Furey and Spencer squeezing down chimneys, scooping up the presents, and fleeing the way they had come. Norfleet laughed to discover that he'd become inescapably obsessed, then turned in for the night.

On Christmas morning, lonely and sheepish but still resolute, Norfleet went to the sheriff's office and met Walter Shay. Norfleet spilled his entire story to Sheriff Shay, sparing none of the details of his own gullibility and describing his enemies as precisely as he knew how. Shay let him get all the way to the end of his speech before replying. "The Sheriff's office doesn't make a general practice of giving every stranger in town a Christmas present," he said, "but I may have one for you!" It took a moment for the words to register with Norfleet. The sheriff beckoned him over to the cells and pointed: there, in adjoining cages, sat Ward and Gerber, the fraudulent secretaries of the Dallas and Fort Worth stock exchanges.

Norfleet's stomach turned, his entire body broke out in a sweat, and he felt a tingle run up and down his spine. And yet, despite his revulsion, his first absurd impulse was to wish his enemies a merry Christmas. After all, for most of the time that he'd known Ward and Gerber, they'd been his esteemed colleagues, crisp, well-dressed executives who had treated him with deference and respect. He marveled at how utterly their affects had changed and how little they resembled their former selves. Ward turned toward him sullenly and sneered like a common thief, "So you found us did you, you damned old fox?" Gerber, the one Norfleet had picked as the killer in the gang, was craven. "Norfleet, for God's sake, don't identify us!" he shouted. "Have mercy on us! Have pity for us! For God's sake, don't, don't identify us!" Keeping his face impassive, Norfleet turned and followed Sheriff Shay back to his office without a word.

As soon as they were out of earshot, Norfleet grilled the sheriff for the details of their arrest. Shay told him an extraordinary, an astonishing, a nearly unbelievable story. A Texan by the name of Cathey—did Norfleet know him?—was in San Bernardino for business and had fallen in with a group of phony stockbrokers. He was just about to close a deal with them, when he read in the newspaper of Norfleet's swindle. Cathey knew at once that he was in the hands of the same men, minus Reno Hamlin as the mule buyer, and he dashed from the hotel room he was sharing with the swindlers and accosted the first police officer he saw on the street. Alas, Furey's crew spotted him talking to the officer and fled the hotel. Furey and Spencer disappeared via the fire escape, but Sheriff Shay managed to intercept Ward and Gerber a few minutes later at the train station. He took the chance of detaining them long enough to wire Sheriff Sterling Clark in Fort Worth, and he received an instant reply to hold them under the warrant that Norfleet had filed after his swindling. In Ward's suitcase, they found precisely the same credentials and documents used on Norfleet. Only Furey, now going by the name of Peck, had bothered to change his alias.

The rapid capture of two of his men did not dampen Norfleet's fervor for the other three. While the Fort Worth authorities readied the paperwork to extradite Ward and Gerber to Texas, Norfleet continued scouring southern California for leads on Furey, Spencer, and Hamlin. He searched the telephone and telegraph records at all the San Bernardino hotels but found no trace of Mr. Peck. He visited police stations in the surrounding cities and towns, and in Los Angeles he had a minor score. While looking through the rogues' gallery of photographs, he identified a picture of Furey and learned his real name for the first time. And while he was in the big city, he thought he'd try his hand at disguise. He left his suitcase at the sheriff's office and sought out a suitably adventurous beautician to wrestle with his mustache. A few hours later, a clean-shaven businessman wearing a neat gray suit walked into the sheriff's office and asked for his suitcase. "Say! how do you get that way? Those things belong to a West Texas cow-man. What'cha tryin' to pull off?" Norfleet beamed in happiness.

Norfleet's escapades in California were soon brought to a close by a summons from the Fort Worth district attorney to appear at a grand jury hearing for Ward and Gerber's requisition. While the two men fumed in their California jail cells, Norfleet caught the next train east to Texas. He sat in the Pullman and thought about his case, his mind restlessly circulating around the same meager facts. And then an elderly man sitting across from him folded up his newspaper, leaned over, and introduced himself as Perry Garst. "I have just been reading about the capture of these fellows, Ward and Gerber. It looks like they're in for it now, doesn't it?" In high spirits, Norfleet cried that they would be if he had anything to do with it, and out came the entire story. Garst was riveted. By the time Norfleet finished his tale, Garst had decided to stop at Fort Worth with him to see how the trial turned out, and in the meantime he leaned in the corner of the car for a short nap.

As Norfleet watched the older man's head tip back into the seat and the light from the window play on his features, his mind suddenly froze. He knew that face. He was sure he had never met Mr. Garst before, but the characteristics of his face were undeniably familiar. And then he had it: Perry Garst was exactly what E. J. Ward would look like in thirty years. His newest friend was, he was instantly confident, the father of one of his mortal enemies, sent to tail him and reel out information from him. Norfleet cursed his own "egotism of the ignorant" for never even considering that the swindlers just might be as devious and obstinate as he.

Garst woke, reached for his suitcase, and drew out an elaborate luncheon of many tempting morsels. He offered them in turn to Norfleet, but, as if compensating for his previous susceptibility, Norfleet turned down everything—the sandwiches with their curly lettuce, the stuffed olives, the cream-filled cakes, the fruits. His paranoia was strengthened when Garst refused to eat his own food, claiming an upset stomach, and choosing for himself only two hard-boiled eggs. It would be difficult, Norfleet thought savagely, to poison two unbroken shells, and this small act told him all he needed to know about Mr. Perry Garst. He resolved to double his caution.

And then, in practically the very next instant, Norfleet broke his own resolution. His natural garrulity simply could not be held back, and he soon found himself in delightful conversation with a woman from Georgia. When he learned that she had been a detective prior to her marriage, he unstintingly granted her his confidence, telling her his tale of woe and giving her precise descriptions of the three men still at large. She promised to keep her eye out for them as she continued across the country, and to wire him with any leads. Norfleet stepped off the train at Fort Worth well satisfied with the progress he had made.

Garst stepped off the train with him but was prohibited from following Norfleet into the grand jury hearing. Norfleet testified against Ward and Gerber, and as he left the courthouse, Garst seized his arm and asked feverishly, "What did they do? What did they do? Did they bill those men?" Norfleet affected nonchalance. He had done his part, he said, and the rest was up to the jury. He began to walk away. Garst's voice grabbed at him again, saying that the hotels were booked up for a convention, so would Norfleet like to join him at the room he'd secured at a nearby boardinghouse? Once again, Norfleet declined, and eventually Garst gave up and took his leave. Norfleet shed his indifference, swiveled around, and did his best imitation of a private eye, trailing Garst into a poor district and up to the door of a disheveled house. When Garst was safely inside, Norfleet dashed back to the courthouse. He buttonholed Frank Evans, a newspaper reporter, and cajoled him into returning to the boardinghouse, hoping to confront Garst with their knowledge of his true identity and publish it as a scoop on the next day's front page. On the way back to the boardinghouse, however, Norfleet got lost, and by the time they found it, Garst was gone, and all traces of his stay had been erased. Norfleet took that as the strongest possible evidence that his supposition of Garst's relation to Ward was correct.

Norfleet's testimony that afternoon secured Ward and Gerber's extradition from San Bernardino to Fort Worth. Sheriff Sterling Clark personally escorted his charges back to Texas by train, and they spent the rest of the winter in the Tarrant County Jail. Norfleet simply couldn't resist visiting the two men in their cells and finding out the sequel to his swindling. Gerber matter-of-factly related how the men had congregated in the grillroom of the St. Anthony Hotel in San Antonio to divvy up Norfleet's cash. So the J. Harrison in the hotel register really was Furey! Cutting up the score, naturally enough, led to a poker game. Which, just as naturally, led to one of the men losing all his money—in this case, Reno Hamlin, fresh from his short stint in jail, who left in disgruntlement. Minutes later he came back, unnecessarily masked with a handkerchief, a six-shooter in each hand. He took the money and vanished. Ward and Gerber were locked up for a crime from which they never even had a chance to profit.

While Ward and Gerber made themselves at home in the county jail, Norfleet had another conversation that deflated his swelling sense of triumph just a little bit. He was at the jail when the pair of swindlers was visited by G. C. Cornwall, a U.S. Secret Service agent who helped identify them as accomplices in the swindling of a Washington, D.C., man, a furniture dealer named Peter Nee. Cornwall told Norfleet that Ward and Gerber were part of the infamous Furey gang that used to operate out of New York. "The photos of all the leaders are right here in this town," Cornwall informed him. "I sent them to the city detective a long time ago and asked him to be on the watch for them and to notify me if they appeared." Norfleet was knocked flat by this news.

How much easier would his search have been had he possessed photographs to show to sheriffs, hotel managers, and retired lady detectives? "You stay here and I'll go hunt them up and bring you enough pictures of that gang to make a big family album," Cornwall offered. But when he returned from the sheriff's office, he shook his head in frustration and told Norfleet that the office was claiming never to have received the photographs. Norfleet got his first inkling of the swindling and sleight of hand performed on the other side of the sheriff's counter. So when Cornwall launched into a lengthy speech intending to dissuade him from spending any more time or money hunting down Furey, Spencer, and Hamlin—pointing out that the Secret Service alone had fifteen hundred *trained* men sniffing out crooks like them—Norfleet was unmoved. The photographs may have been a false lead, but they gave him something invaluable: renewed conviction that only he was responsible for bringing about justice.

His disappointment was soon offset by a miraculous lead. The two swindlers he'd landed in jail would give him no information on the other three, so he found himself once again with a wide-open country to scour. And then he received a letter, forwarded to him at his hotel in Fort Worth, from the retired lady dick. A man had boarded her train in Houston who matched Norfleet's description of Furey down to the smallest pore. The woman moved close to him and eavesdropped on his conversation with a colleague. He started by telling the man that business in Dallas and Fort Worth "was as easy as running a picture show." Clearly, that could only mean one thing. She leaned in closer. He said he was on his way to Miami to play "the game." And then came the kicker, as he remarked in a casual aside, "I think I'll stop off a few days in Jacksonville; so many of the boys are down there, and I like to keep up with the 'gang' and find out who the 'new suckers' are." Indubitably, it was Furey. The wide-open country had telescoped down to a single city. Furey was squarely in Norfleet's sights, and just as soon as he'd acquired a small arsenal of guns, a suitcase full of disguises, deputy sheriff credentials, and arrest warrants for his remaining quarries, the cowpuncher hopped on the next eastbound train.

Let's take stock. First, Norfleet jabbed his finger at random on a map of California and just happened to find two of his swindlers. They just happened to have swept a fellow Texan and longtime friend into the con, a man who just happened to have read Norfleet's newspaper account in time to get wise and kick before he was cleaned out. Then Norfleet just happened to recognize a stranger on a train as the father of one of his swindlers in time to avoid further endangering himself. Finally, Norfleet described the ringleader to another stranger on a train, and she just happened to recognize that man halfway across the country and obtain precisely the information that Norfleet needed to track him down. All this in just twenty pages of his autobiography. Either the world was several orders of magnitude smaller in the 1920s, or something other than strict verisimilitude guides Norfleet's account of these events.

The first question his story raises is: Could he be conning us? His autobiography piles on the improbabilities without ever once acknowledging that they *are* improbabilities. He plays it so straight that it comes to seem like winking. For instance, the lady detective whom he meets on the train on his way to Ward and Gerber's hearing is named Mrs. Ward. "As far I know," he says neutrally, "this Mrs. Ward was in no way related to either E. J. Ward or his probable kin, Perry Garst. It was merely a coincidence." Later, in hot pursuit of Joseph Furey, he approaches a police officer on a street corner in St. Augustine, Florida, who turns out to be named . . . Ward. Norfleet merely writes, "Would I never get rid of the Ward family!"

On the one hand, perhaps Norfleet should be commended for sticking to the truth of his narrative, even when he risks our incredulity with particulars that no novelist could get away with. On the other hand, perhaps these inscrutable details and asides should signal something to his readers. The narrative sounds quite different from Norfleet's early life history. Instead of self-righteousness and moral rectitude, Norfleet projects a hokey humor and an extreme tolerance for moral ambiguity. When he finds himself almost broke in southern California, he takes a jaunt down to the racetracks at Tijuana. He finds a Texas horse on the program and bets his last $90. "It would be a poor Texas horse who couldn't win a little money for a Texas cowman, I thought." According to the autobiography, "my little baby" won and paid out at six to one—this from the same man who banned gambling from his ranch and preached to young men on living up to their mother's expectations. Norfleet justifies his vigilante quest as an attempt to restore his cowboy values that had been so summarily violated by the urban tricksters. But when he leaves his ranch and embarks on that quest, his values begin to drift away from their origins, and he starts to resemble his enemies more than he realizes. Take a man with a propensity for spinning yarns by the campfire, and then immerse him in the deceptive arts of the swindler: suddenly he almost seems to be impersonating himself and daring us to believe him.

This prompts a second and far more beguiling question: If he *is* conning us, do we mind? Arguably, the most defining—and perplexing—characteristic of an American sense of fun is a perennial willingness to make oneself into the mark of a showman, artist, or director. Audiences and spectators have relished the very particular pleasure of accepting an invitation into a story they know might be false, only to be immersed in it completely and then duped at the end by what they thought was true. It is a sensation that is composed of equal parts admiration for the cleverness of the ploy and gratification at a neat resolution, and it has a long pedigree in American culture. It is called humbug, and it all started with P. T. Barnum.

Long before he founded a traveling circus and made Jumbo famous in the Greatest Show on Earth, P. T. Barnum was a hoaxer. He came from western Connecticut, the land of wooden nickels, practical jokes, and Yankee dealings. His "organ of acquisitiveness," as he called it, was activated at an early age; his father died in 1825 when Barnum was fifteen, leaving him to support his mother and siblings by working as a store clerk in a nearby village. Barnum portrayed early market capitalism in the country as ruthless and exploitative. "Sharp trades, especially dishonest tricks and unprincipled deceptions," are not confined to the city, he warned. Women would bring rags of linen or cotton to his store to trade for dry goods, and he would later open the bundles to discover stones, gravel, or ashes. Men would bring oats or corn to trade for nails or rum, and later Barnum would weigh the loads and find them four or five bushels short. In such transactions, each party knew he or she was scheming to defraud the other, and the only question was who had enough savvy and insider knowledge to come out on top. Barnum's brilliance as a showman came from his insight that this same adversarial relationship might be transposed into the field of entertainment. Contrary to popular myth, Barnum never said that there is a sucker born every minute. He was not that baldly cynical about humankind. He did say, "The public appears disposed to be amused even when they are conscious of being deceived." And so he set out to deceive them in a thousand different ways with their full cooperation and a quarter from each of their pocketbooks.

In the summer of 1842, if you were a regular reader of *The New York Herald,* your curiosity might have been piqued by periodic mentions of Dr. J. Griffin, a British naturalist traveling through the southern states with an exhibit on loan from the Lyceum of Natural History in London, the preserved body of a mermaid captured in the South Seas near the Fiji Islands. Dr. Griffin first appeared in a dispatch from a correspondent in Montgomery, then one in Charleston mentioned him, and soon reports of him were issuing from Washington and Philadelphia. One Sunday morning in July, all three major New York papers reported that Dr. Griffin would soon come to the city with his tantalizing catch. For the next few weeks, everywhere you went in the city you would have encountered boys selling pamphlets titled *A Short History of Mermaids, Containing Many Interesting Particulars Concerning Them.* Handing over a penny and opening it up, you would have read that an "eminent Professor of Natural History in the City of New-York" testified to having examined Dr. Griffin's mermaid, and though he found her "far from being the beautiful and captivating creature represented by many pictures," she was most definitely real. "That the animal has lived, moved, and had its being, *as it is,* ADMITS NOT THE SHADOW OF A DOUBT, as all must acknowledge who see it."

When the Fejee Mermaid, as she began to be called, finally arrived in the city and sat in state at Concert Hall, the *Herald* dismissed her in two lines: "Humbug—the Mermaid—and no mistake. We can swallow a reasonable dose, but we can't swallow this." Yet in the very same issue of the newspaper, you would have read the following confusing information: "A committee of scientific gentlemen yesterday examined the mermaid brought to this country by Mr. Griffin, and now exhibiting at Concert Hall, No. 404 Broadway, and reported that notwithstanding they had hitherto regarded the existence of this animal as fabulous, and as an anatomical impossibility, they were now convinced to the contrary, and could plainly discover that the formation and anatomical construction of this creature would allow its being under water a great length of time, but that it evidently remained, for the most part, with its head out of water." So was the mermaid real or not?

When the *Herald* announced that P. T. Barnum had paid $1,000 for the right to exhibit the Fejee Mermaid in his American Museum on lower Broadway, you might decide it was worth the twenty-five-cent admission to see the creature for yourself. You would have headed down Broadway toward the Drummond light slowly revolving on a spear atop a five-story building. In a time of gaslight and tallow, this limelight was itself a wonder, a free attraction anticipating the treasures within. You would have waited in line and then wended your way through the exhibition halls packed and layered so tightly with wonders that you wouldn't have been able to take them all in: wax figures of European royalty, skeletons, taxidermied animals, live animals, dioramas, oil portraits, minerals, gems, optical instruments—and hundreds and hundreds of curiosities, from the miniature to the monstrous, from a straw taken from the mattress upon which Czar Nicholas slept when he visited Buckingham Palace, to a gigantic hair ball taken from the belly of a sow.

Perhaps, like Herman Melville, you would have simply relished the

One of the images P. T. Barnum used to advertise the Fejee Mermaid at the American Museum in 1842

museum's "lean men, fat women, dwarfs, two-headed cows, amphibi-
ous sea-maidens, large-eyed owls, small-eyed mice, rabbit-eating ana-
condas, bugs, monkies and mummies." Melville was a great admirer of
Barnum, and it appeared to him that the organization of the universe
had bent itself to accommodate the American Museum. "If the whole
world of animated nature—human or brute—at any time produces a
monstrosity or a wonder, she has but one object in view—to benefit
Barnum." Perhaps, like Henry James, you would have loved the American Museum's "spurious relics and catchpenny monsters in effigy, to say
nothing of the promise within of the still more monstrous and abnor-
mal" with a "passionate *adverse* loyalty." James remembered that when
he was a boy, he and his family "attended this spectacle just in order *not*
to be beguiled, just in order to enjoy with ironic detachment and, at the
very most, to be amused ourselves at our sensibility should it prove to
have been trapped and caught."

You would have ascended the staircase to the Second Saloon, past
the dioramas and war relics and daguerreotypes. And then at last you
would have come to a tall glass bell sitting on a table and, underneath
it, the Fejee Mermaid. The object at the heart of all those words was, in
Barnum's own later confession, "an ugly, dried-up, black-looking, and
diminutive specimen, about three feet long. Its mouth was open, its tail
turned over, and its arms thrown up, giving it the appearance of having
died in great agony." The mermaid was unquestionably humbug, the
head and torso of a monkey sewn to the body of a fish.

Almost certainly, had you been in that stifling and crowded museum
in 1842, you would have done what thousands of visitors did. You would
have peered as closely as the bell jar allowed to see if you could spot
the seams joining the monkey to the fish. That bend of the waist, that
squint of the eyes—*that* was the foundation of Barnum's genius and
his fortune. He realized that the mermaid's exposé was a single and
relatively insignificant moment in an otherwise lengthy production.
The exhibits were not simply static objects in glass vitrines; they were
occasions for dramas that swayed thrillingly between suspicion and
credulity. Nineteenth-century visitors seemed always to be game for
the intellectual challenge and never to resent the way Barnum played
with their perceptions. As Lawrence Weschler observes in *Mr. Wilson's
Cabinet of Wonder,* the spectator "continually finds himself shimmer-
ing between wondering *at* (the marvels of nature) and wondering *if*

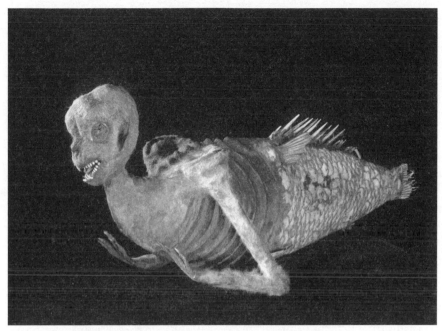

Barnum's Fejee Mermaid as it exists today in the Peabody Museum of Archae-
ology and Ethnology. The museum lists the materials of construction as fur,
ceramic, fish skin, tooth, animal claw, wood, papier-mâche, and wool.

(any of this could possibly be true). And it's that very shimmer, the
capacity for such delicious confusion . . . that may constitute the most
blessedly wonderful thing about being human." So that's why so few
visitors complained about the deceptions. Neil Harris, one of Barnum's
biographers, believes the showman was distinguished by "a peculiar
and masterly way of manipulating other people and somehow making
them feel grateful for being the subjects of his manipulation." Barnum
brought out something livelier and more interesting in his visitors than
simple umbrage.

In his 1855 autobiography, Barnum confessed that he had rented "her
fish-ship" from his colleague Moses Kimball and that it was probably
crafted in Japan, the birthplace of unicorns, phoenixes, triple-headed
snakes, and other fabulous creatures residing in curio cabinets around
the world. Barnum further revealed that Dr. Griffin was, in reality, a
confederate named Levi Lyman. "Dr. Griffin" never set foot outside of
New York. All those dispatches from the South were written by Barnum
himself, then sent to friends in southern cities and mailed north with
the requisite postmark. The woodcuts, the pamphlets, the transparency

outside of Concert Hall had all been commissioned by Barnum. Every notice in the *Herald*—except the two-line declaration of humbug—was an unsigned, paid advertisement written by Barnum. In the first four weeks that the mermaid was on view at the American Museum, attendance almost tripled, and Barnum made more than $30,000 that year.

Yet Barnum's customers were not dim-witted, inexperienced, or overly susceptible. His attractions called forth not their naïveté but their rational skepticism, not their blind faith but their empiricism—just like a swindler. Barnum's critics found his deceptions too uncomfortably similar to those of Samuel Williams, the Confidence Man. Melville, for his part, made sure his readers understood the connection by describing his protagonist in *The Confidence-Man* as an "original character," who is "like a revolving Drummond light, raying away from itself all around it—everything is lit by it, everything starts up to it." But Barnum strenuously—if disingenuously—denied the similarity. In 1865, he published a book titled *The Humbugs of the World* in which he defined humbug as "putting on glittering appearances—outside show—novel expedients, by which to suddenly arrest public attention, and attract the public eye and ear." Humbug is merely publicity, not deception. "An honest man who thus arrests public attention will be called a 'humbug,' but he is not a swindler or an impostor," insisted Barnum, as long as he gives them "a full equivalent for their money."

In fact, as Barnum knew full well, it was precisely *because* his exhibits veered so close to con artistry that audiences found them so exhilarating. Visiting the American Museum was not all that different from running into a well-dressed stranger who asked you for your watch. Barnum's exhibits invited spectators to think like speculators. When they opened the morning newspaper to an advertisement for a mermaid, the issues that confronted them were fundamentally market based. As the historian James W. Cook argues, nineteenth-century urbanites continually needed to pose and answer questions such as "Is this advertised commodity genuine? How much should I pay to find out? Are the remarkable claims in the papers to be trusted? or is this merely another overrated fraud in a vast sea of dubious commodities?" Humbug is the characteristic stance of American capitalism, what Jackson Lears calls "vernacular philosophy for a society on the make." It is a game with its own self-referential rules that begins the instant the viewer recognizes that a deception is being practiced upon him or her.

The value that structures this game is not truth or beauty but irony: the invisible, unbridgeable, yet palpable difference between what is indicated and what is meant. There is no attempt to conceal the fact that the showman controls the game, but the spectator is invited to join as an intellectual equal who fully consents to the rules. And it is flattering to be welcomed into a deception as a knowing participant of guile and cunning.

P. T. Barnum was not, strictly speaking, a con man, but perhaps he softened the moral hardness toward deception and made the swindlers' jobs a little easier. Certainly as the popularity and geographical reach of humbug escaped the city, swindlers found they didn't need to wait until potential marks disembarked at the train station before hooking them and taking off the touch. Beginning in the 1870s, swindlers began to use the mails to draw their victims to the city with circulars offering them "green goods." They'd comb lists of reputable businessmen as compiled by credit-reporting agencies like R. G. Dun or the Bradstreet Company, and they'd send out letters by the tens of thousands to cities around the nation. "Dear Sir," read one such letter. "Your name was sent to me by a reliable person in your town. He said he knew you to be a man who was not adverse to making money in any way, manner, or form, and that he knew you were up to snuff." The letter writer would then wink and nod, saying something like "I am dealing in articles, paper goods—ones, twos, fives, tens and twenties—(do you understand?)." Some circulars would be even more explicit, offering to sell the recipient "the best and safest counterfeit money ever put on the market." The recipient could buy the money for a fraction of its face value: $1,500 for $75; $4,500 for $125; $6,000 for $180; $10,000 for $220; and, for the truly go-ahead man, $30,000 for a mere $400.

The circular would direct the mark to a hotel in New York, where he would be met by a steerer who would swear him to confidentiality and then bring him to a secret office. A distinguished gentleman would show him a sheaf of bills, genuine bills masquerading as counterfeit, and the mark would be so astounded by their verisimilitude he would eagerly part with his own savings, only to discover that the satchel he received in exchange was stuffed with green-colored paper. One steerer, who worked for a green-goods kingpin named Eddie Parmeley, estimated that Parmeley would take the touch off at least fifteen and as many as thirty marks a day in amounts ranging from $300 to $1,000 apiece. For those who could not make it to the city in person, the letter would offer $1,000 in counterfeit for a deposit of $20, saying, "I will trust you for the balance until we meet face to face to show you I have the best of confidence in you." The green-goods men garnered a fortune in $20 bills from the hinterlands.

Another version was the "gold brick" swindle, where a respectable businessman would desperately need to sell a block of the precious metal on behalf of a friend, who had come into possession of the gold during a mining dispute. The mark would be shown a heavily gilded lead block with a slug of real gold in the center, to ensure that a sample taken from it would test as authentic. This was a trap only the wealthier marks could afford, for a $9,000 brick would sell for the still significant price of $7,500.

With a swindle for every income bracket and the means to reach marks in their hometowns, no one need be left out of the busy urban market in fraud. The culture of the city streets—its ethics, its assumptions and conventions, its language—had overrun the urban grid and now extended deep into the nation. Green-goods circulars appealed not only to the mark's greed but also to his unwillingness to be left behind in the sprint into the future. Green goods grew out of humbug, but its structure prefigured the big con, and many of its elements—the steerers, the green-colored boodle, the bribes to policemen and detectives— would soon be imported wholesale into the phony stockbrokerages and betting parlors.

No matter where one lived, by the end of the century it was impossible to be innocent of humbug. Barnum had injected a new stance into American popular culture; winking had become a recognizable cultural code. His success with the Fejee Mermaid proved eminently repeatable, and he went on to present a wild buffalo hunt in Hoboken, a maneless horse covered in woolly fur supposedly captured in California, the wooden leg that Santa Anna had lost on a Mexican battlefield. As this list suggests, Barnum found inspiration for many of his hoaxes in the folklore and mythology of the American West, importing into the urban centers of the Northeast the untamed energy of the frontier. If, in the 1880s, deceptions as serious as cheating at poker on the Texas plains were still punishable by hanging or burying, nonetheless a new and separate exemption had been carved out for deceptive entertainments. Norfleet would have been equally capable of killing a crook and chortling at a Barnum exhibit. Humbugging and running a blazer were two points on a long continuum, with confidence artistry somewhere in between.

So is Norfleet humbugging us with his story of the mark turned ace detective, and if he is, are we entertained or aggravated? How much of our pleasure in Norfleet's adventures is dependent on their truth? It turns out that if we decide to pull a Norfleet on Norfleet—to chase after the man and attempt to pierce through the scrim of the deception—what we find is a kind of reversed Fejee Mermaid.

The unadorned facts of Norfleet's account of hunting down E. J. Ward and Charles Gerber check out. Norfleet did indeed put two notches in his belt almost immediately upon starting his vigilante sleuthing, and independent sources like newspapers and court documents make it possible to fill in dates and details for his adventure tale. There are only a few disquieting inconsistencies.

On December 21 or 22, S. N. Cathey did indeed stop at the Sunset Hotel in San Bernardino. He fell into conversation with Charles Gerber, who invited him for a walk down the street. As they sat down on a park bench, Cathey discovered a lost pocketbook. Inside were the exact same documents that Norfleet had examined in the Adolphus Hotel in Dallas: a code cipher, a letter warning against undue publicity, a membership card, a bond, and a receipt. Gerber suggested they return the wallet to its owner, a man named E. J. Ward, but Cathey balked and the play floundered.

Sheriff Walter Shay did indeed spot Ward and Gerber at the Pacific Electric Depot in San Bernardino just before Christmas, and he did indeed arrest them as they attempted to board an eastbound train. He confiscated their baggage and examined it when he returned to his office, finding the same pocketbook with its now-familiar five slips of paper. Shay, however, claimed that this arrest happened on December 16, five or six days before Cathey's arrival in the city. Certainly it happened before December 23, because by then the governor of Texas had issued extradition papers for Ward and Gerber; therefore, Norfleet couldn't have arrived at the San Bernardino jail on Christmas morning, as he'd so dramatically portrayed.

It is true, though, that Ward and Gerber must have been terrified at the testimony that Norfleet would be able to give against them. They spent over $10,000 and hired two of the best criminal attorneys in the State of California to fight their extradition. It was rumored that at their final hearing in district court, they were going to stage a fake fight and then slip away in the company of their colleagues planted in the audience, but the courtroom was heavily guarded. The proceedings were routine. Their writ was dismissed, and within half an hour they were on the Sunshine Special, headed for Fort Worth. They arrived handcuffed to each other, but otherwise looking the very picture of respectable businessmen. Norfleet was standing on the steps to the jail. As Ward and Gerber passed by him, none of them said a word.

Jesse M. Brown, the district attorney for Fort Worth, wrote in his own autobiography, "Some of the facts recited in [Norfleet's] book are exaggerated." But it is true that in May 1920, District Attorney Brown did indeed prosecute Ward and Gerber separately in two jury trials. Norfleet testified in both trials—wearing, according to the International News Service, "a sombrero and a corduroy suit out of the plains"—and in what remains of the court transcripts, we can see that his testimony tallies perfectly with his later autobiography, sometimes nearly word for word. This is either reassuring or deeply suspicious. On the stand he recalled Furey's words upon sending Spencer out to the Fort Worth exchange for one last gamble: "Today will be the last day that we will be on the anxious seat." He recalled Spencer's fearful cries when he pulled a gun on them in the Westbrook Hotel: "Before my Angel Mother in Heaven, with the Bible lifted up to Heaven, before my Angel Mother, I swear to you that I never did prove false and never will prove false to you." Under oath, he told the jury that Furey quelled his fiery temper by giving him a Master Mason's sign—which, you'll remember, was the second of two versions of how the altercation was smoothed over. Norfleet's wife and son also testified, giving their version of Spencer's visit to the ranch as a representative of the Green Immigration Land Company. Mr. Cathey and Sheriff Shay testified to the San Bernardino chain of events. And the *real* secretaries of the cotton exchanges in Dallas and Fort Worth testified to never having transacted business with Ward and Gerber.

Neither defendant brought a single witness to the stand but instead attempted to stall and obfuscate by filing a small forest's worth of legal motions. Their lawyers bickered with each other about who should be tried first. Gerber even attempted to invalidate his trial by giving up Reno Hamlin. He filed a bill of exception pointing out that Hamlin was also indicted by the same grand jury and arguing that Hamlin should be tried first and, in the event of his acquittal, Hamlin's testimony be used to acquit Gerber. Gerber alleged that "the said Reno Hamlin, alias R Miller, now is and *is* residing in the town of Cleburne in Johnson County, Texas, about thirty-five miles distance from Fort Worth, Texas, where this court is in session, and that he is living there openly and notoriously, and without any effort on his part to secrete himself from the process of this court, and that he can be arrested upon said charges at any time under the orders of this court." Gerber's attempt to turn in Hamlin instead caused the judge to dismiss the case against Hamlin. Gerber must have howled in outrage. And yet, just a few days later, Reno Hamlin found himself unceremoniously dumped in the county jail. The court's dismissal of Hamlin's indictment was apparently a ruse to draw him out into public life, and it worked exactly as planned.

Ultimately, none of these procedural tactics made any difference. Within eleven days of each other, Ward and Gerber were both found guilty and sentenced to the maximum penalty of ten years in the Texas state penitentiary at Huntsville, putting Norfleet's tally at three out of five swindlers behind bars. When Ward heard his sentence, he murmured, "Ten years—the limit," but he smiled at the jurors as they left the jury box. Ward's and Gerber's cases were appealed and Ward was released on a $25,000 bond, but he was almost immediately rearrested and extradited to Washington, D.C., presumably for swindling Peter Nee. The day he was to stand trial in November, he was found in his solitary cell with his head battered, cut, and bruised. He was taken to the hospital, treated, and returned to his cell. Not long thereafter, groans were heard, and when the guards rushed in, they discovered Ward dying for real this time, having done the job right with a surgical knife he'd stolen from the hospital. Ward was the first but not the last casualty in Norfleet's manhunt.

But if we bend toward the vitrine and peer closer at this strange beast of a story, even the tentative, provisional certainty we've just arrived at begins to falter. The bare outline of Norfleet's story checks out, because its details reside in the records of district courthouses, but so much of his story—all of the most interesting parts, in fact—lies outside the historical record. There was no stenographer in the Norfleets' kitchen that winter day just before Christmas in 1919 to transcribe the conversation in which Frank and Eliza hit upon California for his next destination. The Associated Press article about Norfleet's swindling, the one that ran in papers all over the country, the one that Cathey saw in San Francisco in time to break the con men's spell, has not yet surfaced. Norfleet said that the article ended with his direct appeal to readers for clues leading to his criminals' capture. "Letters from every part of the country poured in for three years," he claimed. Perhaps he was telling the truth, and the newspaper article still lies hidden in an archive of a local library somewhere in this huge country. Or perhaps there was no newspaper article. There might not even have been that conversation at the kitchen table. *The Plainview Evening Herald* reported that Mrs. J. F. Norfleet joined her husband in Dallas on December 5, and the two of them didn't return to their ranch until December 23, the day that Ward and Gerber's extradition papers were issued.

The Fejee Mermaid was definitively a fraud, with just enough verisimilitude sprinkled on top to make it perplexing. Norfleet's story is unquestionably true, with just enough embellishment sprinkled on top to make it spicy. Of course, Norfleet had plenty of incentives to embellish his tale besides the cowboy's natural tendency toward spice, and the story of the newspaper article is a convenient one. Perhaps, in 1919, he was not quite so willing to publicize his own gullibility as he was in 1924, when he wrote his autobiography, and the newspaper article exists, but under an assumed name. Or maybe he had virtually nothing to do with the capture of Ward and Gerber, and he inserted a newspaper article into the story to make himself more central to the adventure. Or just maybe he was absolutely crucial to Ward and Gerber's arrest, but his methods were underhanded or illegal enough to jeopardize their eventual conviction. The deeper we travel to the heart of this story of deception, the more entwined become the hero and his villains. These doubts about Norfleet's sleuthing methods arise at exactly the point in his chronicle when he begins to assume the tactics of a master swindler. To get the rest of his con men, Norfleet would become an impostor.

Perhaps, just perhaps, we can profit more from Norfleet's story by allowing ourselves to be his marks than by letting our skepticism ruin the adventure. After all, a willingness to be humbugged characterizes the finest minds. As Barnum himself said, "The greatest humbug of all is the man who believes—or pretends to believe—that everything and everybody are humbugs." The Prince of Humbugs wants nothing to do with such a killjoy. "He thinks himself philosophic and practical, a man of the world; he thinks to show knowledge and wisdom, penetration, deep acquaintance with men and things. Poor fellow! he has exposed his own nakedness. Instead of showing that others are rotten inside, he has proved that he is." In fact, humbug points to more than an individual virtue; it underscores a value crucial to the functioning of American civic culture. As *The Literary World* opined on the occasion of the Confidence Man's debut in 1849, "It is a good thing, and speaks well for human nature, that, at this late day, in spite of all the hardening of civilization, and all the warning of newspapers, men *can be swindled*," because it proves that men still retain the capacity for trust. So, to preserve the very foundation of American society, let us agree to believe J. Frank Norfleet and his extraordinary adventures. Even if the ensuing chapters make that more difficult still.

CHAPTER FIVE

Double-Crossings

Norfleet left Fort Worth after Ward's and Gerber's trials, and with Mrs. Ward's tip as his only lead he headed to Florida. His first stop was Tallahassee, where he managed to gain an audience with the governor and obtain a requisition warrant that would allow him to take his men out of the state without interference from local officials. Then, since he had absolutely nothing to go on, Norfleet canvassed Jacksonville, St. Augustine, Tampa, and St. Petersburg. In each town he visited the sheriff and the chief of police and combed through the photographs in their rogues' galleries. He spent hours at a time hanging out on board-walks and piers, watching the crowds and hoping to spot a familiar face.

In St. Petersburg, he met an elderly couple, the Bockermans, who'd just been swindled out of $10,000 in a real estate deal, and he took a diverting couple of days out of his own manhunt to track down their three swindlers. Twice he located them; twice he approached a police officer and pointed out the men; twice he watched as the police officer thanked him for his service and then sauntered off to "an important engagement." He grew doubly frustrated, at the corruption that didn't even bother to disguise itself and at the loss of time from his own quest. "There seemed to be just two of us, myself and my gun," he concluded. This was an unforgivably disingenuous statement. There were actually *five* of him, because Norfleet had four guns on his person.

He had read in the newspaper a few days earlier that three swindlers had been apprehended in Tampa. By now his search carried him along on its own logic, and so, "one lead being as good as another, I left for Tampa." The train ride gave him time to reflect: clearly, his method of capturing swindlers by emulating a police officer was flawed. He would have to sneak up on the police just as he was trying to sneak up on Furey; he would have to ease information out of people and nudge them into doing what he wanted, and for that he needed to steal a trick not from a detective but from his very prey.

He unfolded the newspaper with the article about the three swindlers, and with hands more accustomed to lassoing and branding than needlework, he carefully cut it out and pasted it inside the first page of the current day's paper. He was making a blute, a fake newspaper clipping designed to elicit both information and trust. The insideman in the big con would often pull a blute out of his wallet and reluctantly show it to his mark. Its photograph would be blurry, or even torn in half, the paper would be creased and worn, and the article itself would be vague, but the mark would rush to fill in the perceptual blanks and see what the swindler wanted him to see. The blute would testify to the insideman's notoriety in the world of finance, and the mark would soon regard the swindler the same way the newspaper did: as dangerously successful. It was a way to invert the relationship between con man and victim, making the mark eager to be included in the swindler's trusted inner circle and allowing the swindler to adopt the position of skepticism, requiring the mark to earn his confidence. Furey hadn't used a blute on Norfleet, but somehow he'd learned the ploy. Norfleet took to calling it "my Extra" and would use it as a conversation starter whenever he arrived in a new town.

As soon as Norfleet disembarked at Tampa with the newspaper under his arm, he looked around for a venerable officer of the law. He "grinned a grin as wide as the prairie," adopted his most exaggerated redneck accent, and approached the officer, unfolding the paper to his article and asking if the man could please explain the words "bunco" and "con." The cop looked at him with incredulity and asked if he really didn't know what those words meant. "No, I don't," declared Norfleet. "I thought mebbe as how you'd learn me?" So the cop, warming to his subject, began to enumerate the various categories of swindles and scams. He was soon joined by two other officers, to whom Norfleet turned and earnestly exclaimed, "I never heered the like of it. Gol dern their hides, if they ain't got more nerve'n a pack of coyotes! I never heered none of 'em howl!" The officers laughed indulgently and then began talking among themselves. "Say, fellows," said one of them, "I just got a tip, personally, that one of the links in the big con-chain has opened headquarters in the Montezuma Hotel, in Sanford." Norfleet bowed away, then slipped onto the next train to Sanford.

When he appeared on the columned porch of the Montezuma Hotel, he was painted in local color. He'd seen from the train the vast fields of celery that grew stoutly in that part of central Florida, lending Sanford its nickname of Celery City, so at the first possible opportunity he'd tramped around a muddy celery field, ruining his leather shoes and staining his pant cuffs up to the shins. Now, in the lobby of the Montezuma, he moved slowly to allow himself to be seen. He checked in under the name of Parkinson, then surveyed the long room and picked a chair in front of the fireplace with a good view of the staircase. He proceeded to peel the mud off his shoes and trousers, shaking his head in rue while keeping an eye on the men who walked through the room. At length, an elderly couple could not resist asking if he'd taken a fall into the mud. Why, no, he had not, he answered loudly. He was a stockman from Blackwell, Oklahoma, he boomed, but he'd heard about the crisp investment potential in celery fields, so he'd come over to Sanford to take a look, and he thought he might well make a purchase.

The lure he'd thrown into the waters of the lobby netted him a fish the first thing next morning. On his way to breakfast he thought he saw a dapper young man with sleek blond hair approaching him. Norfleet readied his face in a pleasant smile, and sure enough the blond man sidled up and began making small talk. Eventually, he came to the point. "I believe I heard you mention a celery farm. I happened to be passing through the lobby last evening and I thought I understood you to say you intended purchasing one." He extended a manicured hand. "My name is Johnson."

Norfleet had his lines ready. "I went out to look at one last night and got mud up to my ears, almost. It's dirty work, this personal inspection, but a man cannot afford to sink forty or fifty thousand dollars into the mud, unless he's sure it's rich mud, can he?" And Norfleet smiled equably, giving time for the figure to enter Johnson's head and find its place in the equation he was drawing up in his mind. When the number clicked, Johnson smoothly moved to the next line, telling Norfleet that he was in luck, because Johnson just happened to know quite a bit about celery farming—"Can't we find a comfortable seat?"—and he'd be happy to advise him on his future purchase. Johnson proceeded to disparage the land and industry of Sanford, stressing the difficulty of growing celery and the risk of the investment, but then he began to talk up the land around Daytona Beach. Why, he was going up to Daytona that very afternoon, and if Parkinson would care to join him, he'd be happy to give him an agricultural tour. It seemed to Norfleet that he was awfully eager to move the action to Daytona, so he protested a little for form's sake but soon acceded to a plan that included checking out of the Montezuma and taking the train up to the beach. Norfleet packed two of his guns in his luggage and two in his suit.

The men fell into a rhythm of conversation with just a hint of an adversarial tone to it. "I was determined that he shouldn't get the better of me with his politeness," said Norfleet. Underneath the courtly pantomime of their conversation, Norfleet admired Johnson's professionalism. "It always amused me to note how well these crooks played their roles. No character actors surpass them. Johnson began to fit into the groove. He had a certain patronizing manner which they all have." Norfleet's nature as a practical joker simply could not resist the opportunity to upset the script in nettlesome little ways, all the while allowing its grand arc to carry him to what he hoped were the winter quarters of Joseph Furey.

So when Johnson jumped up from his seat on the train and stared out the window in total astonishment, exclaiming that he'd just seen someone he knew motoring by, Norfleet said, "I saw him, but he looked about the same as many other men. Was he peculiarly marked?" Johnson was unperturbed. That man, he explained, was Steel, the infamous trader who'd taken $125,000 out of the stock exchange in just one day. And that evening when they arrived in Daytona Beach, Norfleet lagged behind Johnson as they walked down the main street, and he popped into a small guesthouse to book his own room for the night, upsetting the roper's plan of rooming together. But Johnson did not disappoint; he only appeared to let Norfleet off the leash, when in fact Norfleet witnessed him spending the night on a bench in front of Norfleet's room. Johnson knocked at his door promptly at 8:00 a.m. to begin the next stage of the con.

Johnson proposed that they take a walk on the beach, and knowing exactly whom they'd encounter, Norfleet assented. Sure enough, they soon spotted a man walking toward them in apparent oblivion to the beauty of his surroundings, his face buried in a yellow sheaf of telegrams.

He did not raise his head even as his shoulder brushed Norfleet's, so engrossed was the important man in his important work. Only when he had settled down on a large piece of driftwood did Johnson bend down to whisper excitedly to Norfleet that the man who'd just passed was the same man he'd spotted from the train, the stock trader whom he'd had the good fortune to meet once. "I think I'll speak to him and see if he remembers me," he concluded. "By all means, do!" Norfleet urged.

They approached; Steel feigned offense at the imposition; Johnson persisted, and Steel melted into courtesy when he remembered Johnson. As he explained away his initial hostility, Steel's words, or at least Norfleet's version of Steel's words, resonated with unintentional double meaning: "They are so damned clever you know about getting things out of you that you don't suspect you are giving away, that I have to be very cautious with whom I talk. We manipulators, you understand, must protect the secrets of our business. Publicity has ruined many a good man!" The play continued: Johnson asked Steel to submit a $20 bid for him and Steel good-naturedly agreed, striding the few blocks into town to the local exchange and returning within the half hour. The $20 magically bloomed into $40, and then $80. Steel finally invited the men to join him at a private exchange. He explained that some of the members had rented a clubhouse high on the cliffs above the beach where they were betting on horses, and his chauffeur would be happy to drive them up. On cue, Norfleet agreed.

But on the way up to the clubhouse, Norfleet's self-confidence began to ebb. The drive was taking much longer than he'd anticipated, and he was acutely conscious of how far behind lay the safety of town. Every bump in the road heightened the paranoid feeling that he was heading into a trap. He wrenched his mind away from such thoughts and told himself to use what he had. At the next bump in the road, he flung himself against his companions and under the cover of clumsily extricating himself from the tangle of bodies, he felt their hips: no guns. He felt marginally reassured, until they arrived at their destination a half hour later. The club turned out to be a sprawling mansion wedged into the side of a cliff above the sea. It had quite a view, but Norfleet's nerves happened to be a little edgy, and the jagged rocks that broke up the surf below looked not only like a threat but like a foreshadowing of his fate. Steel curtly ordered the chauffeur back to town.

But it was what lay inside the clubhouse that tautened Norfleet's quivering nerves. Across from the front door was a table. Upon the table was a heap of money. And on either side of the money was a man standing guard, each one holding a carbine rifle and wearing a six-shooter. The sight confirmed what Norfleet had begun to suspect, that this go-round of the big con was not going to play out like his experiences in Dallas and Fort Worth. He'd come to expect that the threat of violence undergirding the swindle would, like the profit that was its denouement, be kept offstage until the very last instant. But Steel's exchange was playing by a different rule book, and Norfleet would need to learn it on the fly. Steel and Johnson headed out of the room to enact some private business, telling Norfleet the exchange was not yet open and inviting him to see what he could see while he waited.

He looked around the rest of the room. To the left of the money was a sweaty young man with rolled-up shirtsleeves who was frantically chalking and erasing stock quotes on a blackboard. In the center of the room sat the telegraph operator with the customary green eyeshade. And across from the blackboard sat two businessmen with their eyes riveted on the stock quotations. He recognized none of the faces. The room was silent but for the clicking of the telegraph machine and the booming of the waves below the picture windows.

He headed toward the pile of money, and since no one moved to impede him, he touched some of the bills in their banded packages, astonished to find that they were genuine. For the slimmest of moments, Norfleet allowed his self-righteousness to shade into self-pity: here were hundreds of thousands of dollars begotten in the same manner as his lost savings, a heaping, spilling mountain of money that represented uncountable hours of hard work stolen away. But then he continued his nonchalant survey. He noted that aside from the room which Steel and Johnson occupied, the rest of the story seemed unused, the rooms empty or even boarded up.

Just then, another insistent sound was joined to the steady click of the stock ticker and the booming waves—the buzz of a motor-boat. Norfleet looked down to see a single man sitting in it. The man was heading directly for the dock at the foot of the cliffs under the clubhouse. The stock ticker clicked. The waves boomed. The motor churned, but still no one said anything. To Norfleet, it simply did not feel right. Since he could find no trace of Furey, he decided to leave. He moved toward the front door, through which he could now see the man from the motorboat running up a set of stairs, but before he could get to the door, Steel stepped in front of him, blocking his view.

"We have an ideal location for work, haven't we?" Steel asked. Norfleet replied that it seemed to suit Steel's purposes perfectly. "In that minute of fill-in conversation," Norfleet later recalled, "Steel and I knew that we were wise to each other. I could feel that he knew I knew he was ready to use desperate methods." This gang's method, apparently, was to lure wealthy men up to their club and then "roll" them for everything they had on them. Steel and Norfleet stared at each other. It was as if the gauntlet had been thrown, but the fight could not start until the man from the motorboat finished his ascent up the stairs on the cliff.

At last, the man burst into the room, looked wildly around, and then moved over to Steel. He tried as surreptitiously as he could to slip Steel a piece of paper. The other men in the room studiously went about their business. Norfleet did his part by pretending not to notice, but it was impossible for him to ignore the change that came over Steel as he read the note. He blanched and his hands began to shake. He tried to speak, but his dry throat wouldn't let the words through.

It was Norfleet's chance, and he began to move toward the door. Steel moved with him, synchronizing his backward steps to Norfleet's forward ones. Johnson called out from across the room for Norfleet to join him and start the betting. Without turning around, Norfleet declared that he must be going. Then he saw Steel move slightly to the side, as if trying to position himself behind Norfleet's back. This alarmed him as much as anything else he'd seen that afternoon. Norfleet sidled up to the edge of the room with the wall at his back. Turning to face the rest of the men, he waved his arm in a broad good-bye to the assembled company. Steel lunged. He grabbed Norfleet's waving hand and pulled the shorter man toward him, but Norfleet was ready for him. Norfleet's other hand suddenly held a six-shooter, which he jammed into Steel's solar plexus, drawing out a wince. "Stick up your hands! Hold 'em high!" Norfleet yelled. Most of the other men in the room were frozen by Norfleet's gun, the money guards without cover to reach for their own rifles, but Johnson was coming at him with a rope held taut in his two hands, ready for Norfleet's neck. Norfleet pulled out his other automatic and fixed Johnson in place with it. "Now you two young fellows just walk out of this front door straight to that automobile," he commanded, relishing the look of surprise on their faces when they realized that their car and driver had not, actually, returned down the hill as Steel had ordered. Norfleet had paid the driver to wait for him. As they headed to the car, Norfleet addressed the other men: "If you fellows start anything with me, I'll finish it for you. I hope that's plain to you!" And he backed out of the clubhouse.

Norfleet guided the two men into the backseat of the convertible and shut the door. He climbed onto the running board and stretched over the back of the car so that he could keep his guns trained on Johnson's and Steel's backs. Thus arrayed, they slowly wound their way down the cliff to Daytona Beach. Despite the dire situation, Norfleet felt distinctly cheerier than on the drive up: the menace he'd sensed was now explicit, and that made his strategizing much easier. Yet the game that he'd begun a few days earlier as a celery farmer was nearly played out.

He asked the driver to let them off at a city park of live oaks and Spanish moss. Johnson and Steel sat down on one of the log benches and began imploring Norfleet to let them go. First they tried the sympathy angle: Steel told the sad tale of his eighty-four-year-old mother whose heart would break if her only son went to jail, and Johnson implored Norfleet to think of his invalid wife with their four baby girls. Then they resorted to money: they both spilled out gold, silver, and bills onto the bench. The note that the man in the motorboat had delivered to Steel also tumbled onto the bench. Steel reached for it, but a little puff of wind blew it down to Norfleet's foot. He picked it up and stuffed it in his pocket.

Norfleet relished having the upper hand, but he knew he had no charges against Steel and Johnson, and his recent experiences had taught him exactly how much he could expect from the local police force. Johnson and Steel's importuning was therefore unnecessary, for he had to let them go. He sent them off with a wave of his hand, but as they started to speed walk out of the park, he called them back to retrieve the money they'd thrown at him. The two men paused, suspicious of the request. "Make it snappy," Norfleet growled, "because I've something to teach you the quick-step with if you don't!" Johnson and Steel scooped up the bills and coins, stuffed them back in their pockets, and disappeared.

Norfleet returned to his bungalow, packed his bags, and caught a ride to the train station. Once he was settled into his car on the train, he remembered the note that Steel had received in the clubhouse. He dug into his pocket and pulled it out. It read, "That is Norfleet, himself. Don't get him started. If you do, he'll kill every dam one of you. Don't let him get away, boys. Don't let him get away!—Joe." So Johnson and Steel *had* been working with Furey. They had failed to keep Norfleet in their grasp, and he had failed to detain them long enough to learn how they were connected to his man. He wondered just how close he had come to a violent end in the clubhouse. Many months later, he would have a chance to ask Furey that very question, and Furey would reply, "Johnson might have strangled you with that rope; Steel might have shot you; or they might have bound and gagged you, then weighted and dropped you from a boat a mile or so out at sea; all depending on the circumstances, and the originality, imagination and resourcefulness of the one doing the job." So much for the swindler's pride in committing only nonviolent crimes.

It wasn't long before Norfleet started to catch more tantalizing clues of his prey. He took the train down the Florida coast, and since he had nothing else to do, he resumed his round of visits to sheriffs and police chiefs. In Miami, he met a mayor from a town in Ontario who'd just been swindled out of his savings by three men. When Norfleet showed him Furey's photograph, he shouted, "That's the man who did the job! He's the one who got my money!" He sent Norfleet to the hotel where Furey had been staying, and the landlady confirmed that a man matching Furey's photo had just checked out the day before. Neither the mayor nor the landlady could provide Norfleet with any hints as to where Furey might have gone. But then Norfleet chatted up some federal officers, and they alerted him to a con they'd tried to track in Key West. An Illinois farmer had fallen into the old stock swindle, but on the train home to gather up his savings, he'd gotten suspicious, so he'd gotten off the train in Miami and alerted federal agents. The only way the feds could get involved would be if the swindlers used the mail or telegraphs, so the farmer had tried to entrap them. He had wired his son back in Illinois and instructed him to wire the swindlers to ask if the farmer could send the money rather than deliver it himself. But the swindlers never replied, so the feds could not press charges. The farmer went back to Key West to collect his belongings. As soon as he arrived in the train station, the three swindlers grabbed him, threw him in their car, and drove him outside the town limits for a thorough beating. When Norfleet arrived in Key West, the farmer was only too happy to show him where the fake stock exchange was located, right before he left the state for good.

Grimly, Norfleet began a round-the-clock stakeout. He reasoned that Furey and his accomplices would stay in Key West until they'd made at least one score. The farmer had directed him to a long, three-story office building facing a busy street on one side and backed up against a seawall on the other. During the daytime, Norfleet had no problem blending in with the pedestrian crowds on the sidewalk in front of the building. His only problem was outlasting the storm that had blown in from the ocean. He stood there hour after hour, completely drenched, craning his neck to see past the thick chain of umbrellas slowly moving down the sidewalks. As darkness wore on and the crowd of business-people began to disperse, he worried about finding a secluded place from which to spy, but the storm that he'd been cursing brought him a bit of luck. The wind blew down a fir tree almost directly in front of the entrance to the building. The felled tree was across the street and catty-corner to a fence, making a little triangular pen that was perfect for Norfleet's ambush.

And then he saw him. Just as dusk was shading into night, a man of Furey's size and build entered the offices. Norfleet couldn't make out his face, but he instantly recognized his stride. All Norfleet would have to do now was wait until the con man reemerged, and then he'd run up and arrest him. So Norfleet waited. All night long, he crouched in his corner, and when morning light began sifting back into the sky, he was soaking wet, stiff with cold, aching from immobility, and bleeding from scratches on his arms that he had gotten as he'd held back the branches to peer at the building. The man he'd thought was Furey had not emerged.

Certain his target was still inside the building, Norfleet decided to risk abandoning his post just long enough to gather reinforcements. He went to the sheriff's office, and as fast as he could, he explained the scenario. The sheriff understood at once. Apologizing that he himself could not take on the job owing to a foot injury, he promised to send two of the best men on his force to help Norfleet take down the gang leader. Norfleet returned to his post.

Two hours later, the officers arrived. The larger of the two took command. "You take care of the front," he told Norfleet; his colleague would watch the side; "and I'll go through the place an' if I don't catch him I'll scare him out to one of you!" Norfleet returned to his vigil at the entrance while the other two men took up their posts. Just seconds later, what should he hear but the incredible sound of a motorboat chugging at the back of the building. He dashed around to see Furey and the two officers speeding out to sea, already too far away to reach by pistol shot.

Well, at least he'd been right that it was Furey. Norfleet was not one to stand around cursing the gods. He assumed the trio was heading to Cuba, eighty-one nautical miles to the south. Within hours, Norfleet had a new passport in his pocket and a chartered hydroplane under his feet. Binoculars glued to his eyes, he ordered the pilot to head first to Miami before turning south to survey Havana and all the little islands in between, but he could not spot the three men or their boat. He returned to land, and a few days later he returned to Texas, called home by a telegraph from his son Pete to attend to ranch business.

Back at Hale Center, Norfleet had some time to think. It was the spring of 1920, and Ward, Gerber, and Hamlin were in jail. Furey and Spencer were still on the loose, but he'd followed up and laid to rest every last clue that he'd generated in the months since his swindling the previous November. He had no leads, and Furey knew Norfleet was onto him. Well, there was one lead. In the days after his swindling, on his way to his friend Cathey's ranch in Corpus Christi just before his fateful trip to San Bernardino, Norfleet had stopped in San Antonio. He'd spotted Furey's handwriting in the signature of J. Harrison on the register of the St. Anthony Hotel, and then he'd gone to the police station. The cops, as usual, were unhelpful, but he'd gotten into an intriguing conversation with a girl who had just been arrested, and it was that conversation that seemed newly promising in retrospect. The girl was a pretty, slight young woman with a foul mouth and an arrest warrant for shoplifting. She brayed her innocence as loudly as she could. "I didn't swipe all of the things they found in the room," she cried. "I only copped one piece of junk, a Hudson Seal coat. I swear to God! I never lifted nothin' else." When Norfleet suggested that she simply return the coat, she laughed bitterly. The coat was the one thing she no longer possessed, having sold it to a big spender at the St. Anthony Hotel. Norfleet now recalled that the girl didn't know the man's name, only his room number: room 113. Could that have been Furey? If it had been, would that tiny fact lead him anywhere else?

Norfleet was dying a slow death at home. He was caught between two increasingly miserable circumstances. On the one hand, his swindling losses and the money he'd spent on the manhunt had brought him close to broke, and his absence from the ranch had begun to affect its day-to-day workings. Eliza had taken on the ranch duties but had pared them down to fit her capabilities; she switched from cattle to turkey and hog raising and began to grow crops on a small scale. On the other hand, as he later confessed, "My hot-blooded ambition to accomplish what I had set out to do warped my judgment." His life's work now aimed straight at Furey, and everything else was subordinated to his need to avenge the injustice Furey had perpetrated on him. The winter before he'd met up with Furey, he'd purchased about three hundred cattle at $50 a head. Now the clue given to him by the shoplifting girl grew in his mind and formed itself into a plan. He sold the cattle at $23.75 a head, pocketed the cash, and headed back out into the world. As he wrote, "I turned my attention to trailing a fur coat instead of a live man."

And so he traveled back to San Antonio, but this time he was not alone. He brought with him Jesse Brown, the Fort Worth district attorney who'd proved so helpful with Ward and Gerber's capture. Brown's presence paid instant dividends: the San Antonio chief of police was suddenly entirely willing to help Norfleet on his quest. The three of them went to the St. Anthony Hotel and soon confirmed that J. Harrison had indeed stayed for three days in room 113 last December. Since Furey had not been wearing a seal coat when he'd dashed down the fire escape after Cathey kicked to the San Bernardino police, and since the coat was not found in the luggage he left behind in his mad escape, Norfleet reasoned that perhaps Furey never brought it with him to California. Perhaps he shipped it from San Antonio before he left. The three men combed through the express mail records but found nothing that might correlate with a fur coat mailed during Furey's three days in San Antonio. The parcel post records were off-limits, but Jesse Brown found a federal official who could grant them access. And there it was on the now-dusty record: a package, weighing several pounds, shipped to no one, from no one, during the span of days in which Furey had resided in San Antonio. It was the only package without a sender's or recipient's name. It was not insured, because that would have required a signature. It certainly looked like a package that was meant to slip through the mails unnoticed. It was directed to No. 506 Stanford Court Apartments, San Francisco, California. And as soon as he saw that address, Norfleet headed to California once again. He and Brown left that very night.

The westbound train left them in San Bernardino, and they decided to wait until the next morning to head up to San Francisco. Since they had some time to spend, they stopped in to see Sheriff Shay. He had no new leads for them since he'd handed over Ward and Gerber just after Christmas, but he was glad to see the two men and invited them out to dinner. Brown accepted, but Norfleet was just too restless. While his friends entertained each other, he visited the Stewart Hotel, where he now knew that Furey had stayed under the name of Peck during Cathey's swindle. Norfleet's detective skills had evolved since he'd first consulted the "tattle-tale" in the St. Anthony Hotel. This time, he asked the clerk for the hotel register and the phone log, and by cross-referencing the two, he discovered that Furey had sent a telegraph to "684 Glendale." Furey knew someone in Los Angeles.

Norfleet charged out of the Stewart Hotel, fairly flew up to his hotel room long enough to leave Brown a note, and caught the very next train to Los Angeles. The first thing he did upon arrival was check into the Alhambra Hotel and call 684 Glendale. A woman answered and Norfleet asked, "Who is this speaking?" "This is Mrs. Furey," the woman replied. "Whom did you wish to speak to?" Oh, how Norfleet wished he could have answered her question truthfully! But instead he apologized for dialing a wrong number and hung up. He'd tracked Furey *to his own home*. Norfleet danced around his hotel room as if he were riding a bucking bronco. As he later put it, "I do not think if I live to be one thousand years old that I will ever again feel the same wild thrill of triumph."

For the second time in two days, Norfleet did not wait for Jesse Brown; first thing the next morning, he looked up Furey's address in the phone directory and headed to the suburb of Glendale. Norfleet walked the wide, palm-lined streets, past block after block of modern bungalows on neatly trimmed lawns, and then noticed in quiet amazement as the bungalows gave way to mansions. He turned onto Piedmont Park, made his way down to number 412, and stared at the Furey residence, a large manor with stone pillars and a lush garden. Nothing moved in the early morning haze, and the cowboy just gaped at the columns, trees, and vines. And then Norfleet's appreciation of Furey's real estate turned practical. He surveyed the house for its exits and, in addition to the front door, noted three doors in the rear of the house letting out onto the orange grove, the vineyard, and the garden. Directly across from Furey's manse was a park, and farther down a hospital was under construction. Norfleet decided to pose as a landscape gardener.

For two days, he shaded his eyes to peer up into trees, got down on the ground to sift the soil, drove stakes he'd whittled into the ground, and scrutinized a set of blueprints he'd filched from the construction site trash. In those two days, he saw nothing of interest at 412 Piedmont Park except a young woman who exited the house on the second day. She was about thirty years old, pretty, and well dressed, and she got into her sedan and drove away, then returned a short while later.

Norfleet's breakthrough came on the third day. A little boy in blue linen pants ran out of the front door and began to play on the sidewalk, bouncing a rubber ball into the gutter. He looked to be about eight years old. Norfleet asked himself if it was ethical to pump the boy for information about his father. "It wasn't a pleasant thought," he admitted. "But as I stood watching him springing up and down in play, I thought of the countless other children, hungry, destitute and orphaned, that this little fellow might have his pretty ball and smooth green lawn to play upon." His plan thus justified, he sauntered over. "Well," he called, "that's a fine ball you have there." The boy agreed that it was, and when it bounced over to Norfleet, the boy gladly engaged with him in a game of catch. Casting about for an opening, Norfleet ventured, "You ought to have a nice little puppy to play with. They are great play-fellows for little boys." Jackpot on the first try! "I'm going to have my doggy soon as my papa comes home," the boy informed him. "And he's coming home in a few days too." With a start, Norfleet realized that in a few days it would be Christmas; for the second year in a row, the holiday had almost passed him by in his engrossment with chasing Furey. "That will be fine to have the little dog," he said, already beginning to back away from the little boy. "They are good friends for boys." And he turned and began to walk quickly away. "When my papa gets home my pockets will just stick out with money," called out the boy.

Norfleet made straight for the Los Angeles sheriff's office, where he saw Under Sheriff Al Manning. He described his three-day stake-out and the information he'd obtained from Furey's son, and he asked for help in surveying the home until its master returned. Manning promptly assigned two of his best deputies, Walter Lips and William Anderson, and Norfleet took them right to the Furey residence. They didn't stop, but drove around while Norfleet pointed out the entrances and escape routes. They hatched a plan: Lips and Anderson would dis-guise themselves as telephone repairmen and gain entry to the house while Furey was gone so they could map the house from the inside. That very evening, they carried out the plan, and afterward Lips met Norfleet back at the station. He told Norfleet that everything had gone perfectly and that he'd left Anderson back at the property on all-night watch. He stripped out of his repairman costume in a hurry, eager to eat and then get back to rejoin Anderson. "And believe me, Norfleet," he added, "don't you ever think if Joe Furey shows up there that he'll ever get away. We're no suckers!"

The two deputies followed this routine for the next few days, only one of them reporting back to the station at a time so that the house never went unwatched, yet neither had any news. Norfleet began to grow suspicious. They had warned him to keep far away from the house so that Furey wouldn't spot him and bolt. But could they have had another reason for keeping Norfleet away? Norfleet just had to find out. One evening, he snuck to the Furey house and spied around, try-ing to find a single sign of Furey, Lips, or Anderson. He couldn't see either of the officers on duty. The next morning, he marched into Man-ning's office and told him what he'd done. Manning burst into laughter. "Didn't see 'em! Didn't see 'em!" he shouted. "Why if you could see 'em, so could everybody else! My God, man! They're working under cover." Norfleet cringed. Of course that was true, and he resolved to let the professionals do their job. In the meantime, he had other leads to fol-low. After all, there was still the intriguing matter of the sealskin coat.

Jesse Brown had joined him in Los Angeles, and Norfleet suggested to him that they call Sheriff Shay and invite him up from San Ber-nardino to join the mission to the Stanford Court Apartments in San Francisco, where the package had been shipped. Shay accepted, and the three men took the morning train up the coast. They checked into a hotel, and Norfleet registered under a pseudonym, borrowing the name of E. H. Shaw from a cattleman in Orin Junction, Wyoming. Before casing the apartment building, they made the usual round of calls: to the San Francisco chief of police, to a reporter at *The San Francisco Call and Post* who'd been sworn to secrecy, to the Oakland police station and district attorney's office. None of these visits produced any information, and Norfleet could practically feel the money leaking from his wallet. While Brown and Shay busied themselves by questioning law enforcement officers around the Bay Area, Norfleet took the cable car up the hill to the corner of Powell and California.

Once again, Norfleet was fairly ambushed by luxury. Stanford Court turned out to be an enormous residential hotel built at the top of Nob Hill. The entrance was a circular carriage drive around a fountain that led into a lobby with a grand stained-glass dome. The building teemed with liveried doormen in the public areas and white-capped maids at the apartment windows, and when Norfleet approached the front desk to ask after a resident, he was told that he could not enter the building without a signed order. This would take a bit more care and thought than he had anticipated.

He watched the doormen for a while, then picked out a particularly friendly one, an older Irishman with a florid nose. Norfleet hung around the building until the man's shift ended, then called out to him as he passed by, "Say, do you know where a Scotchman could get a little smile?" The man leaned in close to Norfleet and murmured, "I know where an Irishman and a Scotchman could get a smile—if the Scotchman had the money." Minutes later they were ensconced in a speakeasy, talking like old friends. By now, Norfleet knew not to ask direct questions, so he never did learn the name of the family living in number 506. "All I found out was the license number of the car owned by the people living in the apartment, and that a mother, her daughter and two sons lived there."

The next day, with a new set of doormen on watch, he decided to try again to enter the building. He got into an elevator, but the operator asked if he had permission. Norfleet said no and pleaded ignorance, but the operator took his job very seriously. He blew on a whistle, and instantly two security guards had Norfleet by each elbow and were marching him out of the lobby. Norfleet sorted through his options and decided to fall back on his old redneck routine. They crossed the street and continued marching down Powell, past the Fairmont Hotel, then past an alley in which they could see a service elevator that looked to Norfleet like an entrance to a coal mine. He stopped short. "Well, I'll be dinged," he cried. "What d'ye know about that? I always heered as how Frisco was a great minin' town, but I never expected to see a coal mine dug right off the sidewalk." The guards laughed, relaxing their grip and letting Norfleet lead them farther into the alley. The service elevator opened, and a bellboy came dashing out. Norfleet popped out his eyes. "Why they even got brass buttons on the miners!" he marveled. His guards laughed again. Then Norfleet swung around, his six-shooter in his hand. "Now you better get back to your Stanford Court and attend to your business there if you have any," he snarled into their frozen smiles. They backed out of the entrance and ran off.

Norfleet returned to his hotel, temporarily discouraged about cracking the facade of the great Stanford Court. He thought about the mysterious woman living behind lace curtains, a beautiful sealskin coat hanging in her closet. Who was she? It occurred to him that to catch a woman, he might need the assistance of a woman. And there he was stymied, for where in the big city of San Francisco would a lone cowpuncher from Texas be able to befriend a trustworthy and respectable young woman without raising alarms? He decided to sleep on the matter.

The telephone awoke him the next morning, an unctuous voice asking for Mr. Shaw. Blearily, Norfleet remembered that he'd checked in under a pseudonym. He answered as Shaw and learned that the caller was a reporter looking to interview him about sheep and cattle conditions in the western United States. Norfleet thought to himself, "It would not do to undeceive them as to my identity. That would only bring more publicity down on my head." Apparently, it didn't occur to him simply to turn down the interview request. He was by now far too ensnared in the logic of imposture to break character, and, damn it, Norfleet was enjoying himself. And so he gave the interview, his opinions ranging widely from Hollywood starlets to the advisability of women's clubs. So amiable was he that he was invited to a banquet that very night at the Wool Growers' Convention. Norfleet himself had grown wool, so he could see no problem with continuing the impersonation a little longer. He ate sumptuously that night and gratefully accepted a cup of coffee after the meal, only to discover that it was rather adulterated. Two cups later, Mr. Shaw was invited to give a speech. Norfleet, ever game, got to his feet—"at least that's where my friends told me I stood"—and launched into a rip-roaring polemic on the wool industry and the price disparity between raw wool and finished yarn. His fellow farmers cheered. The next day, Norfleet's speech was printed in all the morning papers with the heading "Wool Grower Pulls Some Wool off the Eyes of His Brother Growers." The convention goers never did find out how much wool was pulled *over* their eyes.

This breezy little side note in Norfleet's autobiography, a story unconnected to his vigilante quest, seems quite deliberately planted, a kind of literary blute that exists to testify to Norfleet's growing mastery of himself, his worldly ability to change shape and smoothly match others' expectations. No newspaper articles with Shaw's interview or his rousing convention speech have yet surfaced. Norfleet seems to be pushing onto his readers this image of himself as a master of disguise, perhaps even falsifying it to inflate his point. But, like the swindler's blute, we aren't meant to bend down and squint at the details, because if we did, we might notice how very different *this* Norfleet is from the rancher at the beginning of the book, the one who lived by cowboy ethics and wouldn't have tolerated a liar—much less an urban sophisticate with liquor in his coffee—for longer than it took to rope him with a lasso. This Norfleet simply wants us to admire his imposture and move on.

After recovering from his encounter with San Francisco black coffee the next morning, Norfleet remembered that Jesse Brown was visiting some friends in town, a woman and her daughter. Might their help be enlisted in penetrating the luxury fortress of Stanford Court? Brown agreed to arrange a meeting, and in an Italian restaurant Norfleet met Mrs. Jesse Carson and her eighteen-year-old daughter, Lucille. Norfleet charmed the two women but said nothing of his quest. He allowed Brown to fill them in on the details that night after he left, and then the next day he made a proposition: Would Lucille be willing to act out a role for an afternoon? She eagerly assented, and they devised a character and some lines upon which she could improvise. Gravely, Norfleet asked Lucille if she was capable of flirting. "She lowered her eyes and admitted that if it was absolutely necessary, she could—a little." She'd be perfect.

The next day, Norfleet lurked in the lobby of the Fairmont Hotel and watched as Lucille, dressed in a little girl's frock that made her look fourteen years old, disappeared into one of the Stanford Court entrances. She did not appear for quite some time, and Norfleet allowed his excitement to grow; if she was still inside, the chances were high that she was succeeding at worming her way to apartment 506.

Finally, she came dashing over and told her story. As instructed, she'd pretended to be on an errand from her mother to collect money for a puppy that she was selling to the woman in number 506. She'd flirted with the elevator boy on the way up, and no one had made a move to bar the girl from entering. She'd knocked at the apartment door, and when a little boy and a young woman answered, she gave her spiel about the puppy. The children called for their mother, and a harried-looking woman came into the room. Lucille showed her the slip of paper on which her mother had written the address, and while the woman examined it, Lucille looked around the living room. She saw no photographs of Furey, but she did see a black derby hat on the coatrack and, artfully draped over a chair in the corner, a Hudson seal coat. The woman told Lucille she'd made a mistake, that the address written on the paper was apartment 501; anyway, she said peevishly, she didn't want any dog because she'd had one that died and she didn't want to get attached to another animal. Lucille drew her out further. How had the dog died? The woman replied that it was a canine flu. Oh, exclaimed Lucille, she happened to have a remedy for such an ailment. Might she send it to the woman? The woman agreed and said to mail it to her, Mrs. Mabel H. Harrison. Lucille made her good-byes and left. She flirted with the elevator boy again on the way down, telling him sorrowfully that she had not yet sold the puppy. She said that perhaps the Harrisons would buy the dog when the father came home. The elevator boy said that the father was an important stockbroker who worked in New York and came home every six months. The family was expecting him home in time for Christmas. Lucille wrote her phone number on a slip of paper and pinned it to the boy's cap, telling him she'd split the profits from the puppy if he'd tell her when Mr. Harrison came back.

Norfleet was overjoyed with the information procured by his new protégée, a girl who was so adept at winning confidence that she could peddle a cure even after the pet had already died from the disease. He remembered that in the suitcase they'd taken from E. J. Ward when they arrested him in San Bernardino, they'd found a checkbook belonging to Furey, in which some of the stubs were made out to M. H. Harrison. Clearly, she was Furey's mistress, and she was expecting him home any day now.

That night when he returned to his hotel, Norfleet found a message from one of the contacts that he and Brown had made, informing him that Furey was currently registered at the U. S. Grant Hotel in San Diego. Norfleet took the next train south, stopping in Los Angeles to check on Lips and Anderson's surveillance operation, and then, when he learned that they'd not yet spotted Furey, continuing on to San Diego. Once there, the tip proved utterly false. Furey was not at the U. S. Grant, nor was he at any of the other hotels. Norfleet hung around for two or three days, taking a quick jaunt down to Tijuana to bet on the horses and augment his expense account, but he made no progress and soon returned to Los Angeles.

He went right to the police department, though it was late at night, and whom should he see but Under Sheriff Manning in huddled counsel with Lips and Anderson, the very officers who were supposed to be staking out the Furey residence. "If someone had dashed a pan of ice water in my face," Norfleet wrote, "it couldn't have struck me with more of a shock than I felt as I entered that place and saw the three of them, heads together, talking in low tones. I knew at once I had been double-crossed." But he didn't let it show. Thinking quickly, if not clearly, Norfleet pretended to have tonsillitis. "Hello, boys!" he rasped. "Has anything developed?" The officers replied that nothing was new, and Norfleet made them repeat it over and over, as if his tonsillitis had also affected his hearing. He reasoned that by playing deaf, he might lull them into thinking they could discuss sensitive matters within his hearing. It didn't work, though he hung around the station for hours. All he managed to confirm, from the contemptuous glances the men threw his way and their references to him as "an old damn fool," was that they were supremely confident in their deception of Norfleet.

It would take a few months, but Norfleet would have his revenge on those deputies. On March 3, 1921, the Los Angeles district attorney, Thomas Lee Woolwine, arrested Deputy Sheriffs Walter Lips and William Anderson and stripped them of their badges. The city was stunned. Only a few weeks earlier, the *Los Angeles Times* had celebrated

Lips and Anderson for capturing the two kidnappers of Mrs. Gladys Witherell. Anderson was an officer widely known to the public because he'd killed several rascally bandits in the course of his career. Walter Lips, for his part, had previously served for five years as chief of the Los Angeles Fire Department. Just one year into his appointment as chief, when Lips was given a gold shield set with diamonds as part of a municipal craze for bejeweled badges, Mayor Owen McAleer noted that he'd earned his title the hard way: "Chief Lips entered the department as a hoseman and by his own energy, brains, honesty and carefulness had arisen to the highest appointment in the department." Both Lips and Anderson were prominent in local politics, and both were said to be candidates for the sheriff's job, the current sheriff having been ousted the very evening before their arrest. Anderson appeared puzzled by the arrest, reportedly asking as the cuffs were snapped on, "What's it all about?" The answer: extorting and accepting a $12,000 bribe from Joseph Furey to let him go after arresting him on Norfleet's warrant in December 1920.

As Norfleet would later learn, Furey did indeed return to his Glendale home just before Christmas, only to be ambushed by Lips and Anderson. Furey tried to escape out the kitchen window, but the officers caught him after firing a shot in his direction, bundled him into a patrol car, and took him to the Long Beach Hotel. Behind the locked hotel room door, they made their business proposition: he could either give them $20,000 and go home to his wife and son, or they could turn him over to District Attorney Woolwine. Furey counteroffered with $15,000 but told them it would take him some time to raise that much money. Lips and Anderson held Furey captive in the hotel for three days. Anderson accompanied Mrs. Furey to the bank, where she withdrew $2,300. Then one of the officers drove her to the local elementary school. She pulled her son, Marc, out of class, brought him back to the bank, and asked him to sign his name to a withdrawal slip. She proceeded to clean out the little boy's account, taking $7,700 and leaving $33. On the third day, Lips and Anderson brought Furey to San Francisco, but not before arranging to clear Norfleet out of town with the false lead in San Diego. Less than an hour after he departed, Furey and the officers checked into the hotel room he had just vacated. Furey got in touch with Mabel Harrison and arranged for her to bring the rest of the money and meet him at the Oakland Cemetery. When Lips and Anderson received the cash, Furey was once again free to leave with Mabel, but the two deputies would have only two months to enjoy their windfall. It would not prove enough time. After their arrest, when the district attorney opened a safety-deposit box that Anderson had taken out under the name of Stafford, it still contained $2,100.

After their indictment, the former mayor McAleer helped post Lips's bond, joining with the former assistant fire chief and Lips's sister to raise the $20,000. Anderson's bond in the same amount was posted by a fellow deputy sheriff and a mysterious woman named Venus Morgan, reputed to be the wife of an oil stockbroker. Before their trials could get under way, the newspapers reported, Lips made a full confession to District Attorney Woolwine. "We were tempted and we fell," he reportedly said as he bowed his face into his hands. Not so, cried Lips to the newspapers the next day. "Neither of us has seen the District Attorney since our arrest over a month ago," he claimed. "It seems this statement at this time is along the lines of the District Attorney's policy, when he said, 'If you can't convict a man, mess him up so he will not be able to walk the streets of Los Angeles.'" Both deputies continued to plead not guilty.

Lips's trial began on June 16, 1921. The first witness was Norfleet, whom the *Los Angeles Times* described as "a small, compact, quiet-looking man" and a "hero." The newspaper marveled over Norfleet's restrained testimony, noting that he could have stolen the show by describing his cross-country adventures but instead opted straightforwardly to answer the prosecutor's questions. The prosecution also called Sheriff Al Manning, the manager of Mrs. Furey's bank, and the manager of the bank that held Anderson's safety-deposit box. But the star witness of the trail was Mrs. Dede Furey, who had been estranged from her husband since four months before her son's birth and who wanted no part of his criminal enterprises. She testified to cleaning out the fund of money she'd been saving for her son's musical education. The International News Service reported, "Her recital of the sacrifice of savings of the past 10 years in order to help her husband was almost totally devoid of emotion."

The defense rested without submitting a single witness or piece of evidence. In his closing argument, Lips's attorney admitted that the deputy sheriff had indeed overstepped his job description in asking Furey for the money and that Lips was guilty— guilty of an excess of pity in allowing Furey to raise bail money before being booked to ensure that he could return to his family as soon as possible. The jury took twenty-seven minutes to find Lips guilty. The decision was appealed all the way up to the California Supreme Court, but ultimately Lips was sentenced to one to fourteen years in San Quentin. Anderson was able to delay his trial for another year, until finally, in April 1922, he too earned up to fifteen years.

But at Christmastime back in 1920, Norfleet did not yet have the satisfaction of knowing the crooked officers would be straightened out under the iron of his sworn testimony. All he knew was that he could not rely on their surveillance and that Furey could be anywhere. And then he got another lucky break. A contact he'd made in the telegraph industry informed him that Dede Furey had just received a last-minute Christmas present from her husband: Furey had wired her a sum of money from Jacksonville, Florida. Was this tip, too, a ploy to get him out of town and out of the state? Norfleet, apparently, never even considered that idea. Three and a half hours later, he was on an eastbound train in blistering pursuit of a nemesis who grew in his mind with each close call and missed opportunity.

CHAPTER SIX

A Small History of the Big Con

In his heyday, newspapers called him the "internationally known confidence man," "one of the smartest confidence men ever to operate in this country," and "one of the most dangerous confidence men in America," yet despite a fulsome chronicle of his deeds in hometown newspapers across the country, Joseph Furey never quite rose to public consciousness as an outlaw. He was born in Vancouver, Washington, in the mid-1870s, and almost as soon as he was able, he started getting himself arrested, serving time in 1895 and 1897. In the first decade of the twentieth century, he booked stays in jail cells in Portland, San Francisco, Kansas City, and Trenton. His prison vacations were always short, and he was always back on the streets within months. As early as 1904, newspapers began identifying him to their readers as "well known to the police as an expert at the bunko game"—well-known if not yet particularly adept.

Joseph was one of a distinguished brotherhood of criminals. His father, Terence Furey, was a respectable citizen in Vancouver, but he spawned five sons who resembled one another in their hulking size and their illegal proclivities. One son, John, managed to avoid a life of crime, but only because he died early of blood poisoning, contracted when he was bitten in a brawl in Portland, Oregon. Tom, Harry, and Edward were as shiftless as their brother and frequently worked with him, but only Edward attained Joseph's level of professionalism and notoriety. Only a year apart and strikingly similar in appearance, Joseph and Edward were frequently mistaken for each other, which perhaps explains why Edward helpfully tattooed his own initials on his forearm.

An undated mug shot of Joseph Furey from a
San Francisco rogues' gallery

At first, the brothers worked short cons that netted them a few hundred dollars at a time. One of them would befriend an out-of-town businessman and lure him into a crooked poker game presided over by the other brother, and the mark would leave $500 or so poorer. They hadn't yet fixed law officials in their favor, which was why their arrest warrants were so numerous, but Joseph Furey invented a successful method of escaping prosecution: he faked his own death. He "died" by gunshot in Boston in 1904, and when the reports of his death reached San Francisco, the police cooled off their search for him. He kept getting arrested, spending time in a southern Indiana penitentiary in 1912, and kept accumulating unfulfilled warrants throughout New York, Washington, D.C., and Florida. He forfeited bail in San Diego in 1912 and was ordered out of Long Beach in 1914.

Interestingly, Furey was given a rare opportunity to step out of the underworld. Had he wanted to, he could have lived a life a lot more like Norfleet's. In 1909, he was living in Warsaw, Indiana. He traveled west to see his family in Washington for the first time in seven years, and as he passed through Montana, he entered his name "just for a lark" in the

Flathead Reservation land draw. Over the objections of the Spokane, Salish, and Kootenai Indians who lived there, the federal government had decided to sell over 400,000 surplus acres in twenty-eight hundred parcels, and in August 1909 it held a lottery to determine who among the six thousand interested buyers could file claims. Joseph Furey was the first name drawn, entitling him to choose a section, a 640-acre parcel worth as much as $50,000, and take possession of it under homestead laws for as little as $1.25 to $3.00 an acre. Seattle-area newspapers were quick to identify the lottery winner as a man with a criminal past, despite his father's protestations that Joseph was a reputable liquor salesman and it was his look-alike brother Edward who was the family rapscallion. Joseph Furey did not redeem his winning ticket for the sedentary life.

In the next decade, his profit margins began to widen. In 1914, Joseph and Harry took $14,000 from a Nevada millionaire using a cruder version of the swindle by which Joseph would eventually con Norfleet. Edward Clifford left his hometown for the first time in forty years in order to deliver his daughter to a convent in Los Angeles. The Fureys lured him into what he thought was a fixed horse race, and they allowed him to win $1,500 before inducing him to wager a small fortune. A friend of the millionaire's grew concerned and alerted the police. Harry was arrested in San Jose, and Joseph was arrested in San Francisco. At first, Joseph calmly accepted the bracelets, assuming he was merely being picked up on suspicion. When he realized the extent of the charge against him, he tried to swallow the millionaire's bank draft. And yet just ten days later both brothers walked out of jail. The mark refused to file an official complaint. The following year, Joseph not only convinced a farmer from Council Bluffs that he had inside information on horse racing, he actually sold the mark the headquarters of his swindling operation for $20,000, leading him to believe that he could take over the fixed-race franchise and reap untold millions. The headquarters were, in reality, the upper three floors of a department store in Peoria, Illinois.

By the end of the decade, Joseph had refined his script into a masterpiece of deception, and he headed his own crew of swindlers who routinely extracted tens of thousands of dollars from their marks. Edward, for his part, worked with Nicky Arnstein, the dastardly husband of the actress Fanny Brice, on a Wall Street heist that netted an extraordinary $2 million. How did these two petty crooks graduate to the highest reaches of their profession?

The answer is simple: they worked under the tutelage of the masters, the very men who invented the tricks with which they conned their marks. In the century's first decade, Joseph and Edward restlessly circumnavigated the country as lone grifters who occasionally worked with each other to take the touch off a sucker. By the century's second decade, their travels grew more focused as their feet found the grooves of an underworld trail etched on the nation's landscape, and they began to work with men whose names were famous in saloons and pool halls but virtually unknown outside of them. Their swindling education follows the historical path of the big con itself: they started in the West and gradually made their way to the big eastern cities.

Confidence artistry is distinct from other criminal subcultures in several ways. It is not defined by ethnic or clan ties and does not owe its cohesion to a shared culture imported to this country by immigrants. While Mafia operatives are deeply rooted in their respective towns and are relatively powerless when they leave their own territories, confidence artists are itinerant and can set up a con virtually anywhere. Confidence artistry is not a crime of vice, though it is related to gambling, prostitution, and saloon keeping. It cannot be fully explained as a corollary to machine politics, Prohibition, and ethnic syndicates held together by violence. If organized crime exploits the opportunities created by a weak central government, confidence artistry profits from a strong economy, by filling in the uncharted terrain that opens up when business innovation gallops ahead of legislation.

The big con of the second and third decades of the twentieth century was, first and foremost, an outgrowth of the railroad boom. The first glimmer of what would become the big con sparked and flared into life at the westernmost stop on the Union Pacific Railroad. In Cheyenne, Wyoming, an aptly named nineteen-year-old called Benjamin Marks hit upon the innovation that would turn the short cons of the nineteenth century, all those green goods and goldbricks, into the underworld corporations, what might be called the con conglomerates, of the twentieth century. Marks, who was born in Waukegan, Illinois, showed an early aptitude for deception by getting himself enrolled in the Union army at the age of thirteen, serving as a dispatch bearer. When the war ended, he went west, landing in Cheyenne in 1867 at the same time that the railroad arrived. The Union Pacific, in its slow dash to complete the transcontinental railroad, had reached the summit of the Black Hills that winter and was forced to wait, gathering men and materials, until construction could resume in April. More than ten thousand people massed in the brand-new town. General Grenville Dodge, the chief engineer of the Union Pacific and the man who platted the city, seemed chagrined at what he'd wrought, calling Cheyenne "the greatest gambling place ever established on the plains" and "full of desperate characters."

Marks hung a tray from his neck and began to deal three-card monte games for the settlers and speculators, but the streets were thick with portable tables, and Marks could barely scoop in a living. He took the radical step of moving his game off the streets, at once jacking up his profits and vaulting the con into an entirely new dimension of urban relations. He rented a storefront in downtown Cheyenne, filled its window with tempting merchandise, and displayed a sign announcing that the price of everything in the store was a dollar or less. Marks never sold a single item. As soon as a potential customer entered the store, "salesmen" would entice him toward the crooked card games under way at barrels behind the merchandise, utilizing the same bait-and-switch, mules-then-real-estate tactic that Furey's gang would someday use to ensnare Norfleet. Marks's Dollar Store took off and spread like a franchise. Soon frontier towns all along the railroad featured their own versions (one of them even turned into a legitimate department store when its proprietor realized he could earn more by selling goods at a dollar—some at a profit and some as loss leaders—than he could dealing monte). Dollar Store proprietors relished the control they wielded over their games. For the first time, the swindle unfolded, in the con historian David Maurer's terms, as "a carefully set up and skillfully managed theater where the victim acts out an unwitting role in the most exciting of all underworld dramas." To Maurer, Marks had "revolutionize[d] the grift."

Marks might not have fully realized what he had invented. Certainly, he didn't stick around long enough to appreciate it. That same year, he moved to Council Bluffs, Iowa, where the Chicago and North Western Railway had just been completed. He set up some tables on the second floor of the Hoffman House on West Broadway, just above a saloon, and got to work dealing crooked faro games. In the 1870s, he shared the plentiful Omaha/Council Bluffs business with aristocrats of the trade like Doc Baggs, Canada Bill Jones, Charley White, George Devol, and Frank Tarbeaux. Business sagged when Tarbeaux unwisely swindled a Union Pacific executive out of $1,200, causing the railroad to crack down on the cardsharps riding its rails. Canada Bill tried to broker a deal, offering $10,000 to the railroad's general superintendent if he'd let them run three-card monte on UP trains, even volunteering to limit their dealings to Chicago businessmen and Methodist preachers, but the official turned him down. Gradually, the gamblers departed Council Bluffs for plumper depots, and Marks had the town to himself. He fixed it right up, placating government officials with cash and establishing Council Bluffs as a "right" or fixed-up town for a little honest wagering. He abstained from drinking and smoking, and he participated with gusto and goodwill in local politics. He soon developed a reputation among sporting men as a square dealer with a kind heart, the sort of man who would make sure you had a ride home if you lost your horse at one of his tables. In 1898, he built a freestanding casino in Council Bluffs that offered roulette, faro, craps, slot machines, and trapdoors in the floor for drunks or cheats who needed time to cool out in the basement pokey.

Marks possessed in full the con man's genius for taking advantage of circumstances and turning them to profit. At the turn of the century, he presided over a lavish mansion on Lake Manawa, outside of Council Bluffs, but what looked like a millionaire's hunting lodge was actually a stage set cobbled together from the detritus of modernity. After the Trans-Mississippi and International Exposition closed its doors in Omaha in 1898, Marks bought one of the buildings, an elaborate two-story log cabin of native pine with gables and verandas that the State of Minnesota had erected. Marks disassembled the building, marked all the logs, and floated them down the Missouri River. When he reassembled them, he expanded the building with telephone and telegraph poles, and he used glass from obsolete streetcars to fill in the windows.

Not coincidentally, Marks's thousand-acre property straddled two counties, and Marks sited his building precisely on the boundary line between them. On those rare occasions when one county's law enforcement chanced to raid the joint, Marks's dealers and patrons simply moved over to the other side of the building and out of their jurisdiction. The first floor of the cabin was entirely given over to gambling, with a little counting room to one side. The second and third floors contained bedrooms in which Marks's wife, the imperious Mary Marks, presided as the town's high-class madam. Mary's refinement and Viennese fashions were so exalted that the socialites of Council Bluffs earnestly desired her company, and they called on her one afternoon to beg her to renounce her career. Mary thanked the women for their good favor but declined the offer. Then she noted that it was getting upon five o'clock and if the ladies would only wait a few moments, their husbands would be finishing upstairs and could walk them home. The Markses' reign in Council Bluffs was never thereafter challenged.

Marks constructed a one-mile horse-racing track near the log mansion, and it was here that he made his second major contribution to the development of the big con —as well as his only mistake. Marks joined forces with John C. Mabray, a con man who had apprenticed in Webb City, Missouri, in the art of faked athletic contests—horse races, boxing, wrestling, and footraces— for the so-called Millionaires' Club. The basic script went like this: A steerer befriends a mark and introduces him to another man who works as the secretary for a group of millionaires, a sporting bunch of men who own, say, a racehorse that they occasionally pit against other horses in friendly wagers. The secretary is disgruntled with his employers and needs some help with a scheme he has cooked up. He has found a horse who can beat the millionaires' horse; all he lacks is someone to represent himself as the horse's owner and place his bet. When the mark sees the secretary's horse gallop around the practice ring, his own heart and avarice gallop in stride, and he agrees to play the part. The secretary tells him to bring along a bank draft for a few thousand dollars, because the millionaires won't do business with anyone whom they don't consider their equal. The match is arranged, the bets are placed, and the bank draft that was only supposed to be a stage prop is inevitably cashed so that the mark may tap into the game with his own money. Often the action is paused while the mark goes on the send for more money, this time in the tens of thousands of dollars. The starting gun goes off, and the secretary's horse leads by many lengths—until suddenly the jockey starts up out of the saddle, gurgles, and dies, falling to the dirt in a splatter of blood.

Loath to be caught at the scene of an illegal race in which a jockey has died, everyone swiftly finds the nearest exit. The secretary whispers to the mark that the millionaires will contact him at home and everything will be set right.

Marks and Mabray turned this swindle into big business by combining it with Marks's earlier invention of the Dollar Store, creating both a space and an administrative structure for the con to be predictably and repetitively managed. They funneled their marks through a big store in Council Bluffs, the third floor of the block-long Merriam Building on Main Street, which acted as the bureaucratic brain of an organization that employed hundreds of steerers, not to mention a stable of formerly respectable jockeys, sprinters, prizefighters, wrestlers, and racehorses, including the bantam champion Harry Forbes and the wrestler Ernest Fenby.

But Mabray was not as careful a businessman as his partner, and a few minuscule mistakes and one large lapse in judgment cost the men their empire. In 1908, a private detective in Council Bluffs opened a let-

John Mabray, left, shakes hands with two crooked sportsmen
and a mark, identified as R. A. Frazer.

ter he'd received by mistake. Addressed to "Friend 39," it read, "Owing to a change in administration here, we move to Council Bluffs, Ia., where conditions are perfect. Drop us a line and keep us posted as to your whereabouts." Instantly alert to the illegalities referenced in these brief words, the detective brought the letter to the attention of the U.S. postal inspectors. The post office inspector J. S. Swenson traced the postal box that the letter referenced, and the trail led to an office in the Merriam Building. Swenson began digging into the Council Bluffs underworld and pretty soon he knew the full story, but he had no jurisdiction until the gang used the mails to defraud their victims. His investigation was forced to pause until someone broke a law.

When Swenson finally unearthed a disgruntled mark who agreed to testify against the syndicate, postal inspectors plotted a raid in Council Bluffs and enlisted the chief of police and the head of the detective bureau in their plan. When the raid failed to go off, Swenson knew just how high up the fix went. His next break came in early 1909 when he trailed the gang to Little Rock, and before Mabray had time to fix city officials, Swenson stormed his house, arrested Mabray and several associates, and confiscated a trunk packed with documents testifying to the new managerial ethos of the big con. A red ledger indexed the names and identification numbers of more than three hundred men working Mabray's swindle in cities around the country. Eighty-eight envelopes held papers and photographs documenting eighty-eight swindles. For instance, it only took a few lines of shorthand and lingo to notate the entire script and cast of characters for the four-day-long swindle of a mark named Dr. C. C. Vanderbeck in 1907 (at the turn of the century, marks were also called mikes):

> Play of 49. June 16. 49 arrived with C. C. Vanderbeck of St. Louis. It is wrestle and "Mike" has $2,500 and his wife is to send three more on Monday. Was interviewed by 12. Will arrange.
>
> June 17. Mike is ready with his $2,500. I will get the balance tomorrow. Met Ogden present, Mike, 49, 12, 13, 36, 66, B. Made match for ten a side and put up two a side forfeit. Bet other three off of him. Turned him five. 36 offered bet of 30 for wine. 49 took 20 of it. Adjourned.
>
> Mike—Dr. C. C. Vanderbeck.
> Guide—49.

Outside—Billy Casey—B.
Manager—James Phillips—12.
Inside—Jack McCormick—A.
C.M.—J. J. Pomeroy—36.
C.M.—H. A. Hill—13.
C.M.—F. Barnes—66.

June 19. Met same place. Present same as yesterday. Gave him five. 49 put in five with him. Turned him five. 13 bet him 2. 66 bet him 2 and 36 bet him three, this louied for 2. He went to bank. 49 and 66 went with him. He drew. Made good and we bet other 500 off him. 66 daved and was $450 short. 66 and 12 to box. Contest. Gave him run off.

Will blow W and then Y.

Once the detectives deciphered words like "louied" and "daved," they added up the amounts recorded in those envelopes to more than $5 million. Marks's Dollar Store had become a million-dollar store.

In March 1910, the evidence in the trunk earned John Mabray the maximum federal sentence of two years in Leavenworth and a fine of $10,000. Thirteen of his colleagues were sentenced with him. Over the next few years, Inspector Swenson indicted eighty-four of Mabray's gang, and most of them served time or paid fines. Ben Marks was also tried for conspiracy, and John Mabray was the chief witness against him, testifying that he kicked up 8 or 9 percent of all receipts to his boss in exchange for police protection. Nonetheless, the local jury could find not a single scrap of evidence tying Marks to Mabray, and he was let go. But the long trial affected his health and broke his spirit for gambling; he and his wife turned their attention to stock raising on their vast grounds until his death in 1919.

Ben Marks's legacy lived on, for if the log mansion and the Merriam Building were the corporate headquarters for a con conglomerate, they were also a training ground for the legions of steerers and ropers who studied under Marks and fanned out to the great cities of the nation to set up their own stores. One of them was Joseph "Yellow Kid" Weil, otherwise known to the postal inspectors as "steerer No. 157," who was convicted in 1909 in Chicago and served a few years before returning to one of the many elegant suites he rented in the Loop for his swindling dramas. Chicago was the other incubator for the con at the end of the nineteenth century and the beginning of the twentieth, and after the Mabray gang was jailed, it became the home of the premier graduate program for the deceptive arts.

In Chicago, the counterpart to Ben Marks's Dollar Store was "the Store," Michael "Big Mike" McDonald's saloon, and it peddled every crooked game the frontier had yet invented, a veritable "department store of gambling." Both Chicago and McDonald owed their rise to the railroad. At a young age, McDonald left home to ride the rails as a train butcher, someone who peddled newspapers, candy, and other comforts to weary travelers, hustling tips and meals. McDonald added to his income with a short con of his own invention, the prize package swindle. He'd flamboyantly insert $5 bills in several of the candy boxes in his cart and tell passengers that every box held a prize ranging from one penny to $5. Mysteriously, no one ever drew one of the $5 boxes out of his cart. After spending some time in New Orleans, McDonald returned to Chicago with a recipe for vice that would prove enduring: separate gambling from prostitution, further separate brace games, or rigged house games, from honest gentlemen's gaming, centralize the gaming interests, and pay regularly and handsomely for protection from police raids. After operating a series of saloons around town, McDonald opened the Store in 1873, spending $15,000 to renovate the five-story building on the corner of Clark and Monroe into the city's most lavish and brazen twenty-four-hour house of games. The first floor was strictly legitimate—a saloon and wholesale liquor and cigar depot—and the second floor was strictly illegal with all manner of card, dice, and wheel games. Like Marks's casino, the Store's plush carpets concealed trapdoors in its floors, and its ornate moldings hid peepholes and secret closets. The third floor hosted out-of-town guests, and the top two floors cosseted the McDonald family in style and acted as a clubhouse for his select circle of friends and politicians.

Most important, the Store was thickly fringed on its sidewalks by bunco men of all varieties who lured traveling businessmen into its hallways. McDonald would buy passenger lists from railroad stationmasters, then dole them out to his lieutenants, who could easily match names to faces by their minute knowledge of regional fashion. A businessman would alight at the Van Buren Street depot only to be greeted familiarly by someone whom he simply couldn't place, and soon they'd be walking arm in arm up Clark Street. Forty percent of whatever the dupes lost at the Store belonged to the men who roped them in, 20 percent went to the police, and McDonald kept the balance. McDonald never held office, but for twenty uncontested years he ran the entire city, installing politicians and collecting the tributes of the grifters who worked for him, men like Tom and John Wallace, Red Adams, Snitzer the Kid, Dutchy Lehman, Black-Eyed Johnny, Hungry Joe Lewis, Appetite Bill, Tom O'Brien, and the brothers Fred and Charley Gondorf. Only when Carter Harrison, the man McDonald had ensconced as mayor, was assassinated in 1893 did McDonald's political power begin to ebb. After that, Bathhouse John Coughlin and Michael "Hinky Dink" Kenna stepped up to take control of the First Ward Levee district and preserve it as a safe haven for vice and larceny, ruling as its joint aldermen into the 1920s. Coughlin and Kenna ran the First Ward as a kind of big store, not only taking a percentage of every underworld dollar and converting it to Democratic votes and police protection, but also curating the Levee as if it were an exclusive social club by making introductions and mentoring young talent.

It was in Coughlin's Silver Dollar saloon that the Yellow Kid met Fred "the Deacon" Buckminster, the former policeman who became his partner, and Billy Wall, the leading con man in Chicago who would tutor him at the racetrack. Soon the Yellow Kid graduated from short cons to the kind of big con that would make him renowned even in the upperworld. By the second decade of the twentieth century, the *Chicago Daily Tribune* dubbed him "one of Chicago's landmarks." His exploits were covered exhaustively, even lovingly, by the metro reporters, and the Yellow Kid obliged them by showing up for every court appearance in exquisite suits and his trademark round spectacles, posing for the flashbulbs, and offering them bons mots on his way back to his chauffeured coupe. "Mr. Weil wore blue over a white shirt studded with gold, a diamond blazer in his cravat, an overcoat of Killarney green, a green velour hat of gay and rakish tilt, and a spanking pair of tan shoes," read one typical article. When Mrs. Anna J. Weil sailed into court one afternoon to post a $20,000 bond for her husband, the gown she wore elicited gasps from the "usual fans" who gathered whenever the Yellow Kid was onstage.

The First Ward was so tightly fixed during the Bathhouse–Hinky Dink era that Weil's untouchability formed the wry subtext, the tacit punch line of every newspaper article about him. He was arrested quite

Joseph "Yellow Kid" Weil in 1923

by accident in 1917, much to the *Tribune's* mirth. A friend had lent Weil his apartment while he was away for the weekend, but when Weil let himself in, he was arrested for attempted burglary. "With the police Weil could reckon," observed the *Tribune,* "but with suspicious janitors not." Once Weil was at the station, the police had no choice but to match him up with the various warrants out under his name, and he soon found himself answering to charges that he'd swindled Albert A. Charles of Kokomo out of an unfathomable sum of money. As he was released on bond, the Yellow Kid played his part perfectly, opening his eyes as round as his glasses: "Why they say he lost $100,000. I never knew there was that much money in the world." In that instance, Weil's bondsman was a former state representative, but just as often he retained the services of the licensed bondsman Cassius McDonald, Big Mike's youngest son.

In 1918, the *Chicago Daily Tribune* yawned and announced, "Ho Hum! Yellow Kid Gang Lands Another 'Hick.'" A stockman from Indiana had mortgaged his ranch and sold his cattle to raise $18,000 to purchase surefire stocks from two of the "Yellow Kid's gang of immunes," one of whom was Joseph Furey, "a long time member" of the syndicate. Furey played the junior partner to a swindler named Edward Burns, and he had clearly been apprenticing for a while by 1918. "Mr. Furey's chances of being captured appear remote," noted the article, because a group of his previous marks had already posted a $1,000 reward, with no results.

And so it appears that Joseph Furey learned tradecraft from one of the con's highest practitioners. According to his self-mythologizing, the Yellow Kid invented the wiretap, but that is almost certainly not true. The wiretap was, after the big store, the second genius idea in the evolution of the big con, a way to make money from horse racing without going to the baroque measure of faking a jockey's death or even staging a race. Chances are, though, that the Yellow Kid cannot claim the title of inventor. *The New York Times* gives credit to Tim Oakes, an ill-fated genius known in the criminal world as "the glass of fashion," who once cleared half a million dollars on the sale of bogus Standard Oil stock, only to die after three years of "queerness" in Ward's Island Asylum for the Insane. Jay Robert Nash, an avid historian of fraudulent crime, believes the wiretap to be the work of Paper Collar Joe Kratalsky, a con man who was unusual for also dabbling in art theft and forgeries, even working with the aristocratic Adam Worth in the sensational theft of Thomas Gainsborough's *Duchess of Devonshire* in 1876. An obscure con man named Curt Jeffreys baldly stole credit in his "Confessions of a Con Man," published in the *Chicago Daily Tribune*. But the real inventor was probably Larry Summerfield, Oakes's partner on the Standard Oil deal, who legend has it was a former telegraph operator and thus well positioned to exploit the medium's weaknesses.

Wiretapping most likely began in New York on December 20, 1885. Bookmakers all across the country were taking bets on a series of horse races in New Orleans, and the results were transmitted to saloons in major cities via telegraph. The first two races went off without incident. At the beginning of the third race, the odds stood at "Bob Swim, even money; Fletch Taylor, eight to five; Fleur de Lis, three to one; John Sullivan, five to one; Judge Jackson, thirty to one." Just before the betting closed, over a dozen young men sprinted into poolrooms around New York and laid heavy bets on Judge Jackson. When the race posted, Judge had won, and the same bright-eyed young men swiftly collected about $8,000 in winnings before bookmakers got wise to the trick. The young bettors had worked in concert with shady telegraph operators in Cincinnati, who had held back the telegraph results of the third race long enough for their confederates to place bets with perfect foreknowledge of the long-shot winner.

Throughout the 1880s and 1890s, wiretappers refined their art—and their Morse code. If the swindlers couldn't bribe anyone inside Western Union to further their schemes, they'd splice the telegraph lines themselves and delay or even fake the transmissions. In 1896, a well-coordinated group of bettors took about $150,000 in fraudulent winnings when rogue tappers seized control of the line that relayed race results from New Orleans and announced that Royal Nettle had won the sixth race. Not until eight o'clock that evening, when it came time to post the next morning's entries, did anyone discover the "slight mistake." Bookies were then instructed to pay out on the true winner, a horse named Plug. In subsequent days, as metro newspapers sussed out more of the story from irate poolroom owners, it became clear that this touch was subtly, even sensually, taken. Days in advance, bettors well armed with funds had begun stepping into poolrooms all around the country to buy tickets for Royal Nettle. The *New-York Tribune* reported that "perhaps not a half dozen poolrooms of consequence in the United States had escaped without loss." Only those few prudent bookmakers who waited for the published race results the next morning before paying out their bets were spared.

The Royal Nettle affair was, according to *The Washington Post,* "one of the most daring and successful swindles ever perpetrated in this country," and a month after Chicago police made a single unsatisfying arrest, the paper ran a breathy exposé of precisely how the trick was done. The average citizen could have no true conception of how complex such a con was, the paper claimed: "None but an expert lineman could do the work." The article went on to describe several other successful wiretap swindles from the past few years, making it sound as if the nation's largest cities were being hollowed out from the inside by teams of tappers: "When the workmen were tearing down the old walls of the Hoffman House, not many months ago, they broke in upon two wire tappers who were busy with their pliers and wires in a vault under the sidewalk." Similar exposés ran in subsequent years in papers from the *National Police Gazette* to the *Los Angeles Times.*

Such articles played so beautifully into con artists' hands that one might even suspect them of having been planted there, for they provided the setup for the big con. The papers demonstrated to the reading public, that teeming multitude of potential marks, that wiretapping *worked*, and anything that succeeded so efficiently in producing magical money could then be marketed as a sound investment. Just four months after the Royal Nettle affair, even those swindlers who were not "expert linemen" were peddling the wiretap, and thus began the era of the wireless wiretappers. In Chicago, four men were indicted on conspiracy charges when they induced George Peck, son of an alderman, to invest $1,000 toward the opening of a crooked poolroom with its own hidden cache of "valuable telegraphic equipment" that purportedly filched Western Union transmissions but that was in reality empty boxes with useless knobs, screws, and wires.

Swindlers continued to splice wires, reroute cables, and falsify race results. As late as 1902, swindlers moved the "old sure-thing" out west and tapped wires at a Los Angeles racetrack. But the game had forever shifted away from racetracks and poolrooms and toward the kind of big stores that con men were, by now, so well practiced at furnishing. In 1905, a consortium of four sharpers shocked and thrilled New Yorkers when they fitted up a fake Western Union office in Manhattan and fleeced a German businessman for an astonishing $96,000, the equivalent of roughly $2.5 million in today's money; the police commissioner, William McAdoo, stated that it was the largest amount lost to date in the big con. In 1907, a Connecticut man named William F. Walker, treasurer of the New Britain Savings Bank, disappeared after having looted his employer of more than $600,000 in order to invest in the wiretap in New York City. The swindlers got about $100,000 of Walker's money, and then they got a handful of arrest warrants for larceny and receiving stolen goods and a thicket of newspaper headlines. To no one's surprise, the gang leader turned out to be Charley Gondorf, "well known about the Tenderloin as a sporting man." What the Yellow Kid was to Chicago, the Gondorf brothers were to New York: notorious, tolerated, even a little respected for their native cleverness. Like Weil, Fred and Charley Gondorf got their start in the great Chicago store under Big Mike McDonald; then they moved to New York to work the wiretap with their own coterie of lieutenants and apprentices. Even after Walker was found, he refused to testify against his swindlers, like so many marks who decline to hold their gullibility up to scrutiny in the courtroom. Connecticut officials were forced to let Charley Gondorf go free, and he rejoined his brother Fred on the well-trodden streets of Manhattan.

Before Joseph Furey could unfurl the perfect con on Norfleet in 1919, there remained one more scene in the swindling script to invent and perfect. The final filigree in the big con was the uncontested invention of William Elmer Mead, the man J. Edgar Hoover called "one of the shrewdest of confidence men." Mead abstained from alcohol, cigarettes, and swearing, and even attended church from time to time, earning him the moniker the Christian Kid. Mead was the Yellow Kid's exact contemporary, and his career almost precisely mirrored Weil's: a scrappy start in short cons, higher education in fixed footraces, and then staggering success with the big con in the first two decades of the twentieth century. His prized gambit, which worked so well it hit the swindling fraternity like a virus, was the wallet drop. Joseph Furey learned it directly from Mead when they worked together in Midwestern towns, and he used it on Norfleet when he planted the leather wallet in the armchair of the Adolphus Hotel. According to Hoover, this technique earned Mead millions over the years. He kept losing his wallet well into the 1930s and might have perpetuated the con forever had he not stumbled into the pathway of another crime. He effortlessly conned a Missouri contractor of a sum reported to be as high as $200,000, but not long afterward he opened up a newspaper and read about a kidnapping: the friend from whom the contractor had borrowed money to give to Mead had been kidnapped. Mead panicked, thinking that the federal investigation of the kidnapping would inevitably lead to him. He contacted a plastic surgeon, the same one who would later operate on John Dillinger's face, and had his fingertips mutilated, then skipped out on the $2,000 bill and dashed across the country to elude the secret agents he thought were pursuing him. In fact, the FBI never connected him to the kidnapping and were not in pursuit—until, that is, they learned of his surgery, which was itself in violation of federal law. "The trick by which he had sought to escape the government was the very thing that brought him into its custody," Hoover noted with satisfaction. "Mead had arrested himself." The FBI turned him over to the postal inspectors, who jailed him for a fourteen-year-old charge of defrauding through the mails, thus ending his career.

Not all con artists ended their lives in jail, unemployed, or destitute—only most of them. Joseph Weil was perhaps the most famous exception. He lived to be a hundred years old, and only about a tenth of his lifetime was spent in prisons. Naturally, he used his enforced downtime to great profit by picking the brains of other arch criminals and inventing new schemes. After spending six years in Leavenworth in the late 1920s, he departed for Italy, where he swindled Mussolini out of $2 million in cash by selling Il Duce mining lands in Colorado. In the mid-1930s, the Yellow Kid went into retirement. In 1948, he published his memoir, and in 1956, at the age of eighty-one, he publicly forswore con artistry in an interview with Saul Bellow. Later that year, he testified before Senator Estes Kefauver's subcommittee on juvenile delinquency, huffing in outrage at contemporary swindlers who used young children to con their elders and protesting that "it was never like that in my time." He appeared contrite for his past, telling the subcommittee, "I see how despicable were the things I did. I found out a man is responsible not only for himself but for other lives he wrecked." The historian Jay Robert Nash befriended him at the end of his life. One time Nash came upon him on a street corner in Chicago's North Side. He was not his usual natty self but unkempt, unshaven, and dressed in rags. Nash immediately offered to help him with a loan to get him back on his feet, but Weil declined and turned away. Nash persisted, until finally the Yellow Kid swiveled around and hissed, "Go away, dammit, can't you see I'm *working*!" Yet even the indefatigable Yellow Kid, who it is rumored earned over $8 million in his lifetime, was buried in a pauper's grave.

Most swindlers in the big con school of artistry never got a chance to relish their five- and six-figure windfalls. As one sharper explained, "Crooked money disappears like lightning. A beer pocketbook and a champagne appetite encourage further depredations." If the law couldn't always catch them, coincidence, ill fortune, drugs, gambling, or their supposed comrades would eventually steal away their profits. Which one of these would be Joseph Furey's downfall?

CHAPTER SEVEN

The Con Never Dies

Following Furey's Christmastime wire to his wife, Norfleet made a second trip to Florida. This time he brought along additional weaponry—his son Pete, then twenty years old. On his way east from California, he dropped in at the ranch just in time to surprise his family as they were sitting down to Christmas dinner, raising a hullabaloo of joy. But Norfleet couldn't help notice that his wife was endeavoring to keep him away from the barn, and soon he'd extracted a tearful confession from her. The last time he'd wired home for money, she'd been so desperate she'd had to sell Hornet, his beloved cow horse, a steed easily worth $350 who'd gone to a neighbor for a mere $75. That did it. With more personal motivation than he'd ever had before, Norfleet gathered up his son, bought a new hat, shaved off his mustache, and headed for Jacksonville. Within forty-five minutes of his arrival, he had Joseph Furey in his sights.

Norfleet and his son had made a list of the city's leading hotels and had come up with eight in total. They split them up and canvassed each of them. When they reconnoitered, Pete told his father that he was sure he'd spotted Furey, whom he recognized from mug shots, in the lobby of the Mason Hotel. They headed back to the Mason and staked it out from opposite street corners, and soon Norfleet did indeed spot his quarry. They trailed him to the Hilton Café, and, secure in his disguise, Norfleet entered with the intention of taking a seat near Furey simply to keep an eye on him. But the headwaiter guided Norfleet to a seat at Furey's own table, and the swindler looked up at Norfleet, looked again, and recognized him. The two men stared fixedly at each other.

In the next instant, Furey rose from his chair, but Norfleet quickly covered him with his gun, yelling, "You can't do it, Furey! You're my prisoner!"

Furey turned away from Norfleet and shouted to the other diners, "Don't let him rob me, men! Don't let him rob me! He'll take my diamonds—Don't let him do it! For God's sake, men, don't let him!" Furey's words electrified the other diners, and the café erupted as they crammed jewelry and wallets into their pockets and fell over one another in their quests for the exit. Norfleet saw Furey's expression change to relief just a fraction of a second before he felt his right arm being wrenched behind his back, his revolver pinned to his own side. Furey lunged past him, but Norfleet managed to grab his lapel in his left hand. Furey bent down and bit like an animal, drawing blood, but still Norfleet held on. "I could have dragged him to Texas," he wrote. "Nothing could separate my grip on him unless someone cut my hand off." With the other man's arm around his neck—Norfleet was incredulous when he managed to glimpse that it was Steel, the insideman from the Daytona clubhouse—the three men were deadlocked.

Then Pete charged through the front door, separating the crowd with a waving pistol in each hand, one of which he jammed into Furey's side. Allured by the commotion, several police officers made their way into the café but froze when they caught sight of Pete, with another gun trained on them as they came through the open door. To the officers, it looked as if Norfleet were a burglar and Pete his assistant, and they came charging at the knotted men with their clubs raised high. Norfleet and Pete began shouting that they were fellow officers with a warrant for the man in their custody, and soon the scene quieted down enough for them to be heard. The officers took possession of Furey, and they all agreed to sort out the matter at the station.

Once there, Furey regained complete mastery. While one of the officers reported on what had taken place at the café, Furey and the sergeant exchanged glances. Then the sergeant turned to Pete and said sternly, "What right had you to have your gun in this man's side?" Pete calmly produced the Tarrant County warrant for Joseph Furey's arrest. "How do you know this is the man?" the sergeant continued, undaunted. Pete handed over Furey's rogues' gallery photograph. "Do you call that a picture of this man?" the sergeant sneered.

Furey stood up and said commandingly, "My name is Edward

Leonard. I never saw either of these men before in my life. I am here on some very important business. Name my bond, officer, so that I may attend to my business without further annoyance." And the officer promptly began filling out the bond form, while Furey stood there and smoothed down his suit, pinching his trouser creases back into place. Norfleet and Pete began to splutter, but Furey interrupted them, saying loudly, "He is writing out my recognizance bond for one thousand dollars." The sergeant obediently filled in the amount.

Norfleet reached into his wallet and produced his requisition warrant for Furey, signed by the governor of Florida. He shoved it at the sergeant, who put down his pen and read it over. There was the tiniest of pauses. Then he sighed, handed the warrant back to Norfleet, and said to the prisoner, "Mr. Furey, I cannot do a thing for you." Norfleet could not stifle his barking laugh. The sergeant had just addressed him as Furey rather than Leonard, and the scene had just fallen irrevocably apart. Norfleet had finally pierced the fix.

With that, Norfleet and Pete took charge of their prisoner and began the journey back to Fort Worth. The head deputy lent them a service car and driver, and suggested that when they got to the Dinsmore Flag Station outside of Jacksonville, they park within a forest just outside the station, to prevent Furey from initiating habeas corpus proceedings or any other stalling techniques. The very instant they crossed the town line, Furey began to plead with Norfleet for his freedom. Norfleet cut him off mid-sentence. "I know all about the suffering humanity, and the rash acts, and I'm not going to take a brainstorm, so you may just as well save your breath. You're going back to Texas!" And the chauffeur pulled the car in to a secluded spot about three hundred yards away from the railroad track.

As Norfleet got Furey out of the car and led him to a tree stump, Furey tried again. "Can't we get down to business?" he said to the cowboy, and offered him $20,000. Norfleet paused. Furey hastily resumed explaining exactly how he could get Norfleet the money. He could hand over the deed to his San Francisco apartment house, or his half interest in a four-hundred-acre ranch in San Luis Obispo. Or he could write a check payable to Pete for the full amount, and Norfleet could send his son back into Jacksonville to cash it that very evening.

And Norfleet accepted Furey's offer.

His autobiography does not offer a single word of explanation for this decision, an act which seemed to undo everything that had preceded it. Was Norfleet's quest, which had dominated a year of his life, really only about money in the end? Would stealing back half of his lost fortune at the point of a gun truly quell the moral fire that had burned in his gut and propelled him across the country all those months? Perhaps there was no moral fire in his gut after all. Or perhaps this exchange between the two men was a further demonstration of Furey's supreme artistry, the way he could read a mark, excite his greed, and almost uncannily discern his price. Perhaps Furey had seen what Norfleet could not quite admit to himself, that Norfleet's quest had begun to affect his very identity. He was no longer a Texas cowboy with his feet planted firmly on the prairie. Maybe, by leaving his ranch and putting on a disguise, he had uprooted his principles and allowed them to become a little less absolute. He had not only adopted the methods of the swindlers; he had also taken on their modern, restless worldview, an identity that was at home anywhere because it seamlessly adjusted itself to the needs of the moment. But of course none of this earns a comment from Norfleet in his autobiography. He simply expects his readers to relate to his opportunistic strategy to regain some of the money he lost in the swindle. Economic self-interest requires no explanation.

As if to compensate for his fall from the moral high ground, Norfleet sealed their deal with a stern little lecture: "I'm going to let you write out that order for the twenty thousand and I'm going to let Pete take it and present it for payment. But I want this to sink into you and sink deep. If you get Pete into any of your traps; if anything happens to him, or if he isn't back here by the time this sun goes down, your light goes out. Is that understood?" Furey agreed, and Norfleet sent his son and the chauffeur back into the dangerous maws of Furey's organization.

It wasn't long before the two men, alike in their garrulity and psychological curiosity, fell to talking. But for the pistol in one man's hand and the handcuffs on the other's, they seemed for all the world like two friends catching up on each other's lives. Furey companionably wished that he'd killed Norfleet the last time he was in Florida as he'd planned. "I have spent seventeen thousand dollars keeping out of your way," noted Furey. "If ever there was a nemesis, you have been mine. I have lost through your damnable hounding as much money as I have made." Norfleet knew that dollar estimate was low, and with pure pleasure he told Furey that the money he'd spent to slip free from Lips and Anderson had been wasted because Norfleet had caught them in their inattention. At this news, Furey railed and shouted at the palm leaves around them, and then poured out the entire story of Lips and Anderson's ambush in his Glendale home: his attempt to scale the eight-foot-tall fence, the fall that plummeted him back into his own garden, the bullets that thudded around him as Lips and Anderson caught up. Gradually, his anger spent itself, and his tirade wound down. And then he looked over Norfleet's shoulder.

Norfleet sprang to his feet and spun around in one motion, putting Furey between him and the trees behind him, his gun to Furey's head. "Go back, men! Go back! For God's sake, go back!" Furey pleaded to his unseen protectors. No one answered. No one moved. So Norfleet gave it a try: "If you over there behind those palmleaf fans don't show up, and pretty quick, I'm going to do some bombarding into your hiding place that'll make you either stand or lie down forever." Silently, four men emerged from the forest cover, four shotguns in their hands, staring at their boss. Furey again ordered them to leave, but the most he could accomplish was to get them to retreat to the main road some hundred feet away.

Norfleet pointed to the long shadows crossing the clearing and said threateningly to Furey, "Pete could have been to Jacksonville and back again by this time." Panic infecting his voice, Furey assured him that Pete would be there soon, and before he'd finished speaking, they could hear an approaching car. But they could also hear that the car was not slowing. It careened past them, swerved around alarmingly, and charged back into the clearing. Norfleet could see that Pete was not in the car. Three men got out, each holding a riot gun, and they joined the four men at the edge of the clearing. By now, the sun was low, enormous, and as red as the bloodshed that Norfleet had promised. "Furey, if you have anything to get off your conscience you'd better begin to unload!" he roared.

"Listen! Listen!" Furey moaned. Sure enough, there was the sound of another approaching car, but rather than feel relief, Norfleet felt his heart cramp in fear: his son was about to drive into seven gun muzzles. In Norfleet's autobiography, when he describes this moment, all the campy bravado drops away, and his words reach for a kind of austere, desperate grace. He secured his grip on the gun at Furey's head and readied his muscles for the battle to come. "The least mistake and God knows what the result. It seems as if all that lived in me left my body. I was suspended between action and inertia." He does not say that he regretted what he'd asked his son to do, nor does he condemn himself for the greed that brought them to this moment, but he does write that as he waited for the car to arrive, he could clearly see in his mind the whole saga, "a long story visioned in the space of a human heart."

Pete's borrowed Cadillac sped into view, but when the chauffeur saw the guns sticking out into the road, he floored the accelerator and the car whooshed past them. Norfleet could see his son in the back and hear him shouting to the driver to turn back, and then he saw Pete lean over and shove "his little persuader" at the driver's head and order him to slow and turn (here, Norfleet's poetic words vanish as he records the black chauffeur's terrified response in offensive pidgin English). Furey continued to implore his men not to start anything; for once, Furey's and Norfleet's interests were perfectly aligned. Pete and the driver returned, and keeping his gun on Furey the entire time, Norfleet maneuvered him into the backseat, keeping the con man on the side facing the gunmen to shield Pete. The driver once again stomped his foot on the pedal, and they barreled to the station to flag down the train to Georgia.

They could hear the train approaching, so Norfleet jumped out of the car and ran to the tracks, waving his arms. A family sat in a buggy waiting for the train to pass, and they watched Norfleet's exertions with a certain bemusement, until finally the man informed Norfleet that the train was a limited and never stopped at this station. Even within his well-earned cynicism, Norfleet still possessed the capacity for outrage. The head deputy had double-crossed him in the only way that the governor's requisition had allowed. Pete and Norfleet decided there was nothing else to do but return to Jacksonville—if they could make it back through the seven-gun salute.

They drove until they could see two cars ahead of them, four guns in one and three in the other. The cars were parallel to each other, with a space the size of a Cadillac between them. Norfleet's driver maneuvered right in between them, and for a second Norfleet and his son were flanked by the gunmen. Norfleet ordered the chauffeur to drive as fast as the car would allow and glanced down at the speedometer. "It registered seventy-eight miles an hour! It didn't seem possible." The Cadillac pulled ahead, but as it did, Furey lifted his hulking mass out of his seat and reached an arm around to the steering wheel. Norfleet turned around and slammed the butt of his gun into Furey's head, knocking the huge man unconscious, but he fell onto the driver's shoulders. The car swerved without slowing, grinding dirt and pine saplings under its wheels, until Furey's body slid back into its seat, the driver righted the car, and they continued on their uneventful way to Jacksonville.

At the station, Norfleet sent a telegram to District Attorney Jesse Brown in Tarrant County: "Have Joe Furey. On way to Texas. Have good man meet me in New Orleans at police station." He then booked them a drawing room on the train to New Orleans. He and his son hustled a bleary Furey onto the train and collapsed, their adrenaline spent.

As the train began its steady journey, Pete revived and related his afternoon's experiences. As Furey had instructed him, he went to room 1000 of the Mason Hotel, where he found several men crating up an enormous array of equipment, the props of yet another phony stock exchange. Pete asked for Weintrot. "He is not here," one of the men answered. "I think he is downstairs. I'll go get him for you." Pete waited and waited, until another man noticed Pete and asked if he could help him. Pete repeated his request for Weintrot; the man repeated the line about fetching him from downstairs and departed. This continued until the room was empty of bunco men, and Pete realized he needed to speed back to the clearing before his father executed Furey. They later learned that fully twelve rooms in the Mason Hotel had been vacated that day.

Furey listened intently to Pete's story. The image of those vanished men seemed to work on him, and he stood and began to pace, a big man caged in a small car fueled by anger. Suddenly he opened the door to the aisle and raised his voice to the other passengers. "Women! Men! Oh, women!" he cried, and he unfolded a tale of the deprivations to which his captors were subjecting him. No food, no drink all day. "For God's sake help a dying man!" They could all see his silver bracelets, but even in captivity Furey was the consummate con man, and he excited the sympathy of a pair of old women, who stopped a passing snack vendor and began choosing a colorful pile of fruits for the starving prisoner. Norfleet and Pete came to the door, and a conductor ambled over to see what the drama was about.

With everyone's attention thus fixed, Furey showed what he was made of. He stepped back into Norfleet's car, put his palms together, raised his arms, and dove through the plate glass window of the moving train. Before anyone quite knew what had happened, Furey was free.

The crowd at the car door was almost as fast as Furey. The conductor pulled the brake cord. As the train slowed, Pete leaped out through the jagged window. Norfleet tossed him his gun, then made his way out of the train to the baggage car, where a porter uncovered his luggage and tossed it next to the tracks. Minutes later, the train continued on its way, and Norfleet saw Pete running back toward him, gasping for breath and Fureyless. "Dad," he breathed, "a switch engine picked Furey up and he is gone!"

Norfleet looked around him and spotted a man in a signal tower. He shouted up to him, asking him to wire to Jacksonville to send detectives out to the switch engine heading their way. Then Norfleet found another engine a few tracks over and asked if they could hitch a ride, explaining as quickly as he could the saga of the escaped prisoner. The engineer leaped at the challenge, so Norfleet and Pete swung up and they thundered off toward Jacksonville. Soon they had Furey's train in sight, and for five or six miles the two trains raced in place toward the station. Norfleet saw Furey's train stop and a policeman approach. He waited, helpless, to see what the officer would do. The officer spoke to the engineer, then brought Furey down off the train and delivered him into Norfleet's custody. Furey was bleeding from his forehead where he'd smacked a railroad tie and limping from a substantial leg injury. Norfleet sent Jesse Brown another telegram: "Furey jumped through train window. Badly injured. Do not know when we can leave with him."

For three more days, their journey continued in this manner as they hustled their prisoner onto and off of trains, in and out of temporary holding cells. Furey kept devising increasingly clever ways to escape, and Norfleet kept scrambling to keep up with and corral his desperate charge. The reversals of fortune that Norfleet relates in his autobiography are so incredible and so relentless that in the retelling they become almost tedious, but they exhilarated Norfleet, each one an instance of his besting a master swindler at his own game. By this point, Norfleet's transformation was complete, and he was taking extreme pleasure in his new persona. Back in Jacksonville, Norfleet booked Furey into the jail for the night, but Furey wasted no time in securing a lawyer and beginning to prepare habeas corpus papers, so Norfleet was forced to repossess his prisoner at midnight. They spent a gothic night in the attic of an imposing colonial mansion where they stopped and asked for shelter. They paused the next evening at another southern city and again stored Furey in jail for the night. When they came to get him in the morning, he was missing; the Humane Society had discovered him in poor health and had brought him to their hospital for care. When Norfleet and Pete showed up, the society claimed Furey could not leave for fifteen days, but Pete brandished a six-shooter and Norfleet pulled out the handcuffs, and they were soon on their way again.

On January 24, 1921, Norfleet's little party arrived in Fort Worth. Police officers assisted Furey from the train to a wheelchair, as he could no longer put weight on his injured leg. Reporters from the *Fort Worth Star–Telegram* were on hand to meet the train, but Furey pulled his overcoat up and his hat down, denying photographers their shot. A waiting car whisked him to the Tarrant County Jail, where, said Norfleet with finality, "we knew the devil and all of his assistants could not get him out." It was discovered that Furey was also wanted in Washington and Florida, and a few days later another mark came forward with a tale about a stock market swindle in Biloxi, Mississippi, that had netted Furey $25,000. Over the next few days, newspapers around the country carried accounts of Norfleet's adventure. The *Fort Worth Star Telegram* got Norfleet's exclusive interview and published it with photographs of the bunco team and a map of Norfleet's gumshoe adventures. "I can go back now to my ranch life," Norfleet declared to the reporter Frank Evans. "I'm more contented now. Maybe I can give my time to ranching and farming."

With Furey in jail, Norfleet had extracted justice for four of his five con men. Furey declined to fight the charges against him, and legal action proceeded swiftly. He made a full confession to District Attorney Brown, and it was his testimony that prompted the surprise arrest of Walter Lips and William Anderson in Los Angeles. He pleaded guilty on two counts of swindling Norfleet, but civil law still offered him the opportunity to defend himself before a judge and jury, and he did so with spirit, acting as his own attorney. On March 14, 1921, Furey's trial began. Furey hobbled into court on crutches, but he wore an elegant suit and nose glasses, and he projected an air of extraordinary poise and breeding.

The first witness was, of course, Norfleet, and the jury and the audience were so riveted that the *Fort Worth Star-Telegram* printed his testimony nearly in full. Then Furey stood up to cross-examine his nemesis. In honeyed words of the utmost courtesy, he asked Norfleet if it wasn't true that the rancher had offered to let Furey go if he would return $20,000 of the $45,000 he'd lost. Norfleet vehemently denied the charge, but then softened under further questioning and admitted that yes, he'd sent his son into Jacksonville to redeem Furey's check for the stated amount. Furey pressed further. Isn't it also true, he asked, that you entered into the stock deal in search of profit and that you actually did earn some money, at which point you could have walked away? Once again, Norfleet was forced to answer yes. But Furey's sophistry earned him no reprieve. The jury took only a few minutes to find Furey guilty on both counts and to dispense the maximum sentence of ten years for each count. Furey asked the judge if he might serve the sentences concurrently, but with a quick glance at Furey's criminal record the judge denied the request. Furey waived his right to appeal, and a week later he moved from the county jail to the state penitentiary in Huntsville.

As if resigned to his fate, Joseph Furey became a model prisoner. The *Fort Worth Star-Telegram* was perennially interested in his goings-on and soon reported that he had organized and was leading the largest Sunday school class ever gathered in the state penitentiary, in addition to his excellent performance in his job as a clerk. And yet there were troubling little signs that Furey did not view his accommodations with complete favor. In May, just a few weeks after Furey took residence in Huntsville, his cell mate, a man named Mark Wheeler, successfully escaped. Three days later, Governor Pat Neff called the penitentiary in a panic and instructed the guards to put an extra watch on Furey. It seems that Thomas Lee Woolwine, the district attorney in Los Angeles who'd arrested Lips and Anderson, had received a tip that Furey was about to saw his way out of jail. Woolwine forwarded the tip to District Attorney Brown, who instantly called the governor's office. It was rumored that Mark Wheeler was part of the plot, as was a $30,000 bribe.

Just three days after the governor's call, two dozen prisoners mutinied and escaped from Huntsville in a volley of gunshots. The riot started when six prisoners charged at their guards with pistols. Then they broke into the prison armory, loaded up on shotguns, and barreled back inside, shooting their way through more guards as they rounded up their friends and escaped through a side entrance. Norfleet claims that Dede Furey and Mabel Harrison worked together to smuggle those first pistols in their handbags during weekly visits to their caged beloved, but this touchingly romantic scene never happened. His colorful account muddles together Governor Neff's phone call and the prison riot, and he puts himself squarely at the center of events. He says Woolwine called *him* to warn of Furey's escape, and *he* raised the alarm in Texas, though he gives no convincing reason why a district attorney would involve a private citizen in an attempted jailbreak. Norfleet asserts that through his concerted action, Furey was placed in solitary confinement while "convicts, resembling stampeding zebras, ran amok, leaped from the high prison walls and, shooting down obstructing guards, fled north, south, east and west." In a nearby field, two women and an airplane languished, their plans thwarted, their hopes unfulfilled. But as the newspaper stated, "Prison authorities said they were unable to establish any connection between the prison [escapes] and the Joe Furey case." And in fact Furey remained securely in jail throughout the fracas, quietly passing through the halls between his cell and the dining hall. According to legend, one of the mutineers offered Furey a pistol, but the swindler looked down his nose at it and replied that he did not run with rabble—he would escape on his own at a later date.

Despite all this nefarious activity that swirled around Joseph Furey that May, when he died the following year, it took a full week before anyone raised an eyebrow. On July 29, 1922, the *Fort Worth Star-Telegram* mourned the death of its favorite outlaw, breaking the news that Furey had died of a tumor in the insane ward, where he'd been committed the previous January after becoming mentally unbalanced. Because his wife had long repudiated him, his body was being shipped to Oakland to lie next to the grave of his mistress, Mabel Harrison, who had died a few months earlier (Norfleet declares that she contracted pneumonia in Huntsville while trying to free Furey). Mabel's daughter, Mrs. J. E. Mannberger of New York, was paying the $400 bill for his funeral expenses.

It was a deputy working under the Los Angeles district attorney,

Woolwine, who first pointed out that Furey had died at least once before. Then the *Fort Worth Star-Telegram* suddenly remembered something Furey had said as he left Fort Worth for Huntsville. "Some day you will read of my death at the penitentiary," he was supposed to have said, "and there will be a new grave in the penitentiary cemetery, but old Joe won't be in it—I'll be gone elsewhere." Woolwine telegrammed District Attorney Brown and asked him to make a positive identification before shipping the body west. Brown replied that unfortunately the coffin was already en route. Identification would have to wait until the shipment reached its destination, which was not Oakland but a funeral home on Sutter Street in San Francisco.

As the body made its way to California, newspapers all over the country traded fact for speculation. *Was* Furey dead? "I doubt it," retorted Woolwine. For his part, the warden at Huntsville snapped, "I'd hate to be as dead as Joe Furey," asserting that they had performed an autopsy at the prison and that Furey had most definitely died of bladder cancer. No, make that stomach cancer. Or was it a hunger strike that killed him? *The New York Times* mentioned that he'd shriveled down from 200 pounds to a mere 115. No further mention was made of Furey's insanity.

While each newspaper advanced its own theory of Joseph Furey's latest con, it was suddenly discovered that the body had already been buried on August 1. The undertaking firm of Halsted and Company announced that it had buried Joseph Furey near San Francisco in Cypress Lawn Cemetery without a service. Only a few people had stood by the grave, including a young woman who represented herself as Furey's niece and who herself became a sudden object of curiosity. It was soon revealed that she was the same woman who had paid for Furey's body to be shipped west, and that she had traveled from her home in the East to take up residence in the Hotel St. Francis several days *before* Furey died. Woolwine now took to calling Furey's death "greatly exaggerated," but the fact remained that he was legally dead in the state of Texas. There was nothing for it but disinterment. While San Francisco and Los Angeles authorities bickered over jurisdiction, Dede Furey stepped into the conversation, testifying in court that if her husband was indeed dead, her son should inherit his estate, valued at $8,000. She was named administratrix for Marc Furey's estate, and the court ordered that she be paid $25 a month for his support.

"Joe Furey is dead. His body rests in a cemetery near San Francisco. These facts were positively established when the body of the nationally known swindler was exhumed Thursday," reported the *Fort Worth Star-Telegram* and newspapers around the country. Woolwine had succeeded in obtaining jurisdiction to disinter the body, and the fingerprints on the corpse's right hand and its Bertillon measurements—a series of eleven measurements such as the length of the left little finger and the length of the right ear, which were said to remain constant over an adult's life—tallied with Furey's prison records. As the Waterloo, Iowa, newspaper put it, "The king of bunco men did not bunco death."

Three years later, the story of Furey's death shifted yet again. The Texas legislature opened an investigation into living conditions in the Huntsville prison in 1925. Dr. E. H. Boaz, a former prisoner who had been convicted of manslaughter but was then pardoned by Governor Neff, testified that in his position as a hospital steward he'd witnessed a number of cruelties against inmates, four of which had directly resulted in death. "Tell this committee what you know of Joe Furey, convict, who died at Huntsville, and who, the record shows, died of bladder trouble," prompted a state representative. Boaz described how he'd seen Furey in the insane ward, where he was under the care of another convict named Fowler, who gave him food only once a week. Boaz said he began slipping Furey additional food, otherwise he would have died sooner. And then one day when he was passing by Furey's cell, "I saw him taken from his cell, thrown into a tub of ice water, hit over the head with a stick of wood and then Fowler threw him on the floor and stamped on him, jumping on his chest and abdomen several times." Boaz said that two or three hours later, Furey died, but he "didn't report the matter, for 'convicts don't talk.'" No mention was made in the coverage of Boaz's testimony of Furey's previous deaths, exhumations, and resurrections, just as no mention had been made in either the Huntsville autopsy or the San Francisco disinterment of traumatic injuries to Furey's body.

Six years after his death, Joseph Furey was arrested for impersonating a federal officer. In March 1928, Harry M. Barrentine, an oil company executive, testified in federal court that he met a man named Edward Miller at a hotel in Kansas City, Missouri. Miller offered to sell him some liquor, but when the two men stepped outside the hotel, Miller seized Barrentine, informed him that he was a federal officer, and threatened to arrest Barrentine for selling narcotics unless he handed over $1,500. A Kansas City police lieutenant testified that Edward Miller's Bertillon measurements matched those of the Joseph Furey who had famously conned Norfleet nine years previously. Miller, defending himself without a lawyer, admitted that he was Furey. As this news rippled its way across the country, the San Francisco detective who had unearthed the coffin three years previously "became choleric" and could barely choke out his statement: "Furey is dead and buried. I don't know who the Kansas City man is but he's not Joe Furey." Once again, everyone stepped forward with his pet theory. The Huntsville warden continued to defend his prison by claiming that Furey's identity had been secured at the time of his death. He mused that there was another man sentenced in 1921 who bore a striking resemblance to Furey and who'd been released in 1926—perhaps this man was the new Furey? J. Frank Norfleet could not bear to remain quietly on the sidelines of this controversy. He stated that without doubt his Joe Furey had died in 1922, even though he undermined his own claim by recollecting, "Joe Furey had been 'dead' eight years before I met him." Norfleet believed that the Furey under arrest in Missouri was Edward, Joseph's younger brother, an assertion that should have been easy to prove with those useful tattooed initials. Whoever he was, the Kansas City prisoner was sentenced to three years, and the newspaper record went forever silent on the confusing chronicle of the Furey crime family.

The next time Norfleet found himself in Fort Worth, a few months after Furey's trial, District Attorney Brown gave him some news that completely shattered the calm he had regained at the ranch: "Reno Hamlin has forfeited his bond and is gone again!" Norfleet could barely believe it. "It was like trying to hold down six keys with five fingers—every time I press one down another pops up." But Furey had taught him that a con that worked once was surely good for another spin, so yet again Norfleet had the charges against Hamlin dropped and the canceled charge publicized in the papers. Then a grand jury quietly issued a new indictment. Next he contacted a friend named Will Flynn, a police officer in Oklahoma City. He'd heard that Hamlin's wife lived there, so he sent Flynn a photograph of Hamlin and asked him to keep an eye out. Days later, in October 1921, Hamlin was arrested on a misdemeanor, and when Flynn spotted him in the holding cell, he excitedly wired

Hale Center. Norfleet found himself in a race with the solicitor general of Atlanta, Georgia, who also brandished an indictment for Hamlin on swindling charges. Norfleet got there first. Hamlin greeted him debonairly from his cell, but his face blanched when he saw the document Norfleet held out to him between the bars, the newer, stronger indictment. Defeated, he waived the legal requirement for extradition papers, giving Norfleet the ability to transfer him to Texas without delay.

Norfleet and Flynn personally escorted Hamlin back to Fort Worth. They walked into the sheriff's office and with no fanfare handed over their prisoner, stunning the Fort Worth police officers. When the deputy sheriff set Hamlin's bond at $20,000, one of the largest in the county, Hamlin gasped. That was a bond he could not post, and at last Norfleet had him fast and tight. Nothing further was heard of him until 1933, when he died in a car accident in Tulsa, Oklahoma. His obituary remembered him as the man who was followed for thirty thousand miles by J. Frank Norfleet, "Texas nemesis of confidence men."

Once again, Norfleet's tally stood at four of five swindlers netted and jailed. Only W. B. Spencer, the phony land dealer, was on the loose. To find him, Norfleet would go where all big con artists eventually went, to the rightest town in America, the home of a store so big and modern and lavish it made Council Bluffs and Chicago look like flea markets. Norfleet went to Denver.

CHAPTER EIGHT

The Making of a Confidence Kingpin

With Furey's arrest, Norfleet became a celebrity, and his name became synonymous with con artistry. For each newspaper article that appeared with his name in it, another dozen telegrams and letters appeared at his ranch—"many of which were from women," he could not help but observe. His fans offered him congratulations and tips, but they also came to him seeking help. After returning home to Hale Center in 1921, he was approached by Judge Adrian Poole of El Paso. Judge Poole dragged with him a young friend, a twenty-eight-year-old named Willis Holman, and the judge pleaded with Norfleet to listen to Holman's story and knock some sense into him.

With no little defensiveness, Holman began to tell Norfleet about a man he'd met in Colorado Springs with whom he'd formed a strikingly deep if sudden friendship. This man had taken Holman to Denver to introduce him to a second man, a stockbroker with a unique backstage view on the inner workings of financial markets. The second man had ushered Holman and his friend into a deal, and Holman had quickly earned $37,000. The money awaited him in Denver; all he needed to do was collect $20,000 of his own money. Norfleet held up his hand and ordered him to stop right there. And then, to the young man's astonishment, Norfleet took over the story. He conjured up the scene in which the secretary of the exchange requisitioned Holman's winnings because he was not a member of the exchange. He told in the minutest detail how Holman's friends had pleaded with the secretary to allow Holman to confirm his bid retroactively, and then even pledged some of their own money against that formidable sum. With unsettling prescience, he described the friends' plans to meet Holman in Denver once his portion of the money was securely on his person. And then Norfleet gave a line-by-line itemization of his own losses at the hands of a matching team of swindlers.

Holman set his jaw and denied everything. It wasn't a swindle, he was sure of it, and he was going to return to Denver to see the deal through to the end. Norfleet sighed. So he told Holman that if he were truly determined to return to Denver, he could count on Norfleet's company for the journey. Norfleet thought it was just possible that Holman's team included his one remaining prey, W. B. Spencer, and the lead was just too promising to pass up. After a night's consideration, Holman decided to give up on his friends in Denver. Norfleet, though, had been infected, and he bought a ticket for that night's train to Colorado. Presumably, it was Eliza's turn to sigh. The ranch was in dire straits yet again, so before he left, Norfleet arranged to sell a large flock of turkeys and some hogs. He also called on his bankers in Plainview to obtain yet another extension on his debts, and then off he went.

Norfleet stopped at Colorado Springs to see if he could gather more intelligence on Holman's team of bunco artists before exposing himself in Denver, but no sooner had he stepped off the train than Captain Irving Bruce of the Colorado Springs Police Department told him to go back home. Captain Bruce warned Norfleet that his amateur sleuthing was not welcome in Denver, because a brash young district attorney was about to bust wide open the swindling syndicate that had been throttling civic life for more than two decades. The district attorney was at the delicate end of a sting that had consumed eighteen months, thousands of dollars, and the best undercover detectives in the country. Captain Bruce told Norfleet that his presence in Denver would only disrupt the swindlers' routine on which the district attorney depended in order to track and net his quarry. So, for the next several days, Norfleet stayed at the Broadmoor Hotel in Colorado Springs, asking questions and piecing stories together. It was here that he learned the full story of the Denver mastermind Lou Blonger, the openly acknowledged boss of the city, the one with a private telephone line to the chief of police, the one whose mistress's lavish home served as a secret rendezvous from which politicians and the syndicate's top executives ran the city. Blonger was what Joseph Furey might have been had he stayed put and dominated a single city, what Big Mike McDonald might have been had he lived into the era of the big con. Could Norfleet stay away from *that*? No, he could not.

Lou Blonger didn't seem like much of a criminal mastermind. His sad eyes and hot-dog-bun nose didn't exactly inspire fear. One reporter affectionately described him as "short, rotund, affable," another as "always a big-hearted spender," yet another as "generous and kind." He was famous around town for his cherry list. He owned a fifty-five-acre cherry orchard just outside the city, and at harvest time he'd give away crates of cherries to the friends and charities on his list, which served as a kind of directory of the innermost circle of Denver elite. The rest of the year, he'd reach into his pocket for anyone in need and pull out a thick wad of bills folded in half lengthwise and then doubled. One recipient recalled, "He would peel off a twenty or a fifty or a 'grand' with the ease an ordinary fellow flips out a dime." At Christmas, poor families all over Denver would feast on turkeys that Lou had sent them.

Each weekday morning, Blonger would climb to the third floor of the American Bank Building on Seventeenth and Lawrence. Behind a plaque that identified his business as mining, he tended to the operations of the Forest Queen Lode, the gold mine on Ironclad Hill in Cripple Creek that he had claimed with his brother Sam in 1892. The mine had quickly proved to be a steady producer, and then in 1909 a rich seam of ore was discovered that began to yield even bigger dividends. By 1911 the operators were shipping close to eight hundred tons of ore a month at a price of $40 per ton, and Blonger's share made him a wealthy man. Each weeknight, he joined his mistress, Iola Readon, in the mansion he had bought her in the country-club district, just down the street from the fashionable Church of the Ascension. Each Saturday morning, Readon would drive him in her purring limousine to the Kentom, an elegant brick apartment building in the Capitol Hill neighborhood, where he would spend the weekend with Cora, his long-suffering wife. In the evenings, he could frequently be seen in dress clothes on his way to the theater in an exceedingly convincing impression of a prosperous businessman.

And yet every last person in town knew him as the fixer. It was perhaps the city's most wide-open secret that Lou Blonger ran Denver. Everyone knew that only a fraction of his wealth came from mining, and everyone knew that though he was the sole person at work in room 309 of the American Bank Building, he commanded an army of men. The ropers, spielers, and bookmakers who filled the corps of the big con were strictly prohibited from entering his office lest they encounter one of the politicians whom Blonger controlled. Each side of the law needed to be able to say plausibly under oath that it had never met the other.

As early as 1895, Denver newspapers had begun referring to him as one of the bosses of the town, even helpfully listing his crew, which back then rather touchingly consisted only of Little Duff Cline, Long and Shorty Washburn, Red Gibson, and Jim Thornton. By 1901 he was "the recognized leader of the gang of bunco men." By the 1920s, at least seventy men worked under Blonger in Denver, though some would later number his international corps of swindlers at over five hundred. They'd work in Florida over the winter, and then in the summer the Denver swindling season would commence. From the first of June to the first of November, three- and four-man teams ran the fake stock exchange or the fake horse race on traveling businessmen, often lining them up like trains in a station and methodically processing them in successive or even overlapping dramas. In 1920, Blonger's crew earned $100,000. In 1921, they more than doubled that, earning over $225,000. And 1922 was shaping up to be their best year yet. By August, when Norfleet sat ready to spring into town, they already had over $270,000 in their pockets or on the send. The ring was said to have earned $1.5 million from its shadow play of gambling and speculation. In the 1920s, the newspapers called him "King" Lou Blonger.

He had come a long way from unremarkable beginnings. He was born in Vermont in May 1849, the same month that the Confidence Man began to appear on the streets of Manhattan. He grew up in Wisconsin, one of five brothers and nine sisters. He left home three days before his fifteenth birthday to enlist in the Union army. After the war, he followed his brother Sam around the Southwest, pacing from one boomtown to another. He arrived in Denver in 1888, when he was thirty-nine years old. At that age, Joe Furey had already been arrested half a dozen times and was a familiar figure to police officers and newspaper editors around the country. J. Frank Norfleet was a married father with his own homestead and the beginnings of a valuable herd of cattle. The men they were to become were already apparent in the men they were. Blonger, on the other hand, had no arrest record, no ties to elders in the con fraternity, no clever innovations on bunco schemes or games of chance. What he did have was the perfect city in which to stage his improbable rise.

The town that Blonger found, when he disembarked at the new Union Station at Wynkoop and Seventeenth, was not terribly different from the ragged camp that had sprung up in 1858 when gold was discovered up in the mountains, but it was on the verge of its renaissance. The man and the city would shape each other. Between 1860 and 1870, Denver gained only ten inhabitants, but between 1870, when the railroads arrived in town, and Lou Blonger's arrival the city grew more rapidly than any other in the country, from 5,000 to 106,000 residents. If they weren't there to mine the mountains, they were there to sell goods to those who did, or to speculate on the real estate of those who would soon arrive. A handful came in the hopes that the dry mountain air would cure their tuberculosis, but the pollution from the ore-smelting factories on the outskirts of the city gave the lie to that civic claim. All of a sudden the city's development was heedless, swift, and dizzyingly profitable. Denver was, in the admiring words of a contemporary writer, "crowding a century into a generation."

Blonger would have left Union Station and embarked down Seventeenth Street, a wide thoroughfare of contradictions. Depending on who was doing the naming, Seventeenth was called either "the Wall Street of the West" or "scratch alley." It was lined largely with three-story buildings in Denver's trademark red brick and yellow stone, but it still lacked sewers and pavement; throughout the day, sprinkling tanks would slowly empty water onto the sand and gravel to keep the street compact. When it rained, one dry goods merchant would hire a porter to stand in the mud in hip-length boots and lay down planks for pedestrians to cross the street into his store.

The first thing a miner, cowboy, or farmer would do upon arriving in Denver after months in the mine or on the range would be to seek out a shave and haircut. A so-called bandit barber on Seventeenth would show him a sign with the reasonable price of two bits, half the going rate in other towns. Then the barber would drape his grateful customer's head in a hot towel and turn the sign around to read "shave and a haircut, eight bits." As he lifted the towel off the man's face, he'd swipe a bit of mud from his boots and display it on the white cloth, convincing the customer to spring for a shampoo as well. In like fashion, the barber would treat his customer's blackheads and dandruff, trim and curl his mustache, and control his split ends. The cost of the haircut could reach as high as $5 or $10. And if he got that far, the bandit barber would shave a tiny inverted V at the base of the man's neck, literally a mark on the mark for the swindlers who worked the sidewalks of Seventeenth Street to detect when he emerged from the salon.

Blonger would have been wise to the bandit barbers. Four blocks from the station, he would almost certainly have encountered the city's most eminent swindler hard at work on the corner of Seventeenth and Larimer, just outside the newly opened Tivoli Club. A reporter for the *Rocky Mountain News* once stood at that same corner and disgustedly noted "a fleet of old shoes, cabbage leaves and potato peelings . . . vainly trying to sail upon a lake of liquid putrefaction." Stench notwithstanding, there was always a small crowd gathered there, and inside the knot of onlookers would be a slender, dapper gentleman with dark hair and a Vandyke beard, his voice raised to the audience as he held out a satchel filled with milky white blocks.

This was Jefferson Randolph Smith, sometimes known as Jeff but more frequently called Soapy after the product he peddled so lucratively, though when the newspapers were in a sardonic mood his moniker would be heightened to Sapolio. "Ladies and gentlemen," his spiel would begin, "I'm out here to do some advertising. The company that I [represent] could plaster the walls of your city [with] billboards, with advertisements, that cost plenty of money. We're going to do it direct, direct to you. We're going to hand out this beautiful soap. The idea is to get this soap in your hands so that you'll speak a good word for it. We don't care how much money it costs to get it there. Money or nothing, I'm going to start giving some prizes out right now." And before the astonished eyes of the crowd, he'd take out a sheaf of $20, $50, and $100 bills and start slipping them into the paper labels wrapped around the bars of soap, then tossing the soap back into his sack. Someone would come forth and hand him $5 for a bar, then fish around in the satchel, pick out a bar of soap, and unwrap it to find his prize. Soon all the people in the crowd would be digging into their pockets for $5, and Soapy Smith would say, "Now, one word before you go. I don't want any of you to show that until you get home. The reason is that I don't want one person to see a hundred dollar bill, another one to see a fifty, and [another one to] reach down and [see] he only got twenty." As his customers grabbed their bars and pocketed them, he would jovially tell them, "Good day, gentlemen. Ladies and gentlemen, I want you to use that soap. I want you to use it. It's worth every cent you paid for it."

Of course no one ever discovered a cash prize inside the penny soap when he or she unwrapped it at home. It was the same con that Mike McDonald would work so well on the railroads before settling in to fix and oil Chicago's machine, but Soapy took it to new heights by hiring a legion of shills, half a dozen of them planted in each crowd to find the lucky soaps. Afterward, they'd further sweeten Soapy's profits by steering men into the Tivoli, which Soapy owned and where he sermonized over its long cherrywood bar and its two dozen green baize tables as what he called a "non-ordained preacher on the vagaries of fortune." There, out-of-towners would be dealt into the Big Hand, a daily poker game run by one of Soapy's best "deck mechanics." Four or five shills would fold good hands and run up the bets on bad ones until the victim felt confident enough to go all in. Soapy kept a business ledger, and in one three-month period he rather unnecessarily broke down his profits and losses for the Big Hand: "Winnings: $4,087, Losses: $0, Volume: $4,087, Win/Loss: +4,087—win/loss to volume: +100%." Figures like this would occasionally bother city officials enough to haul Soapy into court, but he always got off with a bit of Barnumesque showmanship. At one court appearance, he claimed the Tivoli was, in truth, a reformatory for gambling addicts. "After a man once comes to my place he is cured of gambling absolutely. He doesn't want any more of it."

Perhaps Lou Blonger climbed the stairs to the Tivoli for a game of faro, or perhaps he walked two blocks down and two blocks over to the Palace Theatre at Blake and Fifteenth Street, one of the most notorious gambling halls of the West. Inside, twenty-five dealers raked in patrons' money at tables in front of the long bar with a sixty-foot mirror behind it. At the back of the room, perched on his trademark high stool, sat Big Ed Chase, a shotgun across his immaculately tailored lap. The Palace Theatre, which Chase opened in the 1870s, was a magnificent combination of a 750-seat theater, at which a chorus line danced from 9:00 a.m. to 4:00 a.m., and a gambling hall large enough for a crowd of two hundred. Curtained booths on the upper floors allowed senators and city founders to frolic and fondle the "wine girls" in private. Chase hired a string orchestra down from Chicago, and so lovely was its music to the culture-starved families of the boomtown that on summer nights, they'd park their broughams, berlins, phaetons, and surreys in the blocks outside the Palace to listen to the notes that rose above the whir of the roulette and the chink of coins.

Notwithstanding these provisions for the comfort of the refined class, the Palace had garnered a reputation for depravity and violence. In 1888, when Blonger arrived, *The Denver Republican* denounced it as "a thoroughly tough, hard place, frequented by a class of desperate, depraved men and women." Indeed, the previous thirteen months had witnessed four homicides within its walls. But no one ever threatened Chase himself. With his tall frame, his prematurely gray hair, his clear blue eyes, and his perfect suits, the gambling king of Denver was more patrician than thuggish, and he was treated with deference by criminals and politicians alike.

Soapy Smith and Ed Chase had divided the town between them: Smith ran the bunco steerers on Seventeenth Street, fleecing the out-of-towners, and Chase ran the square gambling halls, taking Denverites' money in exchange for an evening of jollity and refreshment. The two men coexisted well enough, as evidenced by the fact that Chase held a stake in Smith's Tivoli Club, but Chase was the lodestar in the city's constellation of power. From his tenure on the city council in the 1860s, when he'd set the fines for gambling so low that they became a kind of backdoor license, to the 1880s, when he had the police force on his payroll and the mayor took a regular 20 percent cut of all gambling profits, Chase had been designing the city to his own purposes. By 1886, the fix was working perfectly: when an amateur crime statistician analyzed the numbers and types of arrests in July of that year, he found that the Denver police had detained 431 people—but not one person had been arrested for gambling. Police regularly staged raids on the city's saloons and gambling dens, but they always made sure to knock out a secret code before they entered to allow the evidence of vice to be swept away.

Lou Blonger surveyed the city's invisible power grid and threw in his lot with Big Ed. He quickly went to work in Chase's vote-fixing organization, escorting tramps and tipplers from bars to polling places so they could stuff ballot boxes on behalf of vice-friendly candidates.

He and his brother Sam opened up the first of a series of saloons just off Seventeenth Street. They owned it jointly with Soapy Smith, but it was Chase to whom they tithed for the privilege of running crooked faro games. Blonger was working his way up in the underworld of Seventeenth Street, but he was succeeding just as the business world was ousting the paid-off politicians and reaching down into the underworld to seize control of the city.

They began with Seventeenth Street, aiming to turn it into a more comfortable home for eastern capital. Already, a prime triangle of land at Tremont Place on which a single cow had expensively grazed was being transformed into the lavish Brown Palace Hotel. Just across the street was the Denver Club, a private men's club that expressed Denver's financial ambitions in red sandstone Romanesque arches and turrets on a manicured lawn. No bandit barbers for the members of this club. Each morning, the "17th Streeters," the dozen leaders of the club, would take turns settling into the chair of the club barber, Fred Basford, and without needing to say a word, they would receive his meticulous attention to their hair and beards. Nor did these men need the entertainments that Soapy and Chase offered. Each evening, they'd stop back in again at the club for dinner at the central table of the imposing dining room, sipping the city's best champagne and discussing their entwined business interests. Men like David H. Moffat, Jerome B. Chaffee, Horace Tabor, and Eben Smith didn't need to compete against each other at faro, because they collaborated with each other in the far more intoxicating game of mining speculation.

One visitor to Denver was astonished to discover that everyone at his hotel, from the owner to the desk clerk, porter, and chambermaid, held claims to mines up in the mountains. The question was how to extract profit from those promising pieces of paper. Moffat, Chaffee, Tabor, and Smith could simply sit in their downtown lairs, receive a steady stream of prospectors and engineers from the mountains who spieled about the invisible richness of their properties, and decide whom to buy out and enfold into their ongoing mining operations. But most entrepreneurs looking to finance the exploration and extraction of gold or silver formed joint-stock companies, hired promoters, and sent them to New York and Boston to chase down the money where it lived.

The promoter would arrive in an eastern city with a prospectus carefully worded to appeal directly to the heart of the second-tier businessman, someone who admired the market manipulations of Jay Gould and Cornelius Vanderbilt in the newspapers but could not himself command enough capital to replicate those feats of enterprise and greed. Western mining, the prospectus would implicitly promise, afforded the proper scope for someone of modest capital and outsize daring. In the 1870s and 1880s, the conservative New York Stock Exchange did not list mining stocks. The chance that any given patch of mountain soil would open up to yield gold or silver was unbelievably slim, and even if it did, the capital required to ship, assemble, and maintain the equipment to work the lode deposits and mill the ore was so steep as to halt the enterprise before it could begin. And then there was the rampant fraud. Promoters named their worthless claims after the famous producers, or salted Colorado mines with Utah gold. Even the 17th Streeters were caught up in the great diamond craze of 1872, when two prospectors found jewels up in the mountains, and it seemed as if Colorado's riches might well be inexhaustible. Soon over twenty-five investment companies were created with a total capitalization of $250 million, and just as soon thereafter a geologist discovered that the prospectors had planted the diamonds.

But the ore specimens that were passed around bankers' offices and gentlemen's clubs were often too tempting to manufacturers who wanted to become speculators. Isaac L. Ellwood, the barbed-wire magnate and Norfleet's former boss, became principal owner of a Colorado silver mine that netted $96,000 in its first six months. On the other hand, Norvin Green, the president of Western Union, spread $100,000 over twenty different Colorado mining properties with little return. Even though men of Ellwood and Green's class believed gambling to be a sin, and even though some of the mining prospectuses felt obliged to acknowledge the risky nature of the endeavor—mining is "essentially a lottery, with a few great prizes and very many blanks," confessed one—everyone still wanted in.

The question, in the second half of the nineteenth century, was how to separate a definition of speculation from the larger, messier classification of gambling, a definition that could perform the moral work of enshrining speculation as a necessary part of economic growth while decrying gambling as a waste of productive dollars. It was a laborious process because, for the first chapter of American history, the two activities were nearly identical, and gambling was an economic mainstay of the developing nation.

Colonists had used lotteries to raise money for capital-intensive building projects like roads, bridges, dams, canals, lighthouses, jails, and schools. They favored lotteries over taxation because they were a voluntary way to pool funds. They held dozens of small, private schemes in cities and towns, including Benjamin Franklin's contest to raise money for strengthening Philadelphia's defenses during the War of the Austrian Succession in the 1740s. Far from being a social menace, lotteries were so crucial to the success of the new nation that by 1776, all but two of the states insisted that they be run by the government, thus monopolizing for themselves the competition for scarce dollars. At the end of the eighteenth century, the annual sale of lottery tickets ran as high as $2 million among a population of four million. By 1815, every town with more than a thousand residents had at least one person making a living by selling lottery tickets for civic infrastructure. Gambling was at once an unremarkable occurrence and the spark for economic development.

As the nineteenth century advanced, Americans began to think more concertedly about the moral implications of monetary acquisition. At issue was not the legitimacy of personal profit itself but rather the emotions that were released in its pursuit. To moralists and reformers, gambling encouraged superstition rather than rationality and undermined the willingness to work hard by offering the fantasy of a quick reward. By 1840, gambling was reproachable enough that citizens agreed the government should have no hand in it, and most states had shut down their lotteries. Yet gambling was tempting enough that it thrived in urban gaming halls, on the ships and shores of the southwestern frontier along the Mississippi River, and in outposts like Denver. Newspapers published exposés of vice districts that were so detailed in their enumeration of the gambling halls that they could also be read as guides to the city's nightlife—Soapy's dive for the greenhorns this way, Chase's lair for the miners and millionaires two blocks over. With a style of gambling for each social class, it permeated the commercialized leisure world, and reformers found it impossible to root out.

Yet it remained increasingly difficult to discern where gambling ended and speculation began. Some of the very same people who had run the state lotteries now worked as stockbrokers in an increasingly lawless system of capital accumulation that promised outrageous profits with a mere exchange of papers. The success of the Erie Canal bond issues in the late 1810s and early 1820s had uncovered a wide reservoir of capital from which public works could now draw, initiating the railroad boom that would define nineteenth-century economic expansion. In 1830, there were only 23 miles of railroad tracks in the entire country, but thereafter the number increased exponentially, from 2,818 miles in 1840, to 9,021 in 1850, to 30,626 in 1860. The railroads integrated local markets into national ones by allowing producers to sell their goods to faraway warehouses and consumers. They powered the Industrial Revolution by creating a demand for homegrown components like rails, cross ties, spikes, bridges, and, eventually, locomotives (the first American commercial locomotive was named the Tom Thumb, after one of Barnum's most successful humbugs).

But more than that, railroad financing swelled the coffers of Wall Street and turned it into a roulette wheel with no croupier. In 1835, only three railroads issued stock on Wall Street. By 1855, the volume of securities available on Wall Street had ballooned by a factor of ten, and more than half of them were railroad stocks. A full third of the tracks built between 1830 and 1890 served no purpose other than lining the portfolios of the financiers who looted their securities, and they were called "blackmail railroads" by those who saw through the deception. Jay Gould's Erie Railway, or the "scarlet woman of Wall Street," was only the most notorious of a list that included the Harlem, the Michigan Southern, Prairie du Chien, and the Chicago and North Western. In 1873, the collapse in value of Northern Pacific's securities caused a panic on Wall Street and the longest depression of the century. In 1884, Moody's credit-rating service calculated that as much as $4 billion in railroad stock had been watered by unscrupulous owners who inflated the value of their assets, much as cattle drivers once bloated their cows with water before weighing them at auction.

The nineteenth century witnessed new ways to profit but also a ratcheting up of the risks within the financial market, and the very existence of those risks began to overturn the traditional understanding of Providence. If, at the beginning of the century, Americans largely viewed Providence as an orderly but unknown plan that gambling unnaturally disrupted, by the end of the century it was everyday life that was itself a gamble, and the judicious appropriation of capital could neutralize its risks. Life insurance and savings banks, once perceived as hazardous uses for hard-earned income, now seemed the very safest hedges against the wide swings of Fortune's pendulum.

A taste for speculation began to creep down from the robber barons to the middle class, some of whom first saw their capital grow upon itself through compound interest and then began to participate in the securities and bond markets during the Civil War. At the beginning of the war, fewer than 1 percent of Americans owned securities. During the war, the Treasury bond drive created a new investor class, and eventually about 5 percent of northern citizens held bonds in denominations as low as $50. Wartime speculation was a dicey business, however. The price of gold went up with each Union victory, so a handful of speculators paid agents on both sides of the war to obtain information straight from the battlefield. Wall Street learned the outcome of the Battle of Gettysburg before President Lincoln did. Lincoln's feelings on the matter ran high, and one day he asked Andrew Curtin, the governor of Pennsylvania, "What do you think of those fellows in Wall Street, who are gambling in gold at such a time as this? For my part," and here the mild president banged his fist down on a table, "I wish every one of them had his devilish head shot off!" Lincoln attempted to stop such speculation, but he succeeded only in driving it underground.

So which was it? Was gambling a pernicious social evil or a respectable pathway from the striving underclasses to wealth? The urgency of this question increased as the nineteenth century progressed and opportunities to gamble propagated. By the 1870s, there was a general if often unheeded consensus that gaming was immoral, and most states, as well as the Colorado Territory, had outlawed it.

Speculation, on the other hand, was hoarded as a prerogative of the elite. Its risks required such detailed knowledge, and its actions demanded such a broad playing field, that only the already wealthy had the reach and vision for it. Norvin Green, the president of Western Union, a man who had doubled his fortune with shares in his own company even as he lost money in Colorado mining stock, firmly believed that the general public had no business in stock speculation. He opposed efforts to nationalize the telegraph and defended its high prices, testifying to Congress that farmers and artisans had no business with the stock quotations it carried and that it should remain a specialized tool of financiers. In his private correspondence, Green considered it his "duty" to warn his friends and family away from mining stock, even as he continued to pour his own money in. He was the president of two mining concerns, one of them the United Claims Mining Company, a steady money loser. When, in a bid to shore up its books, a promoter solicited Western Union managers for shares of stock, wholly without Green's permission, his two interests collided. He could not abide the idea of the "more ignorant" employees throwing their hard-earned money away on what he knew to be an unwise gamble, but neither could he speak out against his own mine and appear as if he had "no faith in the value of the property." At the time of his death in 1893, he was still vainly trying to keep United Claims afloat, but now only with rich men's money.

Blame it on Barnum. The willingness to speculate long after it had become unprofitable was an increasingly common American trait, and it was closely related to humbug, to the tolerance that Barnum had unleashed for minor fraud and perceptual ambiguity. Barnum's hoaxes both exploited and further created a market sensibility that thrived primarily on a willingness to take risks. But even more than that, the growing opportunities to speculate on America's development played into other, less overtly economic mind-sets, such as a reluctance to be left out of national trends that helped Americans define themselves. Most notably, those with the means to speculate found confidence to be more pleasurable than skepticism. It was as simple as that. There was a strikingly noncapitalist impulse at the heart of American economic expansion.

So it was not as easy to keep the middle class out of the capital markets as Norvin Green would have liked. Even as Green shielded Western Union employees from the plummeting fortunes of mining stocks, enterprising businessmen were tapping the Western Union lines that fed into brokerages and stealing stock price quotations from its tickers for use in bucket shops, in order to peddle a new kind of democratic speculation. Bucket shops were brokerage houses at which customers could place bets on the direction of the market without actually purchasing securities or commodities. Beginning in the 1870s, they catered to small-time speculators on the margins of the great financial centers, clerks and newsboys and farmers in from the country who wanted to dabble in finance but lacked the capital to participate in the New York Stock Exchange or the Chicago Board of Trade.

A customer would enter a building adorned with a sign reading "Bankers and Brokers." Inside, he would invariably find a large office dominated by an oak-framed blackboard on which stock quotations were incessantly chalked and erased in columns underneath gold-painted categories like "cotton" and "grain." He would take a seat in one of the chairs facing the board, joining the rows of men already gazing eagerly at the numbers as if at a riveting performance, and there he would sit, listening to the stock ticker transmitting prices from the nearest central exchange. When he felt confident enough to plunge into the action, he would fill out a buy or sell order for an amount as small as five shares, and then he'd put down a margin as tiny as 3 percent per share of stock, much less than the hundred-share minimum and the margin requirement of 10 percent mandated by the New York Stock Exchange. A clerk would then forward his order to the exchange via telegraph. While he waited for the market to move in the direction he'd predicted, he might sample the complimentary luncheon laid out for him, smoke a cigar, or gaze at the illustrations of nude women on the walls.

What happened next depended on the exact form of chicanery in which each bucket shop indulged. All orders were "bucketed"; that is, none of them were exercised on a legitimate exchange. Such orders were side bets between a customer and the bucket shop on the fluctuations of prices on the stock ticker, a zero-sum game in which the bucket shop took the other side of the customer's "trade" and almost invariably profited by it through a menu of tricks. If the price referenced by a buy order went down by even a small amount, the customer's margin would be swallowed up, and the order would be closed out. A bucket shopper could simply fake the prices he displayed on the board. He could "wash down" a stock on which many of his customers were bullish by selling small lots on a legitimate exchange at a low price. In the event of an honestly reported increase in a stock's price, the bucket shopper could adjust his commission to bite into his customer's profit, called "till-tapping." And rival bucket shops could join together to pool their customers' funds and open opposite positions in the legitimate market for their own accounts. Customers patronized bucket shops thinking they were democratic portals into the thrilling world of financial markets, when in fact they were confidence games for the common man.

The legitimate exchanges desperately needed to distinguish themselves from such shamelessly deceptive practices. The Chicago Board of Trade (CBT) soaped up the windows of its exchange, repeatedly tried to prevent Western Union from installing telegraph lines in bucket shops, and hired detectives to discover pirated wire loops within legitimate brokerages. Bucket shops continued to flourish throughout the 1890s, so at the turn of the century the CBT brought the fight over the legitimacy of speculation to the courts, arguing that price quotations were its intellectual property. Though bucket shops violated many state antigambling laws, judges repeatedly denied the CBT a legal victory because it hadn't yet demonstrated how its business practices materially differed from the bucket shop's brand of speculation. In 1903, one judge ruled that the CBT's activities were "so infected with illegality as to preclude resort to a court of equity for its protection." The Chicago Board of Trade's strategy of legitimization was backfiring spectacularly.

In 1905, the CBT appealed its suit against one of the most notorious bucket shoppers, C. C. Christie in Kansas City, to the U.S. Supreme Court. In just a few pithy phrases, Justice Oliver Wendell Holmes reversed decades of precedent to hand the CBT a victory and demarcate in absolute terms the difference between speculation and gambling. He wrote, "People will endeavor to forecast the future and to make agreements according to their prophecy. Speculation of this kind by competent men is the self-adjustment of society to the probable. Its value is well known as a means of avoiding or mitigating catastrophes, equalizing prices and providing for periods of want." He argued that since contracts to buy and sell commodities on the CBT included a clause stipulating the terms for delivery, they were more than "mere wagers," even if that clause was rarely activated. And he ruled that the CBT's stock quotations were proprietary knowledge which it could rightfully protect from the bucket shops' theft. Justice Holmes's ruling, in effect, turned the Chicago Board of Trade into a producer, with price discovery as its labor and stock prices as its valuable export. As Christie pointed out in his refutation of Justice Holmes in *Everybody's Magazine,* there still remained on the books an Illinois statute against wagering, so members of the CBT regularly broke the law each time they executed a put or call option. But it was no use: public opinion had finally turned against the bucket shops, even if the law had yet to catch up. The financiers had accomplished their moral project of separating speculation from gambling and turning stock purchases into a laudable form of investing surplus capital.

The following year, local, state, and federal officials regularly raided bucket shops, causing little flurries of commotion in business districts across the country. The first official to win jail sentences for bucket shop owners was Thomas Lee Woolwine, the Los Angeles district attorney who would later help Norfleet prosecute the crooked police officers Walter Lips and William Anderson. Woolwine and his counterparts in other states were helped along by exchanges in Chicago, New York, and elsewhere that hired their own investigators to dig up evidence and turn it over to law enforcers. In 1913, New York closed the final loophole in its law against bucket shops, and in 1915 the president of the New York Stock Exchange pronounced them dead. Yet their closures were uneven across the country. In Denver, they would not be outlawed until May 1919, and ironically enough the man responsible for shuttering the common man's confidence dens would be Horace Hawkins, Lou Blonger's lawyer.

Blonger's livelihood as a saloon owner was increasingly hard to maintain in the 1890s. The more respectable speculation became, the less tolerance middle-class citizens had for gambling. Organizations like the Woman's Christian Temperance Union and the Law and Order League put so much pressure on the dens of iniquity that public officials were forced to close them periodically, despite payouts from Blonger, Soapy, and Chase. The entire city knew these closures were a symbolic gesture; all they had to do was look across the Platte River to the "sporty municipality" of Colfax to see the selfsame gambling haunts, well lit and bustling, in rooms rented for the duration of their exile from Denver. The town board of Colfax welcomed the gamblers with a detailed contract: they could operate their games without interference, as long as they agreed to be arrested once a month, upon which they'd pay a fine of $50 into the town treasury and be released. And so these "spasms of virtue," as the newspapers took to calling them, were merely a monthlong holiday from drinking and gambling before the cards, dice, and wheels came out again and the kickbacks to city officials resumed. Most gamblers saw the benefit of these spasms of virtue: they allowed the mayor and the police chief to save face, and they drove out the weak competition who lacked the capital to weather a dry spell.

The Blongers were squeezed several times by just such spasms. In September 1891, their saloon on Larimer Street was singled out, and then again in April 1892, just after they'd filed their claim on the Forest Queen Mine. They were undaunted by what must have felt like persecution, and later that year they relocated to a new saloon around the corner on Market Street just off Seventeenth.

In 1894, a new chief of police, Hamilton Armstrong, took office with a strict mandate to shut down gambling in the city of Denver. Accordingly, the big players in the underworld pooled their resources and sent a man to see Chief Armstrong in his office. The representative opened a bag and spilled onto the chief's desk a pile of $100 bills, more than $13,000 in total. The chief didn't touch the money. He picked up a gun lying next to the stack. "You put that money back in the package before I drill you," he ordered, "and tell the men who sent you that gambling in Denver—while I am chief of police—doesn't go!" True to his word, he soon shuttered every gambling den on Seventeenth and its environs, including the Blongers' place, every saloon dark and ornamented with a sign reading "Closed" or "To Let." But Chief Armstrong wasn't yet done. Next, he arrested Ed Chase in his policy shop on Fifteenth Street (the one with a sign out front reading "Loans Negotiated"), which was almost certainly a first for the underworld czar. The following month, the chief arrested Soapy Smith for luring a Kansas schoolteacher into a gambling den and uncoupling him from his money.

In November 1894, fifty prominent businesses, including two banks, petitioned the Fire and Police Board to allow gambling dens to reopen in downtown Denver. The petition strikingly avoided any mention of the "moral, social, and legal aspects of the case," as *The New York Times* noted in wonderment. Instead, it proceeded in the language of cool, rational economic self-interest: if gambling dens remained closed, "many buildings and parts of buildings [would be] rendered tenantless and bring in no rent to the owners thereof." Furthermore, "a large amount of money [would be] kept from coming into the city of Denver and being put into circulation." Rumor had it that the man behind the petition was Lou Blonger. He had mastered the rhetoric of his more respectable peers and could align them with his interests in part because he was not a showman like Soapy Smith. Soapy was soon forced to leave town, and his departure left a power vacuum that Lou Blonger was, by now, perfectly groomed to fill. When the newspapers reported the goings-on of the bunco gangs on Seventeenth Street, they now referred to Chase and Blonger as the vice district's overlords.

The last obstacle to Blonger's career evaporated in November 1895 when gambling was again legalized. Soon, Blonger signaled his ambitions by opening the Elite on Stout Street with his brother Sam. Suddenly the newspapers had only encomiums for the man above the law. The *Rocky Mountain News* wrote, "Nowadays men drink like gentlemen and it is little wonder that when they drink they insist on surroundings befitting them. There are gentlemen in Denver who realize this truth. They are the Messrs. Blonger Brothers." The papers lavished description on the Elite: its mahogany fixtures, marble floors, and the frescoed ceiling that alone cost $8,000. The public froth over dramshops had subsided enough that the city could acknowledge the need for a genteel watering hole, and with its elegant café in the back serving a midday meal, the Elite conformed to the general expectation that imbibing would not be its sole activity and that gambling would no longer be overt. In 1897, Lou and Sam finally warranted an entry in R. G. Dun's credit reference book, where their "pecuniary strength" was estimated at $5,000 to $10,000 and their credit rating was "good," the next-to-highest score. Blonger was reshaping himself as a businessman, and the city accepted the impersonation at face value.

The Elite did not last long, perhaps because Blonger's energies were required elsewhere. At the beginning of the twentieth century, Blonger marshaled men on the street, while Chase sat in a paneled office and ran Denver with a nod of his head. Aspirants for elected office were forced to visit the great man and get his approval before even publicly suggesting they'd like to run. One ambitious young lawyer named Benjamin Lindsey auditioned for district attorney in 1900. Chase's go-between explained what would be required of Lindsey were he selected for the position: "Mr. Chase doesn't want anything but what's fair. He doesn't expect to run wide open all the time. Whenever the District Attorney has to make a demonstration, *he's* willing to pay up. That's understood. You needn't feel worried about that." Chase sensed that Lindsey was unsettled by the proposition, and he selected someone else as district attorney. It was a prescient character assessment: Lindsey would go on to become a crusading county court judge, the founder of the nation's first juvenile court system, a Progressive reformer, and the author of a muckraking exposé of the Denver machine called *The Beast*.

As Chase advanced into his seventies and eighties, he retired from the strenuous work of machine politics, preferring instead to settle into his redbrick mansion on the corner of Colfax and Race, surveying the city from its corner tower, or taking the air in his touring car, a sporty Thomas Flyer, accepting the admiration of Denver's citizens in his goggles and dust coat. By the first decade of the twentieth century, Blonger had become the city's center of gravity.

He stayed almost completely out of the newspapers during this time, but when he did appear, it was always without introduction, as if all of Denver knew his role in the shadow government. The police laughed uproariously in 1898 when a bold young impresario named C. M. Fagen-Bush swung into town and swindled Blonger out of $1,000 in a mining stock deal—"He Buncoed Blonger," read the gleeful headline. The *Rocky Mountain News* reported on the scene in the police station when Blonger came in to make his complaint: "All the detectives were taken with a fit of laughter. Their mouths stretched and their sides shook. Tears rolled down their cheeks and it was fifteen minutes before they could compose themselves." They laughed again in 1902 when a man in a dirty coat submitted to a short con in one of Blonger's joints on Seventeenth Street but reversed the direction of the swindle and took $200 from Blonger with a bad check. "The funniest part of the joke," crowed *The Denver Times*, "is the 'holler' Blonger made to Chief Armstrong. Blonger left the bank for headquarters so fast his coattails could not be seen for dust." The papers gave comparatively little space to Blonger's arrest for assault and battery in the Fagen-Bush affair; nor did they dwell on the beating he and Sam gave to a saloon keeper who wouldn't let Blonger's crew work in his establishment, nor could they work up much ire when a young Kansas fireman committed suicide after writing a check to L. H. Blonger for money he did not possess. The newspapers largely confined themselves to toothless griping at Blonger's connections with Frank Adams, head of the Fire and Police Board, and Milton Smith, chairman of the Democratic State Central Committee. Lou racked up two more arrests for gambling but evaded jail time for both.

In 1904, a shocking speech delivered on the floor of the House of Representatives in Washington, D.C., predicated Blonger's sudden ouster from Denver. Congressman John Shafroth of Colorado's First District stood up before his colleagues and announced that he had been illegally elected. He told them he'd been examining ballots from the 1902 contest between himself and the Republican Robert Bonynge, and "I must say that if I were a Judge upon the bench, considering this case, I would be compelled to find that, according to law, Mr. Bonynge is entitled to the seat." In the suit that Bonynge had filed against him, eight witnesses, including an undercover detective sent downtown on a sting operation, testified to seeing Lou Blonger hand out silver dollars and voting tickets to the drinkers and gamblers who thronged around him on Seventeenth Street. Blonger's crew voted all day long, even interrupting him when he ducked inside for a drink to plead, "Give us some more slips right quick, we want to go back again." Shafroth handed his seat over to Bonynge just three days after his announcement to Congress, and Bonynge served until 1909. "Honest John" Shafroth's reputation soared, and he would go on to become governor of Colorado and then U.S. senator. There were no losers in the election of 1902.

Blonger was never prosecuted for election fraud, yet his position in Denver had become untenable. In February 1904, he announced that he and his brother Sam were packing up their faro boxes and leaving Denver for Havana, Cuba. "What's the use of staying in a business where you can't make anything?" complained Lou. "When you do make a little, the police take it away from you." A businessman to the last, Blonger would go where the profits were unimpeded by a maturing city's need for respectability. Sixteen years after he'd arrived, Blonger left the city of Denver.

CHAPTER NINE

The Machine and the Sting

Hermann H. Heiser of the Heiser Saddlery Company purchased an office building on Welton Street in Denver in June 1915, and the first thing he did was to dispatch a crew to clean the vacant second floor. What they saw prompted them to call the sheriff's office. Walking through the suite of rooms, Deputy Sheriff Charles Thompson found letters and telegrams torn into scraps, a blackboard with faint traces of chalk letters, bank deposit slips, and bookies' tickets for a winning horse named Kootenai. In the east room, which had been fitted as a reception area, he found a wire that started over the hallway door, continued in a manner both covert and conspicuous along the molding, and disappeared into a hole leading to the second room. Picking up the wire's trail, Sheriff Thompson followed it over doorways, along baseboards, and around corners to a hole leading to the third room. And there it was unceremoniously clamped to a radiator. Sheriff Thompson had stumbled upon the imperfectly dismantled set of a fake betting parlor.

As he pieced together the scraps on the floor, he saw both the props of the con men's play and their tidy bookkeeping system. The correspondence appeared to be between the Denver crew and its counterparts in San Francisco, Oakland, Salt Lake City, Wichita, and Chicago. Some of the letter scraps read: "You can fix it—," "Lead the fellow on—," "These guys have the money," "Of course, I won," and, most damningly, "Blonger is always—." The wiretappers had left so suddenly because one of their marks—a British army officer who had come to Denver to purchase horses and mules for the war effort but instead bought into the big con at the price of $85,000—kicked to the federal government. The swindlers had somehow gotten wind of the complaint and had refrained from cashing the bank drafts, so federal law enforcers were currently stymied in their pursuit, but the local police force was on the case, and they knew the man to whom the evidence pointed: "Lou Blonger, well known in racing circles during the last twenty years."

Except the entire scene was fake. Blonger was never in danger, because the contents of the office had been planted and their discovery staged as part of a municipal power play whose target was not Blonger but Chief of Police Felix O'Neill, a close friend of Blonger's (who would one day serve as Blonger's pallbearer). The main conspirator was Under Sheriff Glen "Big Mitt" Duffield, an officer in disgrace for having been caught a few weeks earlier accepting two diamonds from a pair of crooks and letting them escape from the county jail. To rehabilitate his career, he conscripted the help of Isadore J. "Kid" Warner, a con man run out of Denver during Chief Hamilton Armstrong's cleanup in the 1890s and later jailed along with the Mabray gang in Council Bluffs. The two of them strung the wire and tore the incriminating scraps of paper to make the empty rooms look like one of Blonger's stores. The plan was almost upset when Sheriff Thompson was called onto the scene. Under Sheriff Duffield was supposed to "find" the rooms and use them to embarrass and ultimately unseat Chief O'Neill. Like a good spieler, he ad-libbed in a hurry. He sent a public letter to the commissioner of safety, reminding him that he'd reported on the bunco operations of the city several months earlier at the commissioner's request, finding that bunco artists had been at work since the previous December and had earned between $85,000 and $90,000 in that six-month period. With his own reputation suddenly at stake, the commissioner was forced to suspend Chief O'Neill. Duffield readied himself by ordering a new uniform. Sure enough, two weeks later, O'Neill resigned to avoid a messy trial, and the commissioner appointed Duffield in his place— even though the daily papers had widely reported that Duffield had constructed the swindlers' lair and framed its discovery. By faking a fake betting parlor, Duffield baldly conned his way into office.

The convoluted story revealed a great deal more than the unembarrassed nature of the fix. First of all, it disclosed the open secret of Blonger's continued presence in Denver. He'd never left. His sudden exodus to Cuba was a ruse, perhaps a cover for his friends in high places to compensate for the political capital they lost by associating with him. For the next decade, Blonger's name was never even whispered in the Denver press as he seemed to content himself with farming his cherry orchard and managing his mining concerns. Second, it demonstrated how impervious he was to prosecution: not once in the furor that engulfed city hall before Duffield's promotion did it occur to anyone to ask Blonger about the British army officer's enormous loss. Most important, the Duffield story linked Blonger to the big con and tipped off the extent to which his operations had matured into a modern, efficient machine.

Probably by 1915 and certainly by 1920, Blonger had established the big con as Norfleet would encounter it, and he did it by mirroring the era's fascination with speculation on the stock market. His paneled dens with their buy sheets and stock tickers were the missing, necessary link between the bucket shops and the mining exchanges run by the 17th Streeters. They provided a plausible story for how the mark might gain entry to the closeted world of high finance.

Blonger's big con fit into its time like a missing puzzle piece. His organization outperformed Chase's because he required both his marks and his crew to act like businessmen. He created a corporation with bureaucracy, hierarchy, and bookkeeping, and he created in his marks an appetite for gambling that was itself corporate instead of aleatory. Rather than casting bones and exhorting the gods to send luck their way, Blonger's marks mimicked Blonger's own labor: they patiently cultivated their capital and nourished its natural tendency to grow under their expertise.

Many years later, an origin story would be told to account for Blonger's machine, for the way he transformed the big store into a franchise that dominated the city of Denver. As the story goes, Blonger learned what he knew in the Ben Marks–John Mabray school of swindling at Council Bluffs, but he escaped prosecution with Mabray in 1910 through an extremely well-placed pair of defenders, a law partner of a U.S. district attorney and a deputy U.S. marshal, who traveled to Council Bluffs to pressure federal authorities to leave Blonger's name out of the proceedings and to sit through the trial every single day until it concluded, ensuring that Blonger's name was not so much as breathed. Other evidence suggests that Blonger's connection to Mabray's Millionaires' Club was through his able lieutenant, Adolph "Kid" Duff, a short, wiry man with a luxuriant wave of upswept black hair. Duff roamed around the country, with stints in Colorado Springs, El Paso, and Council Bluffs as a member of the Mabray gang, until he arrived in Denver in 1904 at the age of thirty. He soon became Blonger's spokesperson within the syndicate, transmitting the older man's commands down through the hierarchy and allowing the boss a degree of remove from the tapping of the telegraph machines and the exclamations of exchange secretaries.

Duff could always be seen around town, chatting up the steerers or stopping into the bank to do a bit of business, a pair of glasses perched on his nose and attached to a wide black ribbon strung over his ear. Any bunco man who came to Denver looking for work needed the nod from Duff, and so he would ask someone within the syndicate to make the introduction. The two men would climb the stairs to the Lookout, the all-purpose name for Duff's rented office, which shifted location from year to year but was always on the second story and always faced Seventeenth Street. Duff would ask the prospective employee where he'd been based, with whom he'd worked, and how much money he'd made. If the answers were satisfactory and if the current employee could vouch for him, Duff would send the man back downstairs as a steerer, assigned to prowl a well-demarcated territory within the city limits: Seventeenth Street from Union Station to Broadway; Sixteenth

Lou Blonger and Adolph "Kid" Duff, the top of the
Denver swindling hierarchy

Street from the upscale department store Daniels and Fisher to Broadway; the Civic Center; and the State Capitol grounds. The steerers, dozens of them, formed a regular army of flaneurs, loafing and strolling this busy rectangle, chatting up strangers, paging through newspapers, eavesdropping, and peering over at hotel registers.

When a steerer landed a mark, he'd contrive to walk with him down Seventeenth Street. As they passed under the window of the Lookout, the steerer would "give the office," or secretly signal by raising his hat. George "Tip" Belcher, Duff's own lieutenant, would be sitting in the window and would let Duff know that a play had just begun. On any given day, two or three or four spielers would be waiting in the Lookout, and Duff would dispatch one of them to grab a sheaf of yellow telegrams and position himself for his entrance onto the scene as the highly important and deeply distracted speculator who'd recently been in the news for his impossible stock market winnings. The steerer and the spieler would smoothly convey the mark through the play, telling him the tale, giving him the convincer, putting him on the send. The very instant that the mark handed over his cash in the inner office of the stock exchange and then retreated to the reception room, Duff would come in through a side door, wrap the money up in newspaper, and leave the building with it. Tip Belcher would follow him, armed and ready to attack if anyone threatened Duff. The two of them would stash the money in a safety-deposit box near Daniels and Fisher and let it sit until they could ensure the mark had been cooled off. The steerers and spielers were required to sequester themselves at home until Duff called them to tell them the mark had left town.

A week or ten days later, Duff would stage a little ceremony in the Lookout with Belcher and each crew member of that particular play: the exchange secretary would get 5 percent, the spieler 15 percent, Belcher would get 2 percent, and the steerer would make about 45 percent, out of which he would have to tip his bank teller about 5 percent for not going to a bank officer for approval when cashing the mark's large draft. Duff and Blonger each took 10 percent, leaving roughly 13 percent for the fix. Each policeman and detective on their payroll received $50 a week whether the big store made money or not. And then they'd all go to Tip Belcher's private Grafters Club on Fourteenth and across from the Public Market. Even Blonger would make an occasional appearance at the club, granting the lower echelons a rare opportunity to glimpse his visage.

Blonger's highly articulated corporate body did not always function well. A bunco man could be fired for a breach of swindler etiquette like marrying a local girl or making too much money and getting cocky and careless. The system did work beautifully, though, when it was the mark who malfunctioned. If a mark kicked to the police, he'd be turned over to the bunco squad, all of whose weekly payments were up-to-date. The bunco detectives knew precisely where the Lookout and the fake stockrooms were located each season, so they'd walk the victim around town in increasingly dizzying circles yet somehow never arrive at a building he could identify. One time, two con men sat drinking in the Quincy Café when in walked two detectives and a very familiar man. One swindler told the other, "Don't look around. There is a fifty-five grand sucker with two dicks, so come on." The detectives obligingly called the mark's attention to a nickel piano against the wall while the con men slipped outside behind his back. Another time, a mark kicked to the Denver police, and the detectives propelled him around the city streets before sending him out of town, but for some reason it cost Blonger $8,000 of the mark's $19,300 score to keep the officers silent on that one.

One formerly rich mark skipped over the cops entirely. Norfleet's arrest of Joseph Furey in 1921 had been so broadly publicized that when Dr. W. H. Scherrer lost $25,000 to the Denver syndicate, he paid Furey a visit in the Texas penitentiary to see if the convicted con man could help. Furey listened to Dr. Scherrer's tale with sympathy. "Well, Doc, you are a pretty good sport. I would like myself to have taken you on for about ten thousand, but they shouldn't have trimmed you for twenty-five thousand. That's too much." He continued, "I used to work in Denver. You go there and see the Boss." Furey refused to elaborate further, so Scherrer headed back to Denver, employing first the district attorney, Charles Fox, and then a Pinkerton Agency detective as his go-betweens. Blonger had been expecting him, having already heard of his conversation with Furey, and he proceeded to give the doctor the runaround, promising him a $10,000 refund while whispering to the DA and the Pinkerton detective that he'd pay them $2,000 to make Scherrer go away. Scherrer never got his money.

The year before Norfleet was swindled in Texas, a mark named

Albert Backus came to Denver and returned home to Okmulgee, Oklahoma, $8,500 poorer. He proceeded to spend his own money to chase down the three-man crew who'd taken off the touch, one of whom was William Elmer Mead, the inventor of the wallet drop whom Hoover would later arrest for mutilating his fingertips. Backus actually found one of his swindlers, a man named J. P. Kinsman, among the celery fields of Sanford, Florida, the same place where Norfleet met Johnson before being lured to the sinister clubhouse in Daytona Beach. Backus had Kinsman detained, but the Denver DA refused to issue extradition papers, and Kinsman was released. Three years after his swindle, Backus was still writing to the Denver DA's office, pleading with it to prosecute his men or dismiss the criminal case so he could proceed with a civil action. A letter from 1921 reads like an anguished cry into a void: "I offered a $1,000.00 reward for arrest and conviction, and spent a good deal of money in tracing them, but I have lain off until a change in the district attorney's office should occur at Denver, hoping that some day the State of Colorado, would have officers who would have an interest in the prosecution of those who rob tourists at Denver."

By the early 1920s, Lou Blonger seemed invincible. The men who

Denver district attorney Philip S. Van Cise in 1921

accepted his money included not only detectives in the Denver Police Department but the district attorney and even staffers in the Denver office of the U.S. Department of Justice. He was a close personal friend of Harry H. Tammen, co-owner of *The Denver Post*, the most powerful of the city's four dailies. Blonger had created a black hole in the center of the city into which truth slid and vanished. If he harbored any vulnerabilities, no one had found them during his twenty years of indomitable rule.

Philip S. Van Cise didn't intend to be the one to take on the power-monger of Seventeenth Street. In fact, he had been elected district attorney almost by accident. For one thing, his demeanor made him a most unlikely political candidate. A contemporary described him as "abrupt, incisive, a bit inclined to deal with people as if he were a drill sergeant," and "the sort that repels familiarities"—and that from an admirer. His family remembers him the same way: he simply couldn't be made to care what other people thought of him and never modified his words in order to cultivate someone else's impressions of him. If he didn't like someone, he'd simply cut that person off. As a result, people either loved or hated him. He was the polar opposite of a salesman or a swindler, congenitally incapable of glad-handing like Blonger or shape-shifting like Norfleet.

He'd distinguished himself in his father's law firm in the eleven years since he'd joined the bar, and he'd further burnished his credentials with a stint in the Colorado National Guard. He then served as an intelligence officer during World War I in France, where he attained the rank of lieutenant colonel, and from then on he was the Colonel to his friends and law associates. Even so, he had nobody's backing when he entered the Republican primary for district attorney in 1920 at the age of thirty-six. He was the long shot in a race against two other candidates, one backed by the political machine and the other by a U.S. senator, but the two more powerful candidates split the votes between them and Van Cise emerged as the surprise victor in the primary.

A few days later, the Colonel got his first glimpse of what he had taken on. A man named Leonard DeLue, a former police inspector who was now head of the city's largest private detective agency, called upon him at his office, and after congratulating him on his win, he got right down to business. He had a friend, he told Van Cise, who controlled at least fifteen hundred votes in the general election. Would Van Cise meet with him? At first, Van Cise turned DeLue away. It took Van Cise a little nudging from colleagues to understand that this was how the game was played, and eventually he agreed to meet the power broker in DeLue's office. When he opened the door, there sat Lou Blonger. He smiled affably at Van Cise and introduced himself as a veteran of the Civil War. "I wear the same G.A.R. button that your father did," Blonger told the Colonel. "We old soldiers feel mighty proud of you young fellows." Then Blonger smoothly asked how Van Cise's law practice had fared during the war. When Van Cise was forced to admit that he'd given it up to enlist, Blonger had his opening. He informed the candidate that it would cost $25,000 to win the general election. "I like your style," he told Van Cise, "and I want to help you, and because you are the only soldier on any ticket, I'll put up that twenty-five thousand. You can either have it now, or call on me as you need it, and you don't owe me a cent." The district attorney's yearly salary was $5,000.

Van Cise mustered the appropriate amount of deference and replied, "This is the first time I ever ran for office, and I don't know much about the game. I don't need your money now. I want to get through without any outside help. But I may need it, and if it costs as you say it does, I will certainly call upon you. I don't know just how to thank you." The two men smiled in perfect agreement, and then Blonger continued to the next phase of his campaign. He explained that his friends' grandsons were, like Van Cise himself, just coming into manhood and venturing into business on their own. He sighed as he explained that many of them sold mining stocks which, while perfectly legitimate, would occasionally land them before the district attorney on some irritating complaint or other. "Now, Phil," said Blonger, "what I would like to have you do is agree with me that whenever I have to go on a man's bond, you will fix it at a thousand dollars. Then I can just have a regular arrangement with a bondsman and not have to bother at all." So there it was, and it was just plain insulting.

"Phil" could no longer play the part that was being offered to him. "Blonger," he said, "my hunch would be that the safe rule to follow is to fix the bond at double the amount which the defendant is said to have stolen." And with that, the meeting was over. Blonger had no further use for Van Cise. On election night, Blonger's downtown district went firmly for the Democratic incumbent, William E. Foley, but the race was so close that even Foley's own gambling hall would not make book on his reelection. Van Cise had run an aggressive campaign—his slogan was "A Fighting Man for a Fighting Job"—and the suburbs overwhelmingly tipped the polls in his favor. As the *Post* reported the next morning, "His victory is chiefly due to the almost unanimous support of the best element of Denver's citizens."

Before being sworn in, Van Cise decided to take his political education into his own hands, and he paid a call on someone whom the entire city viewed as a man of integrity, despite the curse words that detonated inside each one of his sentences. Hamilton Armstrong was in the midst of his fourth nonconsecutive term as chief of police in a town where few men lasted long at the job. He was the one who had temporarily shuttered the establishments of Blonger, Chase, and Soapy Smith, and he kept up his reputation for direct action. Once, he stormed into the home of a Capitol Hill socialite during one of her soirees and without a word smashed a roulette wheel in her living room with a firefighter's ax, then gathered up the shards of inlaid mahogany and walnut to give to the janitor to feed the furnace at city hall. If he caught a police officer drinking while on duty, he wouldn't wait for a trial board to weigh in on the matter; he'd simply snip the man's copper buttons off his blue coat and send him home unemployed.

Yet when Van Cise came looking for advice, the chief took a subtler approach. He beckoned over one of his captains and asked him to give Van Cise a tour of the town. "What do you mean, Chief," asked Captain August Hanebuth, "how much shall we see?" "Everything," answered the chief pointedly. And so for the next few nights, Captain Hanebuth took Van Cise on a tour of the Denver underworld as seen by a police officer. Van Cise trailed along as Hanebuth strode up to saloon after saloon, knocked, waited a few minutes as scrambling and dragging sounds came from the other side of the door, then entered into a room of poker-faced men holding nothing but drinks. In Chinatown, when the two men gained access, the bars were eerily empty, tobacco smoke hanging in the air, with no sign of the means by which their patrons had vanished. Van Cise was mystified. He had seen nothing on the captain's tour of everything.

A few days later, the chief spelled it out for him. Did Van Cise know anything about Lou Blonger? It was then that Van Cise learned that the man with the ridiculously generous offer was the boss of the entire town. Chief Armstrong served at the pleasure of the mayor, who reported to Blonger through Adolph Duff and two insiders, Abe Silver, the constable, and Hal Crane, chief deputy sheriff. Any attempted raid would be quashed beforehand or thrown out of court afterward. "But, son," said Chief Armstrong, "if you are on the level, I will get you the dope and you do the work, and we will smash the whole damn bunch of them." The day before Van Cise's inauguration, Chief Armstrong died. The official cause of death was heart failure, but *The Denver Times* headline read, "Heartbreak Kills Armstrong"—heartbreak over his ineffectuality as a reformer in a fixed-up town. "I am being jobbed," he told his friends. "I am being double-crossed on every side; I am so tired of it I will be glad when it is all over."

The mantle now passed to Philip Van Cise, and on his first day he tacked up to the wall of his office a vice map of the city, coded for districts particularly plagued by bootlegging, gambling, prostitution, and "general lawlessness." That same day, Union Station witnessed an unusually large exodus from the city, when fifty or sixty of the city's best-known gamblers and bunco artists fled the town in groups of five or ten for St. Louis and Chicago. "We are laying off temporarily to see what Van Cise is going to do and who is the next chief of police," one of them confided to the *Times*. "We hope to be back in town in sixty days if all goes well."

They did come back, all of them, fooled by the con that Van Cise was running on the entire city. He pretended to be a naïve young lawyer still running to catch up with his superiors, but all the while he was devising a sting operation to take down Blonger's syndicate. Van Cise started by gathering his facts, using what he'd learned under Chief Armstrong's tutelage to guide his self-education. Now that he knew what to look for, Van Cise found Blonger's tracks all throughout the district attorney's filing cabinet. There he was, the invisible presence who finessed Robert Ballard's bond down to $2,500 when he was arrested for swindling a Dallas florist named Nitsche out of $25,000; the one who'd posted bond on the handful of cases that had come before judges in the last two decades; the one who collected the $12,000 that the Reverend Albert S. Menaugh stole from his church back home in Goshen, Indiana, to bet on the stock market. After meeting Blonger's crew, Menaugh returned home from Denver, confessed to what he'd done, and pleaded with a judge to be sent to jail. His parishioners refused to prosecute him, so he went home and swallowed poison.

Van Cise made a list of all the victims who'd been denied justice in the Denver courts during Blonger's reign, and he wrote to them to convince some of them to testify in the distant future. He visited other law enforcement officials who'd made public stands against confidence men, officials at the federal level in the Secret Service or the U.S. Postal Inspection Service, and he used the evidence they'd gathered to educate himself in the con man's script. At first he said nothing to the others in the DA's office, unsure of whom he could trust, but soon two men, Fred Sanborn and Kenneth Robinson, impressed him with their brains and honesty—and their service in the war didn't hurt. He brought them into his confidence, and together they bided their time.

In August 1921, eight months into his term as district attorney, he read in the *Rocky Mountain News* about a moving-picture proprietor named George Kanavuts from Sapulpa, Oklahoma, who had been trimmed of $25,000 and had complained to the police, with no results. To ignore this incident without being on Blonger's payroll would reveal too much to the underworld, so Van Cise opted for a bit of theater. He called the detective department to ask where the investigation stood. Captain Bacon informed him that he had two of his best men on the case, Pete Land and George Lusk, and at Van Cise's request he sent the detectives and Kanavuts over to the district attorney's offices. "Who were the men, and what have you done to catch them?" Van Cise asked the detectives. "It's the same old racket about the stock market," Land responded. "We tried to locate the place, but though he has taken us all around town, he can't find the building where it occurred. And he can't describe the men." Van Cise turned to Kanavuts and told him, "There's nothing this office can do to help you. These are the two wisest dicks on the force, and if anybody can locate your men they can." And he escorted the three men out, sending Land and Lusk back to headquarters to report on the district attorney's ineffectualness. Once the detectives were out of sight, Van Cise brought Kanavuts back and amended his earlier statement. "We can't do much more now, but give us some time and we think we will get your men. We will keep in touch with you, and don't give up hope. Will you keep away from the police department and never tell them anything and only work with us?" With nothing to lose, Kanavuts agreed, and so Van Cise secured his first cooperating witness.

As a former army intelligence officer, Van Cise was more qualified than the average lawyer for the job at hand, and as his resolve and knowledge grew, he began to orchestrate a military-style campaign to bring down his enemies. First, he refined his understanding of who might be dangerous to his campaign. Unlike the Progressive reformers who had done so much to clean up and open out civic life in Denver, Van Cise was forced to consider the press as one of his enemies. Several times he had gone to the editors of the dailies and asked them to suppress stories if publicity would have damaged the public good, but for this case even that backdoor maneuver wouldn't work, since everyone knew of Blonger's close friendship with Harry Tammen, co-owner of the *Post*. Therefore, everything Van Cise did must be cloaked in secrecy, even—no, especially—from his own employees. He installed a secret telephone line and purchased a secret safe for documents related to the conspiracy. And, he reasoned, if he were hiding information, others were probably seeking it. Surely the Blonger syndicate, after their failure to buy Van Cise, would be trying to find a way to burrow inside his office. So Van Cise hired someone to spy on him. He called the detective department and asked it to dispatch one of its officers to act as his investigator. When a man named Oliver Smith arrived, Van Cise beckoned him over and told him, and only him, that they were going to raid the red-light district on the twenty-eighth. "Keep that date open, because you boys will be busy." When Van Cise began to hear of the raid through the grapevine, including from Abe Silver, the constable in Blonger's employ, he knew he had an open line to the boss, and he began to pipe false information down into the underworld.

Van Cise next sought to widen his band of conspirators by considering where his best evidence was likely to originate. He asked the president of the First National Bank to comb through his draft register for large cash withdrawals to out-of-town men, and from that he found three more marks who agreed to provide information. Van Cise wrote to other police departments to gather photographs of known swindlers from rogues' galleries, painstakingly matching aliases and nicknames, filling in the gaps where photographs had been removed or records expunged, eventually compiling an index of 631 bunco artists. The federal postal inspectors were unable to open any of Blonger's mail, but they readily agreed to copy all of the information on each envelope that they delivered to him in the American Bank Building. Western Union and the Postal Telegraph Company agreed to save Blonger's communications and produce them whenever Van Cise secured a court order. The janitor in Blonger's building was willing to deliver the contents of Blonger's wastebasket every single day. The local telephone company collected data on Blonger's long-distance calls.

But more was needed. To prosecute a group of criminals on a conspiracy charge, Van Cise would have to submit airtight evidence linking them to one another and divulging each of their roles in Blonger's corporation. It wasn't enough to sit in his office, sifting through Blonger's detritus for clues; he needed to penetrate Blonger's organization and ride invisibly through it, no matter how dangerous. So Van Cise hired three private detectives from out of state. First came Arch Cooper, a lazy, sociable fellow, which made him perfect for loafing about the underworld and making friends among Blonger's lower corps. Next came Andrew Koehn, a navy man with a photographic mind and an incredible eye for detail who was assigned to watch the executives. Last was Robert Maiden, a fearless, sometimes heedless man, who worked under Koehn to follow bunco men from the Lookout.

All three men filed daily surveillance reports in careful code, using numbers for the bunco men—Lou Blonger was number 9, and Adolph Duff was number 1—and false names for themselves. Maiden's reports show a particular relish for the job, as well as the tedious business of incrementally collecting data without exciting the suspicion of preternaturally cautious men:

> #1 and another stranger came to 17th and Arapahoe and split. #1 watched to see if any one was about. He went into McPhee and McGinnity, 1624 Arapahoe. Stayed about two minutes and went down Arapahoe to 19th and doubled back on Curtis to Champa 9. Appeared to be looking at buildings but watched everything and everybody. It is impossible to get within a block of him without his attention.

Maiden haunted Loritz's cigar store, Clayton's diner, the newsstand at the Albany Hotel. He followed "the bunc with the undershot jaw," "the blind bird," "the Miami bunc." As he wore grooves in the sidewalk, he began to decipher the map his own footsteps were drawing. "I saw the bunc that limps come out of 1515 Grant. It looks as if the entire place is a bunc hangout and I don't believe that any mistakes would be made if the whole place was pinched."

Van Cise took one further measure to penetrate Blonger's organization, a treacherous step that nearly cost him the entire campaign. He installed a bug in Blonger's office in the American Bank Building. He obtained a key to the office from the building manager and had Cooper and Koehn sneak in one night to make a map to scale of the office's contents. They ascertained that the chandelier would be the best hiding place, so they found a similar one and performed tests on it until they optimized the placement of the bug, then they sneaked in again to install the Dictaphone. They drew the wires up through the ceiling to the unused attic above, where they connected them to two wet batteries that needed constant maintenance. Van Cise asked his friend Arthur Jones, an executive at the General Electric Company, if he knew of a trustworthy electrician. Jones thought hard on the matter, and then insisted that he do it himself, so for the next year he would regularly change from his business suit into work clothes and crawl forty feet through the dusty attic with pans of water and zinc for the wet battery.

The Dictaphone wires continued from the attic outside the building to a telephone pole on the sidewalk and then across the street to a room that Koehn had rented as an observation post, where he could both listen in and spy on Blonger's conversations. This perfect setup was Van Cise's first big mistake. After two weeks of listening to monotonous, generic business conversation, Koehn was jolted awake when he heard Blonger rage to a colleague, "See that room across the street where the shades are down? The District Attorney has two detectives over there. They have a tap on my telephone and hear every word we say." Blonger said that he'd have a friend at the telephone company check out the room across the street, and he swore if he found anything, he would sue the district attorney. Koehn scrambled to clean out the room while Van Cise called his own friend at the telephone company and arranged to have him send a friendly crew to the lookout who would neglect to find the wires from across the street.

Van Cise had violated one of the most basic principles of observation posts that he'd learned in the war: never locate them too close to the subject. For the second round in his offensive, Van Cise located the listening post around the corner and out of sight of Blonger's office. He then constructed an authentic observation post in an old loft across the street from the American Bank Building, punching a hole in a windowless brick wall through which he fitted a telescope, then built a black-painted box around the spy hole.

The last plank in Van Cise's campaign was to pay for it all. He couldn't ask the city for a penny without tipping off the machine, so his only recourse was to raise a secret fund from private individuals. He drew up a list of fifty wealthy Denver philanthropists, and then he began to show that list around town, asking his fellow lawyers and bankers for testimonials on each of the men. After cross-referencing these recommendations and rejecting anyone with a single slight against his reputation, Van Cise was left with thirty-one names. One by one, he made appointments to see them in their plush lairs. He'd open the meeting with a well-rehearsed spiel about Blonger's stranglehold on Denver civic life. He'd show the blute, a suitcase full of evidence that he'd borrowed from federal indictments against con men: documents like a $100,000 bond of the Metropolitan Bonding and Security Company, stationery stamped with the Masons' seal, buy and sell tickets on the International Exchange, and a newspaper clipping about a young trader making a fortune at a regional brokerage house. Then Van Cise would end with the convincer, a sheaf of letters from Blonger's marks proving that the con really did work but that the victims of the con were also the very men poised to help end it in the city of Denver. All thirty men on his list—and one woman—responded unhesitatingly by pulling out their wallets, and their donations totaled almost $15,000. A year later, a prominent businessman who had not been on the list of thirty would hear of Van Cise's campaign and would rush into his office. "Colonel, is there anything wrong with me?" he would ask in dismay. "Haven't I lived a long and upright life in this city? Haven't I contributed to every worthy enterprise in the history of Denver? Why didn't you come to me and ask me for funds? Why was I left out?" Van Cise would calmly explain that they simply hadn't known the man well enough at the time. Somewhat mollified, the man would ask how much more money was needed to fund the sting, and he would instantly write a check for the full amount.

Though his naïveté was diminishing by the day, Van Cise still had much to learn about his enemy, and early in the conspiracy he made another costly error. Blonger's wastebasket had yielded the information that Adolph Duff would be stopping at the Baltimore Hotel in Kansas City for a month or so. Van Cise saw an opportunity to get more information on Duff without exciting his suspicion. He wrote to his counterpart in Kansas City, explaining his secret campaign and asking that he find a pretext for detaining Duff, photographing and fingerprinting him, and then letting him go. A few days later, Blonger's wastebasket informed him that Duff had skipped over to St. Louis, "as our friend Van Cise has all the dope." Much later, Van Cise would learn the path of his letter: from the Kansas City district attorney, to the chief of police, to the captain of detectives, to two detectives on the squad, then to Duff himself. In just one sheet of paper, Van Cise had given up nearly his entire strategy. Luckily, it only took another sheet of paper to cover up his mistake. He wrote to the Kansas City DA again to convey the sad news that his investigation had been halted because the city council had refused to allocate the funds.

Like Norfleet before him, Van Cise soon learned to turn his ingenuousness into his biggest asset. Blonger was suspicious of Van Cise but complacent in his estimation of the district attorney's abilities. Van Cise decided to bumble the suspicion right out of Blonger. He learned that Blonger had purchased the Anna Gould mansion, a former brothel that had been vacant for several years. The red-light district was a perennial scourge to city reformers, and so with very little exertion Van Cise cooked up a plan to get the churches to raise funds for a raid against all the whorehouses on the row. Then he called Petie Beers, owner of the A&B Taxi Company and the center of the underworld grapevine. Van Cise waved a fistful of checks from the churches and threatened to shut down the whorehouses that Beers and Blonger owned. Beers was astonished, because neither he nor Blonger owned a brothel, but he dutifully passed the threat up the hierarchy. That afternoon, Van Cise heard the result of his little scheme on the Dictaphone. Blonger said to Duff, "What do you think that goddamn fool is up to now? That fund that we thought he was raising to attack me with he is getting from the churches to shut up the row, and a fat chance he will have." Blonger was mystified by the whole affair. "Now, how did he find that out about Beers being the tip off? That fellow is funny. I can't make him out. At times he is right; other times he doesn't know anything, just plain dumb." One of the detectives on the force told Duff that there was a Dictaphone in Blonger's office, so he and Duff tore the room apart, but when they didn't find one, they figured the detective was only trying to squeeze them for more money.

When the swindling season approached in 1922, Van Cise's second year in office, he began to see the effects of his campaign. That spring, a spieler approached Duff and Blonger for work, and they granted him permission but warned him that no one was likely to make much money that summer. Van Cise wouldn't take their bribe, they told the spieler, but they would do the best they could without him. As Lou handed one of Duff's minions the boodle for the season, he sighed and told him to try to get along with as small a bankroll as possible, only five hundred $1 bills. The summer approached, the city streets bristled with tourists and businessmen, and the chatter in the underworld increased as steerers and spielers moved back to town, ready to assume their places on the Denver stage—but the big store stayed closed. Arch Cooper met a new man in town who told him, "There is nothing doing here yet as everybody is scared to death of the D.A." The standoff seemed to grow worse when the postal inspectors contacted Van Cise and asked his permission to nab a con man named Walter Byland whom they sorely wanted for a 1918 swindle, a plan that might have scared the swindlers away for the rest of the year. Van Cise soon figured out a way to work the situation to his advantage. He allowed the federal authorities to arrest Byland the instant he came to town—and then he studiously ignored him. For two weeks, Blonger let his man sweat it out in jail, until finally Duff said, "Hell, the District Attorney is dead from the neck up. If he wants any con-man, he wants Walter. And he doesn't even know who he is. Let's spring him." Their lawyer posted bond, and soon Byland was free to steer for Blonger.

Then Van Cise repeated the stunt. Arch Cooper had identified the Black and White Cigar Store on Eighteenth as one of the gang's meeting places. Conveniently, it was also a bootlegging joint, so Van Cise pulled off a nighttime raid, arresting the owner and detaining the two customers in the back with glasses raised to their lips. Luck was with him: they happened to be Audley Potts and William "the Painter Kid" Sturns, both known members of Blonger's gang. The next morning, in their presence, Van Cise searched their wallets and found bonds from the Metropolitan Bonding and Security Company, buy and sell forms, and the rest of the usual paraphernalia. After conscientiously studying them, Van Cise turned to his associates and said, "Why, these seem to be respectable businessmen of rather large means. I see no reason to arrest them." Later on the Dictaphone, Blonger delivered his own lines right on cue: "That fellow don't know anything. The damn fool had both Potts and Painter, and read all their stuff, and doesn't know a con man's layout when he sees it. He's just a big bag of wind, and will never get wise to anything."

Only one thing was left to do. Van Cise abandoned the scene. Or at least he loudly announced to various city officials that as he had not had a break since he took office, he would take advantage of the fine weather to spend a month in the mountains, far from the reach of telephones and telegrams. In truth, he was holed up in a mountain resort sixty miles away, in constant communication via mail, telephone, and wire. As a bonus, his assistant Kenneth Robinson had persuaded one of their wealthy patrons to give him the use of his Packard, and he was able to make regular deliveries of the documents and reports that Van Cise needed.

The deception worked perfectly. Within days of Van Cise's departure, the underworld passed along a message: the season would open on July 26, and the new Lookout would be at 729 Seventeenth Street. Suddenly Blonger's schedule was booked solid with meetings with police captains and Hal Crane, the deputy sheriff, in his office, and the mayor and the manager of safety at city hall. The bunco hangouts were thronged; on one day alone Andy Koehn trailed twenty-three swindlers to their various hotel rooms and boardinghouses. Van Cise's heart gladdened to hear that Duff and Tip Belcher had been spotted outside the Denham Theatre building handing out checks to their crew. They must be feeling safe to be so brazen, and the money must be flowing.

In his mountain hideaway, Van Cise was as busy as Blonger. Once again, he marshaled his military expertise to design a plan for what he began to call D-day and H-hour, the moment so long in coming when he could swoop in and arrest Blonger and his entire gang. He was confident that he possessed enough evidence to tie the men together. All that he needed, the last merest detail, was evidence tying them to the business of swindling. He must catch them in flagrante delicto. With his growing powers of persuasion, Van Cise recruited two men to pose as suckers, a Houston lumber dealer named Hoxie Thompson and a wealthy Nebraska farmer named J. W. Bryan. Van Cise instructed them to act conspicuously like themselves in all the preferred con man fishing grounds. As soon as one or both men snared a bunco team, Van Cise would name D-day and H-hour.

Van Cise called up the governor of Colorado and divulged the entire plan to him. Governor Oliver Shoup then gave him command of fifteen Colorado Rangers, who would aid Van Cise's deputies in making simultaneous arrests at Blonger's office, the Lookout, the fake exchanges, and the cigar stores and lunch counters. Van Cise tapped a handful of World War I veterans to serve as drivers. And then he cast around for a jail in which to house his charges. The city jail would never do; as soon as the first prisoner arrived, the tip-off would go out, the swindlers would vanish, and the raid would be over before the day had gotten started. Van Cise thought about it for all of three seconds before the solution came to him: his church. The First Universalist Church at Colfax and Lafayette was temporarily closed and without a minister. No one would think to look for Blonger and his corporation at the First Universalist. With that final detail, the trap was set, and Van Cise was poised to pounce on the Denver underworld with one terse phone call.

That's when Norfleet strode into town.

CHAPTER TEN

The Raid

Tap, tap, tap. As Norfleet hobbled down the street, his back hunched over and one hand clutched to his hip, the sound of his cane on the pavement echoed the sound of another cane behind him. Without looking, Norfleet knew he'd succeeded in drawing the attention of Bill Mooney, a veteran of the swindling fraternity whom he had recognized by the deep scar on his cheek, visible even underneath the blue-tinted glasses he'd adopted in his disguise as a blind man. Walking slowly to ensure he didn't outpace Mooney, Norfleet made his way toward the post office. He was careful to keep his hand on his concealed gun and his Panama hat on his shaggy bowl cut. Norfleet approached the general delivery window, and as soon as Mooney was in earshot, he squeaked out in a high voice, "Any mail for L. A. Mulligan?"

There wasn't, of course, so Norfleet headed back out to the street. He stopped by the entrance and waited as his follower emerged, passed him, and made his own way down the street. In only minutes, the Denver underground would learn that a new mark had arrived in town.

Norfleet hadn't even left the vicinity of the post office before the first steerer approached him. Norfleet recognized him, too: Fred Soloman, an especially smiley representative of the tribe who introduced himself as Whatley. Norfleet responded with his own pseudonym and an elaborate personal history that touched on all the important points: his background as a hick cotton grower in Ferris, Texas, the black gold under his fields, his wife back home ready to sign a lease to an oil company. That afternoon, each man parted from the other satisfied that he'd performed his role well. Norfleet felt he'd learned enough about the Denver crew to warrant calling Colonel Van Cise on his secret emergency telephone line. It was the least he could do for the district attorney and his covert campaign against the bunco men.

When Van Cise first met J. Frank Norfleet, he was decidedly underwhelmed. He had, of course, heard of the Texas sleuth—everyone had. They had even exchanged letters when Van Cise had taken office, and Norfleet had helped him understand the complex network of bunco artists that stretched across the nation. Van Cise was expecting a "he-man," but, as he later wrote, "Norfleet did not look the part. Instead of the steely gray eyes of fiction, he had watery blue ones. Instead of the powerful, crushing grip, he had a soft and flaccid paw. Instead of being tall and broad-shouldered, he was a little fellow about five feet six inches tall, weighing about one hundred and twenty-five pounds, and had a soft, drawling Texas voice."

Norfleet had sneaked into Denver, just as Captain Bruce of Colorado Springs had begged him not to do, and he had made a beeline for the district attorney's office. His plan was to contribute his expertise to the sting in return for first dibs on W. B. Spencer, should he be unearthed in town. But Norfleet found the DA's team harder to crack than a swindling syndicate. First he met Roy Samson, the former superintendent of the FBI who had resigned his post to join Van Cise's team. Samson spirited Norfleet down to a room in the basement of his office building and wasted no time telling him, "For God's sake keep out of sight. If the con men find you are here, you will spoil the work of fifteen months." Samson promised Norfleet that he'd find Spencer for him, but only if Norfleet would agree to their conditions: "Don't go out-of-doors in the daytime, and if you go around at night, keep off the main streets and out of leading hotels."

When Van Cise finally granted him an audience, it was only to further tighten the restrictions on his movements. Van Cise ordered him to stay away from the district attorney's office, the hotels, the Civic Center, and the capitol grounds. He was expressly forbidden to speak to any police officers, almost none of whom could be trusted. If Van Cise could have found a pretext for locking Norfleet up, he might have. Instead, he gave Norfleet a secret telephone number only to be used in an extreme emergency. Under no circumstances should Norfleet communicate with him through normal channels. And with that, Van Cise let him out of his sight, assuming he'd lie low. Norfleet had neglected to mention anything about a Mr. L. A. Mulligan.

But that August day in 1922, when he heard Norfleet's voice on the line, Van Cise had to admit that Norfleet was onto something. Van Cise's phony marks had been fishing for weeks without catching any swindlers, and here Norfleet had caught two with his first cast, making him instantly indispensable. Van Cise invited him to a planning meeting of the sting operation that night at Roy Samson's home. The entire team was there, and they were thrilled to hear of Norfleet's success. They gave Norfleet full permission to carry on with his con, and everyone recognized that the power dynamic within their team had flipped: now Norfleet had the upper hand. As Norfleet later wrote, "I offered my services to them under the condition that I be allowed a free rein and an unrestricted hand in dealing with the situation. I made it clear that I wished to act on my own judgment entirely, but would depend upon their support when the time came."

It's tempting to speculate on what Van Cise might have felt when he realized how much he depended on the famous rancher, so fired up with his own righteous fury and so confident in his ability to outsmart the sharpest of the nation's criminals. When he published his own memoir in 1936, fourteen years after D-day and twelve years after Norfleet's own autobiography, Van Cise was scrupulously professional when describing this moment, calling Norfleet's arrival "the greatest kind of luck" and lauding Norfleet for being "as brave and fearless a man as ever rode the Western plains." But Van Cise's memoir does not quite interlock with Norfleet's to form a seamless whole in their relation of the events that August, and their points of difference, though minuscule, tell their own story of a tussle for ownership over the operation.

Van Cise claims, for instance, that he stripped Norfleet of his guns before sending him back out in disguise, because he was unwilling to risk that the ever-meticulous Denver police would detain him for concealing a weapon. Van Cise writes that Norfleet entered the swindlers' game the next day "as helpless as a child." Norfleet, for his part, says he was armed to the teeth. Surely, knowing what he did about the Furey gang and what they would have done to him in Florida, Norfleet carried a gun, and just as surely he lied about it to the man who would be his colonel.

On their most picayune disagreement—really, just a pen stroke of difference between the two accounts—it is Norfleet who must be doubted. Throughout his autobiography, Norfleet refers to the alias he used in the sting as "Mulligan," but in Van Cise's memoir the name is "Mullican." Van Cise saved a note that Norfleet scribbled to him during the sting: it is signed "Mullican." Perhaps Norfleet simply had trouble remembering his alias. Or perhaps Norfleet changed his pseudonym ever so slightly from an unusual name to a more generic one because, back in June 1920, six months after he was swindled, he had sold seventy-seven hundred acres from his ranch to recoup his losses, and his buyers were W. M. Mullican, Lon A. Mullican, and Clark M. Mullican. Norfleet did not want his autobiography to reveal that when he was casting about for a country bumpkin to impersonate, he settled on the fine personage of L. A. Mullican. Yet in most respects Van Cise's memoir and the documents that have survived from his long surveillance agree with and sometimes amplify Norfleet's story.

Norfleet's sting properly began the next morning, when he put on his bunchy suit and his too-small Panama hat and headed for the Brown Palace Hotel on Seventeenth Street, the elegant anchor of the city's business district and the main pond in which the steerers fished. Robert Maiden, one of Van Cise's private detectives, was watching him, and he recorded in his surveillance notes that Norfleet first entered the Brown Palace on August 22, 1922, at 11:10 a.m.

As soon as he did, Norfleet saw a steerer lounging in a club chair, but first he would play his big entrance to the hilt. He walked into the atrium under the stained-glass ceiling eight stories above him, a room that had held royals, millionaires, and Roosevelts. He stood for a moment in his homespun shagginess, letting his incongruity sharpen, and then he pounced on a man who had just entered the atrium with his two young daughters.

"Well, well, I thought I knowed you," Norfleet exclaimed, pumping his hand. "You're Mr. Woolridge from down my way in Texas, ain't you?" But the man laughed and said that no, he was Jennings from Nebraska, and he took his leave, shepherding his girls through the tables of ladies sipping tea. It was enough. Norfleet heard a voice with a familiar twang behind him.

"Are you looking for someone? May I help you, sir? You seem to be

a stranger!" He turned to see a sleek, dark-haired businessman with a
neatly trimmed mustache. From his years of studying rogues' galleries,
Norfleet knew him to be Leon Felix, but the man introduced himself as A. C. Davis from—wouldn't you know it?—Houston, Texas. He
guided Norfleet over to the front desk, and together they ascertained
that Mr. Woolridge had not yet checked in. Felix took Norfleet by the
arm and steered him out of the hotel to an elegant Cadillac parked on
Seventeenth Street. "Guess we Texans will have to throw in together,"
he said, and he offered his services as a tour guide for the lonely cotton
grower so far from home. For the rest of the day, as they laced through
city parks, museums, and the zoo, Felix gently pumped Norfleet for
information like an oil rigger relentlessly performing its job of extraction. Norfleet took the first opportunity to fumble out of his pocket
the letter he'd forged from his wife: "The drillers have struck oil in the
corner of our field. They have quit drilling, and the company is leas-
ing every acre of land they can get around this well. I am now holding
down a lease on 236 acres of our land with my signature and I recom-
mend that you come home at once and sign this lease so we can get
the money and then you can go back to Denver and stay as long as you
please." He could almost see the calculations behind Felix's eyes as he
read the letter.

It wasn't until the next day that Felix began to turn the conversation
toward himself. On a drive up to Lookout Mountain, Felix declared,
"It's too slow waiting for your money to grow. Not for me. I like mine
quick!" Out came the scripted story of the reckless young speculator on
the stock market, the judge who helped him with a side deal, the thousands of dollars in frictionless profit. As they returned to town, Felix
parked the car under a shade tree near the capitol to finish his story.

Norfleet looked down the street. Yes, there was the next character
in the drama, a man who he would later learn was named Arthur Cooper. Seconds later, Felix seized his arm and pointed urgently at Cooper,
walking toward them with his face buried in a bouquet of yellow telegrams, a tall, blond fellow in a crisp blue coat, white flannel trousers,
straw hat, and an enormous diamond stickpin that glinted in the afternoon sun. The instant he passed the Cadillac, Felix whispered hoarsely,
"Speak of the devil, and his image appears! There he is—the mysterious
stranger. I can hardly believe my eyes. But it is true!"

Norfleet, mustering all the cornpone he had inside him, shouted,

"Tackle him! Tackle him! Find out how he does it! Get him to learn you how."

Cooper was letter-perfect as he huffily rebuked them and then softened when he realized they were friends whom he could trust. He introduced himself as P. J. Miller, and only minutes later the three men were headed to the exchange, an imposing brick building at the corner of Eighteenth and California. Cooper took $40 of Felix's money and transmuted it into $120, then invited them into the sanctum. There Norfleet was introduced to the third player, the secretary of the exchange, a Mr. Zachary, whom he did not recognize but whose inky-black hair, florid complexion, and extravagant waxed mustache would be easy to remember. At the end of the afternoon, Zachary counted out $201,500 into Norfleet's arms, then just as quickly repossessed it and sent the three men on their way.

From this moment onward, Norfleet knew, few of his experiences would be routine. The swindling script would continue to structure his relationship with Felix and Cooper, but he would simultaneously need to record every detail as evidence for Van Cise and be prepared to improvise his way out of a situation that was rapidly seeming like captivity.

Norfleet counted his steps as he was ushered into a nondescript hotel somewhere in downtown Denver. Thirty-one paces from the front door to the stairs at the rear. The stairs turned to the left, then deposited him at a landing and an elevator. Up to the third floor, down a corridor utterly lacking in identifying details, to room 310. Norfleet burned the map into his mind. They entered a large room, comfortably furnished for the three men, with an adjoining bathroom. There was a folding bed just to the left of the main door. If Norfleet took that bed, he would be hidden from anyone entering the room until the door was closed. Norfleet casually strode to the window. Outside, he saw the back of the Brown Palace Hotel, as well as several billboards. He added them to his mental map.

The men settled into the room, and Norfleet sat patiently as the two swindlers began to give him the breakdown. Cooper told him about a rich uncle who could lend them the entire $100,000 needed to bail out Norfleet's winnings, and Felix jumped in to say that if that idea didn't pan out, he had $50,000 worth of Liberty Bonds to lend to the cause.

Just then, they heard cries of "Extra! Extra!" floating up from the street. Felix fetched a newspaper, and the three of them crowded around to read the breaking news. Felix and Cooper were disappointed to learn that it was only the latest installment of the labor dispute unfolding in the Colorado coalfields. The governor believed that a riot was about to erupt, and so he had sent the Rangers out to quell the uprising. Felix and Cooper returned to their unpacking, but the news ratcheted up Norfleet's inner turmoil by a few more notches. Those Rangers were supposed to come to his rescue in a few days. The governor had just commandeered his saviors.

With the appetites of innocents, Felix and Cooper made plans for dinner. They contrived to eat in shifts, one man guarding Norfleet in the room while the other ducked outside. When Felix brought him back a sandwich, Norfleet was catapulted into a new bind. He could not eat the sandwich for fear of poison, but he could not be seen to distrust his friends. Thinking quickly, he improvised a toothache, which provided him the excuse he needed to bring the long summer day to a close. There he was on the bed, a forlorn Texas hick with an agonizing toothache, and underneath that, a hardened rancher with an outsize grudge. And underneath that? Did Norfleet lie there and think about how he might someday narrate this moment? After all, it doesn't make sense that the men trying to extract money from him would poison him before he'd even sent home for the cash. Certainly his life would have been in danger had they known his true identity. But death by poisoning was unlikely at this stage of the script. Norfleet's narration prompts the suspicion that he amplified his own personal danger in order to charge heroically out of it. Van Cise's version lends credence to this suspicion. He says that he gave Norfleet precise instructions to fake a toothache and get in touch with the district attorney from the office of Dr. William Smedley of the Smedley Dental Group later in the week. The other patients sitting in the waiting room would, in reality, be Van Cise's men, planted there to identify the swindlers. Norfleet's flash of genius was preordained by Van Cise.

Felix and Cooper eventually fell asleep, but Norfleet could not afford to relax his guard. Like a hunter in the woods, he set up a blind to spot his enemies before they saw him. He placed a chair at the end of his bed, which stretched lengthwise behind the door. He sat in the chair with his right side against the wall, allowing him to survey the entire room and the door and concealing the death grip he had on the revolver strapped to his right hip. All through the night, Norfleet watched for the unknown, monitoring the room and his own paranoia. When the tension and fatigue threatened to break his concentration, he knocked his head against the wall or stood and quietly paced. When one of his friends awakened, he says he threw himself forward on the bed and pretended to sleep, his right hand burrowing the gun under the pillow. It is, admittedly, difficult to picture.

Norfleet watched morning arrive with bloodshot eyes. If there was any benefit to be had from the situation, he thought to himself, it was that his haggard appearance supported his story of ill health. Felix and Cooper inquired about his tooth, but Norfleet knew that they only cared if he was well enough to carry out their scheme. Norfleet accordingly recalibrated his pain. He was suffering too much to eat, but by all means, gentlemen, let them proceed with business!

Cooper stepped out to retrieve the telegram they had been awaiting, and when he returned, his face had gone sour. His rich uncle was in Mexico, out of reach. Felix's Liberty Bonds would only cover half of the money. On cue, Norfleet pulled out the letter from his wife. Cooper, his voice at once smooth and commanding, suggested that perhaps Norfleet might conduct his business by telegram and the whole affair might be concluded in just a few days. Norfleet deferred entirely to his friend and sat down to write, in big, loopy script, a message to his fictitious wife. Cooper sent the telegram, and the game was on.

For the rest of the day, Felix, Cooper, and Norfleet continued this courtly masquerade with the deadly undertow. Felix and Cooper pretended to be Norfleet's friends, finding yet more creative ways to make his captivity feel like pampering. Norfleet pretended to trust his friends unconditionally, all the while forgoing food and sleep, nursing his spurious toothache, and clutching his concealed revolver. Under the direst strain, none of the three actors broke character. Later, Norfleet attested to the monumental effort that lay behind his impersonation of the gullible farmer. "It was a mad fight against hunger, sleep and these murderous wolves." His feigned neuralgia took the greatest toll on him. "Had the suggestion produced the genuine malady," he wrote, "it would have been more easily borne than the constant struggle to simulate pain and suffering."

Yet he had many reasons to congratulate himself for his toothache as he pretended to await his wife's bank draft. That day it seemed as if all of Denver's underworld passed through the hotel room. Again and again, a secret code was knocked onto the door—two loud raps, then two quiet ones—and it opened to reveal yet another swindler, stopping by to check out the newest mark and ensure he was not a plant. Norfleet remained shielded behind the door, his hands cupping his throbbing jaw to delay recognition, his eyes hurriedly scanning his visitors' faces and matching them up to his mental database. He did not fear spotting a swindler whom he knew. He was confident that he could pull his gun out faster than any fancy talker. In fact, his hope bloomed anew each time the door opened that the man he had trailed to Denver would walk through.

No, his greatest fear was that now that his notoriety had spread throughout the criminal world, he would be recognized by someone he didn't know. His entire life now rested on the meager disguise afforded by his phantom pain. The irony was that Norfleet didn't actually have a tooth left in his head. In one version of his story—but only one—he claimed that he had pulled all his teeth out at the beginning of his manhunt in favor of false teeth, which he could pop in and out to alter his appearance in an instant.

Norfleet knew that his grace period was dwindling. If he did not receive a letter from Mrs. Mulligan, he would have called his own bluff, and the searching glances would become far more penetrating. His only chance of rescue was decisive action—but what? He paced past the telephone he was not allowed to use to dial the district attorney's secret number. He eyed the satchel at the foot of Felix's bed which was stuffed with a "small artillery" that he found no opportunity to sabotage. The hotel stationery lying on the desk gave him an idea. He sat down to write to Mrs. Mulligan back in Ferris, making a point to borrow a stamp from Felix and seal the letter before his eyes. Later, in the bathroom, he loudly splashed his feet in the tub while he flushed his wife's letter down the toilet and wrote another one to Van Cise, giving him as many details of his location as he could and ending with: "If I am bumped off before you can get to me this is my true statement."

That afternoon, Felix drove Norfleet to the post office to check for remittances from his wife. Robert Maiden was on duty, and he saw a Cadillac pull up to the post office, with Norfleet and Felix in the front seat. Maiden saw what Norfleet did not: Felix gave the office to a man standing at the window of a hotel across the street. That man in turn signaled to a large man standing just outside, and they both headed inside the post office. Maiden's senses bristled at the danger, and he hurried into the post office, watching the two men watching Norfleet and Felix. He saw Norfleet hobble his way to the *M* window at the general delivery counter and call for his mail, the large man directly behind him in line. Norfleet was able to slip Van Cise's letter into the outgoing slot without Felix noticing. Maiden saw all four men exit the post office and the mustached man whisk Norfleet away in the Cadillac.

Back in the hotel room, the clock ticked implacably through his hunger, his maddening fatigue, and his phony toothache. Norfleet found himself near his breaking point. And just like that, he would later say, the solution came to him. Wildly, he announced that he could not stand it anymore. In a matter of seconds, he convinced them to take him to the nearest dentist, just a few blocks away from their hotel. At the reception desk, Norfleet's plan brought instant dividends. "Name?" inquired the receptionist. "L. A. Mulligan." "Address?" Norfleet cast about confusedly; "310—310—Oh! where do we live boys?" he asked his companions. Felix and Cooper faltered, until finally Cooper said reluctantly, "Er—er—Hotel Metropole."

A few more seconds, and Norfleet was on the phone to the district attorney, relaying his precise address and room number. He had barricaded himself in an examining room with the dentist and secured his complicity before making the secret phone call. Lying back in the chair amid the steel instruments and the enamel sink, carefully staying in character, and speaking elliptically lest his end of the conversation be overheard, Norfleet helped Van Cise plot the ambush of the largest ring of confidence artists in the country.

The dentist turned out to be an ace improviser. He led Norfleet back out to the waiting room as if escorting a dying man to his grave. Felix and Cooper asked if he had managed to fix Norfleet's tooth. No, said the dentist grimly, his condition was so dire he would need to come back later in the evening for another treatment, and he'd phone Norfleet at the next opening in his schedule. As they returned to the hotel, Norfleet noticed two men nonchalantly talking in the lobby; Van Cise had acted quickly. One of the men pressed the elevator button for Norfleet and turned to meet his eye. Norfleet rose up to the third floor a little safer than when he had left it.

But the outing had made Felix and Cooper nervous in direct proportion to Norfleet's internal relief. Sensing that their hermetic seal on the situation had begun to leak, they rounded on Norfleet and demanded to know when he might expect word from his wife. Norfleet mumbled and stalled. Felix and Cooper furiously gestured behind his back and came to a wordless consensus. Pulling out a Colorado and Southern rail schedule, they selected a midnight train to Ferris. Surely Norfleet would be well enough by then to travel back home with them and conclude the land lease in person. Behind his cupped hand, letting his misery gush out as the pantomime of pain, Norfleet assented. His window of rescue had just contracted to mere hours.

The phone rang and the dentist summoned Norfleet back to his office. Norfleet assumed his position in the dental chair, and at the welcome sound of Van Cise's voice on the line he poured out the sorry details of his plight. He beseeched to know how soon before midnight the DA's men could spring him loose. Van Cise crisply outlined a rescue plan: the deputies who would act without the knowledge of the Denver Police Department, the Rangers on their motorcycles, the church that would sacrilegiously be pressed into service as a holding pen for the con men on their way to the county jail. It would all go down, he told Norfleet, at six o'clock the next morning. *If,* he added, the Colorado Rangers made it back from the coalfields in time. Norfleet must find a way to forestall his journey without exciting a modicum of suspicion. His companions must be in that hotel room the next morning, and they must not be on guard. Van Cise ever so gently tightened the pressure on Norfleet. "Don't let them kill my men!" he barked.

Next, the district attorney gave marching orders to the dentist: "Norfleet must give all the appearance of a suffering patient. Dump everything in the shop on his tooth and mouth so you can smell it for a block and fix it up swell." Cooperative to the last, the dentist administered a pharmacy's worth of unmarked drugs to his healthy patient and turned him loose.

Norfleet stumbled down the dark city street between his two companions, headed for the train station despite his protestation that his condition had worsened since his two dental treatments. In just minutes, his years of hunting, his weeks of preparation, and his days of unrelieved agony would be for naught as he sped away from the only people who knew his true identity and could release him from his disguise. Surreptitiously, he leaned down and sniffed from a vial the dentist had given him. As he would tell it later, "Large cramps wrapped their arms about my stomach and bent me over. I gloried in being able to act natural for the first time in nearly a week." He vomited prodigiously, staggered, and keeled over in a dead faint, the first time his eyes had closed in two nights. When he came to, he saw the dour faces of Felix and Cooper hovering above him, and he heard the whistle of the train departing for Texas without them.

The three men trudged back to the Hotel Metropole, Felix and Cooper in bitter disappointment, Norfleet in utter dread at the night awaiting him. But he had come this far, and his native stubbornness and resourcefulness did not desert him. For the third night in a row, Norfleet began his dance of wakefulness as Felix innocently slept and Cooper spent the night elsewhere. He paced, he knocked his head into the wall, he doused his head in hot and cold water. But the bodily mortifications of the past days had accumulated, and he could feel his consciousness disobediently slipping away from him. Norfleet had one desperate, stupid, brilliant trick up his sleeve. He ducked into the bathroom and sprinkled tobacco leaves into his eyes. "In an instant I thought my head had hit the ceiling!" he wrote in his memoir. "Water gushed from both eyes and daggers pinned my quivering eyeballs to the back of my head. I was awake!" He had nothing left to do but watch the clock and wonder who would enter the door the next morning.

Meanwhile, as Norfleet tortured himself, Van Cise convened a meeting of all the Rangers, veterans, and detectives at the home of Roy Samson. Beginning at seven o'clock that night, they made a list of all the swindlers they'd identified through surveillance and mug shots, then mapped the offices and watering holes where the bunco men congregated, and choreographed the raids at each locale. They finished at two o'clock, and each man headed home for a few hours' sleep before reconvening at six o'clock in the morning at the First Universalist Church. The first sortie would be to room 310 in the Metropole to arrest Leon Felix and Arthur Cooper and rescue Norfleet. Van Cise reminded his men of the swindlers' secret knock.

Two loud knocks, then two soft ones. Leon Felix blearily lifted his head from the pillow, saw Norfleet still asleep, and rose to open the door. In came the muzzles of two guns, followed by Detective Kenneth Robinson and a Ranger in plain clothes. As Norfleet sat up in bed and beamed, Robinson said calmly, "Put your hands up, you're under arrest," and handcuffed Felix. "Davis," Norfleet asked, "do you know who I am?" In Norfleet's account, when Felix heard Norfleet's true identity, he "jumped about a foot into the air, let out a yell and keeled over on the bed in a dead faint." Van Cise's version is simpler: " 'My God!' said Felix, falling back upon the bed."

While Norfleet and his rescuers waited for Cooper to arrive, Norfleet devoured the two chicken sandwiches that Robinson's wife had sent along. Robinson phoned the church and told Van Cise, "The weather's fine." About an hour later, Cooper gave the secret knock. Norfleet opened the door with his left hand, keeping his right hand hidden until Cooper was through the door, then jabbed his gun into Cooper's stomach. Cooper responded with far greater resignation than his colleague and refused to say a word after he'd been handcuffed. Much later, a fellow swindler would tell Van Cise that Cooper had never wanted to pick up Norfleet and had even offered to bet $1,000 that Norfleet was "wrong" because he seemed so jumpy and would whip his head around to the door at the slightest noise. Now Robinson called Van Cise and said, "Number Two party ready to go to church." Van Cise told him, "Wait an hour for other worshipers, then come in."

While they waited, Robinson, Norfleet, and the Ranger inventoried the two men's belongings and confiscated every scrap of paper, from the blank record slips of the International Exchange to a small black memo book that listed Cooper's debts and credits with his fellow spielers. Cooper's pockets also held several hundred dollars in cash, a platinum watch, and other jewelry. As Robinson began to write a receipt for each item, Cooper spoke up for the first time. "There is no need of mentioning that diamond stickpin in the receipt. You have included plenty without it," and he gestured toward the three-carat jewel that had first caught Norfleet's eye outside the capitol. Robinson ignored the offer. In Felix's bags, they found a small quantity of opium.

In the late morning, a car arrived at the Metropole to transport the prisoners and wardens to their holy jail. The car slipped into a small alley behind the church, and the three men led the prisoners into a back door, out of sight of the haughty residents of the neighborhood and anyone passing by who might be inclined to notify the underworld grapevine. Though Felix and Cooper were the first two arrests of the day, by the time they arrived at the church, another twenty men had been apprehended.

Prisoner number three had been Kid Duff, whom Roy Samson quietly arrested as he left his apartment to walk to the Lookout, just after Robinson phoned to say that Norfleet's men were in bracelets. "By God," Duff exclaimed, when Samson flashed his badge and his gun, "your District Attorney isn't going to get away with this! If he thinks he can pick up a reputable businessman on the street and arrest him this way, I will show him what's what." Samson ignored him, and once they arrived at the church, he cut through the businessman's masquerade by reaching into Duff's inside pocket to collect his personal effects. He pulled out a list of names, and after one glance at it he raced upstairs to show it to Van Cise.

The list was a perfect copy of the one that Van Cise had drawn up the night before, which he'd completed just a few hours prior to Duff's arrest. Duff's version was not a carbon copy, but a typewritten copy of the first page of Van Cise's two-page document, with most of the sixty-five names that the district attorney's crew had identified. Van Cise and his assistant Fred Sanborn were electrified by what the list's almost instantaneous transmission implied about Blonger's organization. Sanborn recalled that, while he and a deputized veteran had waited in the car for Duff to emerge from his apartment, they'd seen an under sheriff drive by and, upon spotting Sanborn, wave, circle the block, and return the way he'd come. Van Cise brushed aside the details for the time being. He was far too confident in his own men to suspect a leak. All he knew was that if his men had waited but a few minutes more, Duff would have broadcast their intentions to the entire conglomerate. It was now time to crumple up their carefully wrought plan. "Shoot the works and don't wait for Blonger's arrest," he told his team. "Hustle on every con-man in town, before they light out on us."

Fred Sanborn had been detailed to hook Blonger, and he'd been waiting outside the Kentom Apartments all morning, planning to trail Blonger to the American Bank Building so he could arrest him inside his office and seize its contents. But Blonger had spent the night with his mistress and arrived at his office undetected. Fortunately, Van Cise still had someone listening to the Dictaphone, and word soon reached Sanborn that his quarry was ready for his big moment. Sanborn entered room 309 with two other men and said, "The District Attorney wants to see you at once, Mr. Blonger," then he watched as Blonger silently took down one of the two coats on his coatrack and moved to close the roll-top desk at which he'd been sitting. Like the greenest of marks, Blonger had just telegraphed to Sanborn the location of his most incriminating document. Sanborn searched the coat still hanging on the coatrack to find a small bank-deposit book showing a balance of $10,000. What interested Sanborn was that Blonger also used it as an address book. The penciled names and phone numbers ("Randle York 3201," "Duff Champa 2074," "Lookout Champa 7453") materially tied Blonger to the lower corps of his organization, providing precisely the link Van Cise had hoped to find between the ropers and spielers who'd been observed in the act of swindling and the boss who never spoke to them. Blonger did not protest as he was led out of the office.

Roy Samson, for his part, sped back downtown to the Lookout, where he encountered Louis "Thick Lips" Mushnick coming out the door. Samson pointed him back into the room with the muzzle of his gun, packaged him up with Tip Belcher, two spielers, a bookmaker, and a steerer, and sent the lot of them to the church. He swept clean every desk drawer, confiscating account books that tallied the victims' totals and the banded stacks of the gang's boodle, $2,108 worth of bills made to look like $135,000. Then Samson posted a Ranger and a deputy within the Lookout to apprehend any swindler who came in for his day's orders, and throughout the afternoon they caught five more men. Samson next visited the stock exchange in the Denham Theatre building where Norfleet had earned his $201,500, but it was deserted. Other teams swooped in on swindlers' hotel rooms and apartments. They hit the tip-off headquarters on Seventeenth Street. They plucked swindlers right off street corners as they zoomed around the city. Two men stood on Seventeenth dividing $1,400 between them when they looked up to see Van Cise's deputies. The swindlers began to run but were caught after only a few yards. Such was life in Denver that the sight of a pair of men clutching a handful of bills being chased and caught by two other men in plain clothes caused no stir whatsoever, and no one reported the event to the police.

As each man arrived at the church, he was first brought to the minister's study, where five deputies sat behind a desk to book the prisoners. As the swindlers stood there, they could not help but look above the desk to a sign that displayed Psalm 1:6: "For the Lord knoweth the way of the righteous, but the way of the ungodly shall perish." Nonetheless, they breezily handed over false names and addresses along with the contents of their pockets and were not overly troubled by the obviousness of their own lies. "If your name is Bob Williams, how does it happen that your belt buckle bears the initials J.S.R.?" a Ranger asked a prisoner. "I had a very dear friend who died suddenly and his wife gave me his belt as a memento," replied "Bob Williams" easily. The men handed over fake bonds, jewelry, keys to rooms in the city's finest hotels, dice, playing cards, and cash. One man who claimed he was a waiter carried on him $1,312. Almost to a man, they possessed train tickets for cities like Omaha and Chicago. Each man relinquished his shoes, and some of them were further stripped of their clothes if they had tried to secrete drugs, and the Rangers collected opium, morphine, and hypodermic needles. Their possessions were placed in burlap bags, one per man, and they were each given an itemized receipt. Norfleet and two of Van Cise's detectives sat behind a curtain to identify the swindlers without themselves being identified, and Norfleet was gratified when Mr. Zachary, the exchange secretary with the lavish mustache who'd denied him his $201,500 payout, was brought before him and identified as Len Reamey, bookmaker.

Then the prisoners were led upstairs to the kindergarten room. As they sat in miniature red wooden chairs, Van Cise further questioned them and matched them to the photographs he'd collected from rogues' galleries around the country. The prisoners were photographed against a brick wall, and they resisted mightily, producing some truly gruesome images. Tip Belcher looks inebriated, with his eyes closed and his mouth sagging open, and he had to be held upright by a man behind him with an arm around his neck. In Duff's photograph, two men are restraining him as he struggles to get out of the frame. Duff's eyes are also closed and his mouth wrenched in a grimace, revealing his gold teeth, while one man clasps his arms down and another man holds on to either side of his forehead. Lou Blonger, though, hunches calmly against the wall in his undershirt, his face in profile and his long nose pointed downward.

After their inspection with Van Cise, the men were led down to the church's assembly room in the basement, where a section had been roped off to corral them under the Rangers' guns. Only when he

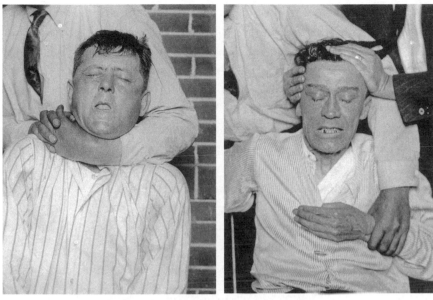

Tip Belcher, Kid Duff, and Lou Blonger on the day of the raid

reached the basement and saw his men penned like cattle did Blonger lose his poise. His head bowed and his muscles seemed to soften as he sank into a chair. For the rest of the afternoon, he sat alone and silent within the milling group, "like a great, gray spider spinning out his thoughts of other days," wrote Frances Wayne, one of the *Post* reporters and the only woman in the room. The rest of the men soon grouped themselves by kind, and Wayne detected three distinct castes. There were five young men in the remnants of flashy clothing who looked as if they'd come from lower-class backgrounds and had something to prove. Then there was a slightly older, more sophisticated group of men who cast contemptuous glances at the five young bucks. And lastly, there were the elder statesmen who might have been mistaken for prominent businessmen in any city in America. But for all the dignity on display in the basement, there was plenty of ignominious behavior. Prisoners outnumbered guards two to one, and several men tried to sidle past the ropes and out the door, but the Rangers took a regular census and no one escaped. Others tried to buy their way out. One of Van Cise's deputies reported that bribes ranged from $100 to $500 or "any amount asked," not to mention jewelry and watches, if the officer would help them secure a bondsman.

From out of the bustle, one diminutive figure emerged. J. Frank Norfleet descended to the church basement, grabbed a straight-backed chair along the edge of the assembly room, and proceeded to hold forth, while Frances Wayne of the *Post* and Eugene T. Lindberg of the *Times* transcribed his every word. He began at the beginning, with the fateful day in November three years previous when he encountered the Furey gang, and he brought the story right up to the present moment, a kind of practice run for his later memoirs. The transcript of Norfleet's statement that ran in both papers perfectly matches his book—except for one embellishment. When one of the reporters asked Norfleet how he was paying for his manhunt, given the financial embarrassments into which the Furey gang had placed him, Norfleet replied, "Why, I put over a deal in California while I was out there first looking for Furey at San Bernardino. I cleared $100,000 on the deal, and that's how I got the money to keep up the chase." He tossed off this detail, never to be repeated or elaborated, exactly like a con man bragging about taking off the touch.

Despite all the reporters milling about the assembly room, not a single word about Van Cise, Blonger, or Norfleet was published in the newspapers that day. Van Cise's campaign to exclude the press from the sting had worked right up to the midnight before the raid, when an anonymous caller telephoned Forbes Parkhill of the *Post* and told him, "The Rangers are coming to town early in the morning." Parkhill thought the call referred to the Industrial Workers of the World, whom the commanding officer of the Rangers, Colonel Patrick Hamrock, had lately taken to denouncing. Parkhill headed to the capitol building first thing the next morning, and as he lingered in the halls, he noticed a number of the district attorney's staffers, all of whom fled before his approach. He overheard one of the deputies say on the phone, "I'll see you at the church." Finally he confronted Colonel Hamrock, and when the colonel steadfastly turned away all his questions, telling Parkhill that it was "Van Cise's party," the reporter tried a bluff. "If you won't play ball with the *Post*," he said, "I'll have to go out to the church myself." Colonel Hamrock blanched. Afraid that Van Cise would think he tipped Parkhill off, he decided his safest course was to bring Parkhill to the church himself, and thus Parkhill gained exclusive access to the headquarters of the raid as it progressed.

But Van Cise forestalled the biggest scoop of the reporter's career by calling up the paper's managing editor, summoning him to the church, and persuading him to hold the story off for one day so he could net as many swindlers as possible. Meanwhile, a reporter from the *Times* overheard Parkhill on the phone say, "I'll be at the Universalist Church," so the process repeated itself, with a reporter demanding access to the raid and Van Cise calling his managing editor to beg for another day of silence. The next day, August 25, 1922, both papers splashed banner headlines above the masthead and told the story of the raid from several different angles. "When the first reports of the wholesale arrests spread thru Denver this morning the whole city gasped," wrote the *Times*, "as people recognized in the prisoners friends and acquaintances who posed as brokers, capitalists, planters and other persons of wealth, firmly intrenched in magnificent houses and secure social positions." Two days later, the *Rocky Mountain News* criticized the *Post* for omitting Lou Blonger's name from the list of prisoners in the church jail and noted Blonger's friendship with Tammen, but regular readers might have interpreted this as professional jealousy, for the *News* had missed the raid entirely. Many years later, Parkhill admitted that Tammen had ordered Blonger's name suppressed at first, but the very next day the story was too big to continue that practice, and the *Post* became the most complete source for the turmoil into which Van Cise had plunged the city of Denver.

Thirty-four of the city's busiest swindlers, including the kingpin and his lieutenant, were captured on that mild summer day. Despite Van Cise's efforts to place an airtight seal around the operations, word of the raid did leak out as the day progressed, and a few dozen con men escaped the Rangers and deputies. That morning, as Norfleet paraded one of his men through the lobby of the Metropole, he attracted the notice of a man loafing in the corner, a former city detective who'd recently finished serving jail time for blackmail and robbery. The ex-convict recognized the man in cuffs and called in the tip to the police station, which then called Blonger's office. The phone in the Lookout also got quite a workout that day, because that afternoon, when the swindlers' wives and girlfriends hadn't heard from them, they began to call Duff and Belcher, and when they couldn't get either man on the phone, they began to call each other, sounding the alarm. Van Cise estimated that about forty swindlers evaded arrest.

Robert Maiden, in his zeal to scoop up swindlers from the sidewalks around the capitol, had arrested three innocent men, and they were let go. One of the men, a shoe clerk from Parkersburg, West Virginia, was guilty of nothing more than reading a letter from his wife on a bench near the capitol. He managed to escape the car at Sixteenth and Broadway but was chased by two Rangers, cuffed in the ear hard enough to draw blood, and dragged back into custody. That night the newspaper called him a "desperate character." He was forced to spend the night with the bunco prisoners before his identity was obtained and he was let go with a curt apology from the district attorney. But on the positive side of the ledger, at least five marks escaped the penultimate act of the big con in which the touch is taken. They'd gone home to fetch their money in amounts ranging from $5,000 to $50,000, when the raid prevented them from handing it over and proceeding to the blow-off. At the end of the day, the prisoners were divided into two groups and sent to the county jails in the nearby towns of Golden and Brighton. Van Cise had one more major target on his list and wasn't going to take the chance of lodging his guests at the Denver County Jail.

For the second straight night, Van Cise went without sleep. He had been combing through Kid Duff's memo book when he saw the following notation: "Call French at Estes Park." Jackie French, the Beau Brummell of the bunco men, was one of the swindlers Van Cise wanted badly, a bookmaker who had one famous week in February 1922 when he made $120,000 from one mark, $200,000 from another, and $25,000 from a third. After the last of the Denver bunco men were secured, Van Cise and Roy Samson drove to Estes Park with a couple of Rangers, and at three o'clock in the morning they found French at the Stanley Hotel, the fanciest place in town, along with at least $2,000 worth of diamond jewelry. In the predawn hours, French was reunited with his Denver colleagues, while Van Cise headed downtown to prepare for the arraignments the next morning.

Norfleet was only too glad not to return to the Metropole on the evening of the raid. He checked into the Columbia Hotel, where he planned to stay as long as Van Cise needed him for the criminal proceedings against the Blonger gang. His three most recent antagonists, Davis, Miller, and Zachary had been unmasked as Felix, Cooper, and Reamey and were locked up behind bonds of $25,000 apiece. But Norfleet began to get antsy. Glad as he was to help cripple the bunco operations for the entire city of Denver, those men were never his targets. Norfleet came to Colorado in search of W. B. Spencer, but he was not one of the men scooped up in the raid. Norfleet had no doubt that any of the men now behind bars could lead him to Spencer. The interrelatedness of the bunco network was everywhere on view in the documents that Van Cise had seized. Duff's little memorandum book contained Charles Gerber's address, and the district attorney's team counted Gerber as one of the men who got away, before they realized a few days later that Norfleet had long ago sent him to the Texas penitentiary. Though he had never met Duff before, Norfleet decided he was his man.

He read in the newspapers that Blonger and Duff, alone among the thirty-four men, had been able to post bond and would be released the next day. Patrick "Red" Gallagher, another one of those men who is "well-known in sporting circles," pledged half of his interest in the Lewiston Hotel as security for the bonds, and the courts waived the requirement that each criminal supply two bondsmen. Norfleet stationed himself outside the jail, and as Duff emerged with Gallagher, he moved in and, without bothering to introduce himself, asked, "Do you think Spencer is worth all of this tribe we have taken in, and all the others I'll get while I'm hunting for him?" Norfleet says Duff was aghast at the idea that the entire raid might have been avoided had Norfleet located Spencer. "My God!" he burst out. "Why didn't you come to me, Norfleet, and tell me what you wanted. If you had come to me first you could have had your man and your money back within three days!" Gallagher glared at him meaningfully, but Duff went on to say that the last he'd heard, Spencer was staying at the Empire Hotel, run by a woman named Mrs. Franklin.

Norfleet thanked him courteously, then dashed over to the Empire, only to learn that Spencer had checked out the morning of the raid. Later, he would find out that Spencer had actually been detained in the middle of August by city detectives while working in an unsanctioned part of town. They were about to take him in, when Duff walked by. "He's all right," Duff informed them. "He's working for Blonger and me in our mines and is a pretty good fellow, but doesn't know much." Yet somehow he knew enough to avoid Van Cise's men a few days later. But Mrs. Franklin had a consolation prize for Norfleet. Spencer had left behind his suitcase with a note instructing her to forward it to him in Salina, Kansas. The suitcase was stocked with the usual con man paraphernalia, labeled everywhere with the name of Harris, the same name Spencer had used with Norfleet three years previously in Dallas. And there, amid the papers, was Norfleet's gun, missing since Spencer had confiscated it in the Westbrook Hotel in Fort Worth. Curiously, Norfleet does not mention being reunited with his gun in his memoirs; the detail only appears in Van Cise's book. Norfleet left for Salina that very night.

CHAPTER ELEVEN

Pure Speculation

From *The New York Times* to *The Oakland Tribune*, the nation's newspapers trumpeted the smashing of Lou Blonger's swindling ring. "Bunko Trust Broken When Arrests Made," they cried. "Supposed 'Sucker' Traps Swindlers." The joyful headlines were tempered by a fair bit of background exposition within the articles themselves, because no one outside of Denver had heard of Blonger. But everyone had heard of Norfleet, and he cast a long shadow over the ostensible protagonist and villain of the drama. *The Denver Post* portrayed Philip Van Cise as the hero, but newspapers outside of Colorado focused almost exclusively on Norfleet, and Van Cise seemed only too happy to shift attention away from himself. "They picked the wrong bird for plucking when they picked Norfleet," he said in his statement to the national press. "They tried to work a $50,000 swindle on the man who caught Joe Furey." Two days after the raid, Norfleet gave a statement of his own to answer the question that was, apparently, on America's lips: What would be next for the famous manhunter? Why, he'd keep at it, of course. "I know 24 men in Texas and elsewhere who have been robbed, broken-hearted, and some have died because of the villainy of these confidence men," he said. "Somebody's got to fight them to a finish and I'm the man that's willing to do it." Norfleet was by now issuing his comments with a showman's flair. He looked forward to the day when the quest was over, he told reporters, and he could return home to "let Ma make a fuss over me and feed me some of those biscuits and waffles and corn pone and baked ham that Ward and Gerber ate before they took us in to the tune of $45,000."

It was shameless, really, the way Norfleet pandered to his audience. Already by 1922, the script for Norfleet's drama was as established as Blonger's swindling script, and Norfleet fully inhabited the role of the good guy who had snared the charismatic outlaw, a kind of white-collar cops-and-robbers tale. He was a descendant of the Pinkerton detective and an ancestor to the G-men and the hard-boiled detectives. And he was a cousin to the stockbroker, a figure very much on the minds of readers in the 1920s for whom the new era of high finance was a frontier as untamed as the West.

The newspaper readers who sat in their armchairs and thrilled to Norfleet's dangerous deeds could defend their interest in his racy story by the notion that the telling of the tale itself extracted a further measure of justice, because broadcasting their swindling methods in the newspapers warned away potential victims of future cons. Based on this very logic, the 1920s witnessed an explosion of articles about confidence artistry, especially in the monthly magazines that catered to middle-class readers. Suddenly, like never before in American culture, confidence artistry became an urgent and endlessly fascinating topic of conversation. Virtually every issue of *The Saturday Evening Post* or *McClure's* contained an article from a state attorney general exposing the latest fashion in financial chicanery, or a confession from an anonymous mark about how easily his confidence had been purloined. Each one of these articles was framed as an object lesson in what to avoid. After all, as the business editor of *The World's Work* observed, "If there is one thing that financial crooks fear more than an active, conscientious officer of the law it is the light of publicity." Yet if that were true, why were so many financial crooks publishing their tell-all memoirs at precisely the same time that Norfleet was unearthing them from their dens?

It turns out that con men were as ruthless about exploiting the new market for swindling stories as Norfleet was. Prior to the twentieth century, virtually the only swindler who published his autobiography was Stephen Burroughs, the New Hampshire impostor and counterfeiter who wrote *Memoirs of the Notorious Stephen Burroughs* in 1798. Then, in the first three decades of the twentieth century, dozens of con men joined up with journalists, ghostwriters, and sociologists to boast about their deeds and divulge the secret knowledge of their underground caste. Over and over, they spelled out the precise steps by which they ingratiated themselves with marks, told them the tale, and sauntered away with their money. Their stories were serialized in the very same magazines that warned against stock swindles and Spanish prisoners, and ostensibly issued under the very same premise: if you learn the tricks of the trade, you will be inoculated against the disease of susceptibility.

But the swindler autobiographies actually sabotaged this logic, right there on the page for all to see. They informed their readers, in a tone so sly that no one seemed to have picked it up, that revealing their secrets was exactly what paved the way for yet more swindling. The stock swindler George Graham Rice, in his saucy 1913 autobiography, *My Adventures with Your Money,* wrote, "A little knowledge is a dangerous thing, and the man who thinks he knows it all because he has accumulated much money in his own pet business enterprise is a typical personage on whom the successful modern-day multi-millionaire Wall Street financier trains his batteries." As the con man William C. Crosby wrote in the memoir he co-authored with Edward H. Smith and serialized in *The Saturday Evening Post* in 1920, then later reprinted as a book called *Confessions of a Confidence Man,* "The average professional man possesses that perilous little knowledge of many subjects alien to his immediate calling. He has nearly always some idea of the working of mechanical and electrical devices. He is progressive, informed, sanguine. He feels the kinship of the quasi-scientist with the sciences. But he is seldom well enough equipped to discover the fraud lurking deep in the dark vitals of a new idea. Thus he is an excellent target for the arrows of con."

Swindlers' autobiographies cultivate that "perilous little knowledge" in their own readers that will fill them with so much self-confidence that they can afford to give some of the surplus to enterprising strangers. Thus do swindling autobiographies only *seem* to reveal anything about their profession. One con man anonymously reviewed another swindler's 1937 testimonial, *The Professional Thief,* with a great deal of bemusement: "While apparently written in frank and candid form the topics discussed are factual without being really expository. There is little doubt as to the authenticity of this work, yet it can be stated positively that the reader will know very little more about the actual profession of thievery upon his completion of the book." The swindler autobiographies cannot have been accused of committing deception, but nor did they commit truth.

Those serialized swindler autobiographies were all part of a very big con that played out in the 1920s. The American economic landscape had changed enormously in the previous few decades, but the terms for talking about capitalism had not yet caught up. Only the confidence artists were fluent. Part of the reason why Norfleet's story gained so much traction was that his quest helped update the discourse about speculation and swindling, markets and morality, that legitimated mainstream economic activity. Everyone was talking about swindling in the 1920s because everyone, for the first time in the nation's history, had a stake in the financial markets.

Charlie Chaplin was nervous as he waited to go onstage. It was 1918 and he was the nation's darling, having made movie audiences laugh throughout the grim war years. But this was no quiet film set. He was

Charlie Chaplin making his first speech for the Liberty Loan drive in
Washington, D.C., on the first anniversary of U.S. entry into the war, April 6, 1918

standing in front of the State, War, and Navy Building in Washington, D.C., beside a hastily constructed platform of boards covered with flags and bunting, and the crowd waiting to hear him speak on behalf of the war effort, alongside Mary Pickford and Douglas Fairbanks, was large and expectant. To ease his nerves, Chaplin turned to the tall young man who stood beside him and confessed that he'd never done this sort of thing before. "There's nothing to be scared about," the man told Chaplin. "Just give it to them from the shoulder, tell them to buy their Liberty Bonds; don't try to be funny." Chaplin was grateful for the advice, and when it was his turn, he leaped onto the stage and poured his nervous energy into his words, not even stopping to breathe: "The Germans are at your door! We've got to stop them! And we will stop them if you buy Liberty Bonds! Remember, each bond you buy will save a soldier's life—a mother's son!—and will bring this war to an early victory!" But so forceful were his words that he slipped on the flimsy platform and catapulted onto the handsome young man, who turned out to be the assistant secretary of the navy, Franklin D. Roosevelt.

The Liberty Bonds with which the federal government financed World War I hurled the nation into a new phase of capitalism with equal enthusiasm and ineptitude. As Chaplin's inclusion demonstrated, America's participation in the war was fostered on the home front with two modern tools: mass media and public debt. The Treasury Department staged four loan drives in 1917 and 1918. When the first, which was intended to raise $5 billion, was undersubscribed, Secretary of the Treasury William Gibbs McAdoo launched an aggressive publicity campaign to market the bonds. Actors, bankers, and even Boy and Girl Scouts exhorted Americans to "capitalize patriotism," as McAdoo put it, by buying war bonds with yields between 3.5 and 4.5 percent. Veterans toured the nation in railroad cars to spread the word. Chaplin and his colleagues divided up the country between them and went on tour to stage massive rallies. Chaplin financed and starred in *The Bond* (1918), a series of skits about the bonds of friendship, love, marriage, and, most important, Liberty Bonds. Goldwyn made a silent film whose premise would have been almost blasphemous just a few decades earlier: *Stake Uncle Sam to Play Your Hand* (1918) depicts a card game in which Italy is losing to Germany until Miss Liberty Loan comes to the rescue.

McAdoo's troops created enormous social pressure to own Liberty Bonds, and by the end of the subscription period the Treasury had raised about $24 billion for a war that eventually cost about $33 billion. Far more important than their effect on their issuer, however, was the Liberty Bonds' effect on their holders. Before the war, only about half a million people owned securities of any kind. By 1918, that number had ballooned to seventeen million. Many of those were people who had never even stepped inside a commercial bank, much less a brokerage house. The Liberty Loan program arguably had the greatest effect on ethnic communities among the working class. At the height of the bond campaign in 1918, 46.5 percent of all subscribers were foreign born or had foreign parents. One study of six hundred mothers working at unskilled jobs in Chicago packinghouses found that 84 percent of their families owned Liberty Bonds. Because the bonds were available in small denominations and payable in installments, millions of people could participate in the financial market for the first time. The Treasury Department's Foreign Language Division, in particular, mobilized pastors, priests, and presidents of more than forty thousand ethnic organizations to persuade their members to demonstrate their patriotism to the United States and help free their homelands by buying Liberty Bonds. Later, corporations would use the same strategy to secure their employees' loyalty, granting workers shares of corporate stock to encourage the middle and working classes to invest in the capitalist system on the terms of the financiers.

The war economy had largely completed the process begun in the previous century by the Erie Canal bond issue, the railroad stocks, the Chicago Board of Trade, and the bucket shops: the slow redefinition of the American adult from a saver to an investor. In the nineteenth century, an ethic of money management that stressed thrift merged with a larger moral ideal of Christian and republican values that were repeatedly summed up in the term "character." To have character, as one reverend explained, was to possess "INTEGRITY . . . INTELLIGENCE . . . INDUSTRY . . . ECONOMY . . . and FRUGALITY . . . ENERGY . . . and TACT." The middle-class adult was expected to finance his or her household almost solely on cash, saved and hoarded from steady labor; living within one's means was the imperative. Gradually, it became common to purchase the new, mass-produced consumer items of the industrial era on credit, but this violated the Victorian value system that made a distinction between "productive" credit, which used borrowed money to increase one's capital, and "consumptive" credit, which merely drained one's resources and weakened one's self-control.

The nineteenth-century understanding of the money economy could be precisely mapped onto the reformers' distinction between speculation and gambling. Productive credit was like speculation that was supposed to lead to greater financial security, and consumptive credit was like gambling, a pure waste. Yet while American culture sought to differentiate speculation from gambling, the opposite trend played out in the value field of money and finance. The two kinds of credit began to blur and combine, enlarging the sectors of the economy in which it was permissible to extend one's capital. Debt was transformed from a potential route to dissipation into the very tool by which a discerning investor might exercise perfect self-control in the pursuit of profit and productivity. The long inflation from 1897 to 1914 actually rendered the savings account a poor financial instrument for the preservation of wealth. The forced austerity of World War I—in which the government limited the spectrum of shoe colors to white, black, and tan and declared wheatless Mondays, meatless Tuesdays, and porkless Thursdays and Saturdays—meant that Americans saved more than ever before, at a rate that had reached 9.1 percent by 1917. The war fueled the economy, but for a time the dollars backed up. The stock market began to rev: in 1915 and 1916, General Motors had risen from $55 a share to $114, and American Woolen had jumped from $12 to $50. Jobs were created, real wages rose, and purchasing power skyrocketed as the cost of consumer goods fell; between 1914 and 1926, the amount a dollar could buy grew by 50 percent. When Americans were urged to put their surplus capital into Liberty Bonds, the barrier for entry into the world of finance was at a historic low. They had the money, and the moral strictures against speculation had melted in the heat of the expanding economy.

What happened next was utterly predictable in hindsight. Within the first few months of the war's end, confidence men had stolen $400 million worth of Liberty Bonds from Midwesterners alone, according to the Treasury Department. The war had pushed the stock market up to unthinkable levels, but the true increase was elsewhere in the nation's economy; as one con man estimated in *The Saturday Evening Post* in 1922, "The war and the activities incident to it increased the output of American suckers tenfold." Even he was a little chagrined at his own success, saying, "I'd hate to know the gross suckerage of this country right now."

In 1918–19, Louis Guenther's muckraking series of articles in *The World's Work*, "Pirates of Promotion," revealed exactly how the new market for securities was diverted and siphoned off. A letter would arrive in the mail from a brokerage house such as the Ratner Securities Corporation. "Send us your $100 Liberty Bond—or as many more as possible," it would begin. "We will loan you the full face value on these bonds, if they are used to purchase good, dividend securities under the Ratner plans. . . . Do not waste the power of your Liberty Bond. If idle in a safe-deposit vault, it is non-creative. Give your bond the constructive element to which it is entitled. It will do its duty to 'Uncle Sam' twice and to you twice." Why be content with 3 or 4 percent yearly interest, the letter would say, when savvy investors earn four times that much? The brokerage would accept the bonds as collateral for a leveraged purchase of the industrial, mining, or oil stocks it was actively promoting. Its house organ might tell of the Kathodian Bronze Works, for instance, or National Bituminous Coal and Coke Company, or Geyser Oil. It might offer early investors favorable terms for lending their capital to a grand enterprise in its nascent phase—say, a hundred shares for $10, with an option to buy as many as five thousand more shares at ten cents apiece regardless of future price swings. To demonstrate its good faith, the brokerage would guarantee to buy back the original shares in sixty days if they hadn't increased in price. But sixty days later, the investor would receive another letter crowing about the success of the first issue and explaining that the next issue would now be priced significantly higher because of vigorous trading.

Sometimes the "brokerage" would actually execute the investor's orders to purchase stock in one of the companies. Sometimes the company in question might have an actual mining lease on some acreage in the West, or an oil rig lazily raising and lowering its arm somewhere in Texas. Sometimes the company's stock might even appear on the New York Stock Exchange or the Curb outside it, where less regulated trading occurred. But there was never a market for the stocks that these get-rich-quick promoters dealt in; it was never possible to sell them, only to buy more and more of them.

Yet if the stocks could not be sold, the names of the people who bought them were highly fungible. The phony promoters made almost as much money by compiling and selling so-called sucker lists as they did by swindling money from the suckers themselves. Like the commodities on the Chicago Board of Trade, these sucker lists were sorted, graded, and priced with precision: the "sold once" names went for two cents apiece; next in value was the "quick" list of middle-class people who had just inherited money; the list of "selected clergy" was prized because religious leaders invested church money and acted as financial advisers to many families, so it went for four cents a name; at the high end, the clerk at a venerable New England bank pilfered and sold a list of its customers to a name broker for twenty-five cents a name.

"Sold once" did not, alas, mean "twice shy," as the monthly magazines' editors and writers learned to their anguish. Guenther's *World's Work* series, as well as George Witten's articles in *Outlook*, Edward Jerome Dies's series "The Fine Art of Catching the 'Sucker,'" also in *Outlook*, and Albert Atwood's articles in *The Saturday Evening Post*, seemingly had little effect in slowing down the steady transfer of wealth from the new population of marks to the ever more resourceful swindlers. Soon, *The World's Work* was exposing the "reloaders," whose genius consisted of approaching the "sold once" and using their worthless stock as the lever by which to extract yet more money from them. A reloader, sitting in a "boiler room" with a telephone and a sucker list, calls a mark and offers to buy his original shares in Kathodian Bronze or National Bituminous at a favorable price, because he has another client who would like to purchase a significant stake in said company. The caller suggests, however, that it would be easier for him to buy the shares if they came bundled into a larger block, and he asks the mark if he'd like to buy more shares at his original price and resell them at the higher price. By the time the mark has purchased new shares, the broker is looking to buy back an even larger bundle, and the mark must spend more money to chase the elusive jackpot.

The swindlers' term for running a mark into financial ruin was "dynamiting" him, and it happened with demoralizing regularity. One mark estimated that stock swindlers stole an average of $1 billion a year for each year between 1919 and 1929, a number that was surely inflated. But was it? In 1905, the *Chicago Tribune* tabulated the yearly loss to bucket shops at $100 million. In 1926, the New York attorney general claimed that $500 million was lost every year solely in his state alone. *The New York Evening Post*, that same year, concurred in setting the national figure at $1 billion. But time and again, columnists insisted that the swindlers stole far more than just money. As a writer in *Harper's* put it, "Every dollar so lost makes timid and distrustful a great many other dollars." The president of the New York Stock Exchange elaborated this point in *Collier's:* "The swindler steals money, but he steals something far more valuable—the investor's faith in his own country. He is the enemy of every farmer, every teacher, every worker, every professional man, every law-abiding citizen."

Between 1880 and 1920, the same forces that prompted the evolution of the big con propelled into being a new phalanx of workers in knowledge trades, the professional-managerial class. The nineteenth-century Industrial Revolution had transformed American business within and without its factory walls. Small, traditional family firms had merged and grown into large, articulated corporations that were distinguished by two deceptively simple innovations: they were made up of many different operating units, and they were managed by a hierarchy of salaried executives. What resulted was managerial capitalism, which prized efficiency above all else. Frederick Winslow Taylor pioneered the study and merciless exploitation of time as a managerial tool in his book *The Principles of Scientific Management.* By measuring the time it took to perform a given manufacturing task, a manager would set a standard for production that would then determine workers' rates of pay, thus vastly increasing the output of each employee. Henry Ford pioneered the assembly line, vertical integration, and the $5 day, which effectively doubled the rate of pay for wage workers in 1914 and also spurred production.

Managerial enterprises had so efficiently organized their internal operations that the supply side of the economic transaction threatened to outstrip demand. American capitalism had succeeded in figuring out how to make products, and the stores and catalogs were awash with new goods like automobiles, kitchen appliances, and canned foods. Now the rapacious economy needed to manufacture consumers who would soak up all this excess. Industrialism required a new attitude toward money and spending to keep its factories humming. Manufacturers turned to aggressive marketing and advertising techniques to create demand and consolidate customers into predictable blocks. Old professions like traveling salesmen transformed overnight to meet this new economic mandate. New professions like advertising and market research sprang up to stimulate consumption; pollsters and sociologists found new ways to measure what happened in the marketplace; a new cohort of "managers" in all sectors of the government and economy began to regulate the changing class structure. The business writers who spoke out so forcefully against the evils of the swindler were not just trying to warn citizens away from shoddy financial deals; they were also trying to shore up the rhetoric of industrial capitalism, a new faith in the power of money to bring about the American dream. Everyone began to pay attention to the stock market.

The New York Stock Exchange (NYSE) was both a symbol and a concrete calculation of the growth that enfolded everyone into its game. You could turn on the radio to hear the latest stock price of Radio (as the Radio Corporation of America, or RCA, was then nicknamed), and the number would always be higher than the last time you checked. In 1921, a share in Radio went for $1.50. By 1929, after splitting several times, that original share was worth nearly four hundred times its original cost. The mesmerizing numbers on the NYSE seemed transparent and self-evident. They told a story of increasing prosperity, of *democratic* prosperity, at least for everyone who stepped onto the climbing escalator. That first step could work like a springboard, vaulting you up into unprecedented heights, if you borrowed the money you invested and traded on margin. The new faith held that it was not self-repression that led to success but self-leveraging, not thrift or the sublimation of desire into hard work, but risk, speculation, investment, and consumption.

And yet, even within this heady era, there remained a seed of doubt in the market as the true forum for success, and this doubt coalesced in the figure of the stockbroker. To people who were not part of the financial elite, the stockbroker's role in the creation of wealth was opaque and faintly sinister. He hoarded, manipulated, and dispensed information, ostensibly working for his clients' interests, but probably only furthering his own at their expense. The broker's reputation was marred by his conceptual association with bucket shops and swindlers, but also by the way he was so completely identified with the market. The monthly magazines published confessions, exposés, and stories that stereotyped the stockbroker as a cunning but weak-complexioned, socially maladjusted man with only one overriding interest. From 10:00 a.m. to 3:00 p.m., he could be found shouting on the exchange floor, and after that he would retire to a club to drink up his profits. He was the antithesis of the family man, because his obsession with money left him unfit for domestic life, nor did he seem to create anything of value. The stockbroker symbolized a life spent in pursuit of money—money as an increasingly abstract concept divorced from productive enterprise—and to many people that kind of life was not a worthwhile one. When the Liberty Bonds inducted American citizens into the world of investment, many wondered if the postwar era meant the end of the stockbroker. After all, the federal government had successfully sold its wares directly to the public; might not corporations now decide to do the same?

Instead, this era witnessed the entrenchment of the stockbroker, because the financial elite commenced a strenuous campaign to rehabilitate his image. The NYSE sought to legitimate itself by excoriating the fraud on its fringes, much as the Chicago Board of Trade had done with bucket shops at the turn of the century. In 1919, the NYSE launched the Business Men's Anti-Stock Swindling League, an alliance of commercial bankers, leaders of industry, trade associations, and the American Federation of Labor, who banded together with NYSE publicists to broadcast news of spurious stock promoters and shepherd investors back to the brokerages with seats on their exchange. *The World's Work* prefaced its "Pirates of Promotion" exposé with an essay on the necessity of the stockbroker to the efficient allocation of capital. The editors portrayed the heroic broker as a kind of financial explorer: "It is his business to discover the little wells of capital and lead them through rivulets, streams, and rivers into the great reservoirs where they are made available for financing the growing business of the country." But he was "a conserver of capital as well as a discoverer of it. Because of his greater responsibility to the source of the capital, he can serve the corporation better than it could itself."

Still, the American public's skepticism toward the stockbroker persisted. Four years later, when Lou Blonger's gang was netted and jailed, the *Denver Times* editorial staff interpreted the events as a parable with a now-familiar lesson: "The man with money to invest who does not consult reputable bankers and brokers in regard to the propositions into which he is urged to put his savings need not sneer at the 'sucker' who drops a fortune in the con game."

Con men preyed on the old middle class, precisely the same

group of people who chafed under the management of the new professional-managerial class but who were nonetheless tempted by the allure of the stock market, almost always to their peril. In 1918, the Federal Trade Commission collected data on the trading done on the Chicago Board of Trade from 1916 to 1918. It was the doctors, dentists, lawyers, clergymen, and teachers who performed most dismally, second only to those in the "manufacture and mechanical" category at the bottom, while "capitalists and retired" sat at the top of the list.

As the monthly magazines that addressed themselves to the middle and professional classes saw that their efforts to educate readers in the new economy were failing, their tone became shriller. They pointed their fingers right at their readers. Thomas Lee Woolwine, the district attorney of Los Angeles who had helped Norfleet catch the two rogue cops on Joseph Furey's payroll, wrote an article in *The American Magazine* about the big con called "Would You Walk into a Trap Like This?" Woolwine could not make his point emphatically enough: "Perhaps you think you would never 'fall for' such a game. Maybe you think your father wouldn't, or your mother, or wife, or sister, or brother, or friend. Don't be too sure. The man in this story never dreamed that he would be caught by confidence men. Neither did his family dream that he would. But he was. Remember that *it is always easier to see stupidity in the other fellow than it is to see it in yourself.*" And when none of their efforts to publicize swindling operations had any effect on the overall quantum of susceptibility in the American populace, the monthlies simply threw up their hands. As one author fretted, "This ignorance and credulity shows itself at a time when men of all-round soundness of judgment have taken a long step forward, and when positive knowledge is increasing at a rate never before known." Another writer ended his long, detailed exposé of financial frauds by complaining, "It seems quite hopeless, this article."

It was. In addition to the $1 billion lost each year to the con men, novice investors continued to shovel their money into the maw of the stock exchange. A Harvard study in 1928 found that fully 97 percent of margin traders on Wall Street lost money, 2 percent broke even, and 1 percent realized a profit. By the end of the decade, *The Saturday Evening Post* pointed to the only possible remedy: public schools in Brookline, Massachusetts, had begun educating all of the grades above kindergarten in "the fundamentals of sound investment" as well as preparing "future salary earners to budget their incomes and manage their personal incomes with thrift and good sense." American adults, as the next decade would soon show, were already a lost cause.

Amid all these hectoring, desperate articles, the charismatic Norfleet stood out as someone who remained unconstrained by the rhetoric of the day. Like an outlaw, he slipped in and out of magazines and newspapers just long enough to bedevil the notion that American managerial capitalism was one smoothly integrated system. He was not the smarmy swindler, nor the pathetic mark, nor the colorless bureaucrat. He had no use for any middlemen or experts and didn't abide by anything that common sense couldn't solve. He believed in money but was not mastered by it. He was an uncategorizable exception, a mark who appeared onstage whenever someone claimed a victory in the fight for the definition of American modernity. And of all the actors in the drama, he was the one having the most fun.

CHAPTER TWELVE

The Showdown

Norfleet arrowed to Salina, Kansas, as fast as the train could shoot him, but once he arrived, it took him just a short while to ascertain that W. B. Spencer was not there, and had not been there in the last few weeks. He nodded to himself, realizing too late that the suitcase in the Empire Hotel had been a ruse, typical for criminals on the run. Norfleet did what anyone would do in such a situation: he went to Ogden, Utah. There, he just happened to encounter a railroad officer who told him that a man answering Spencer's description had passed through a few days previously, bound for Helena, Montana. From Helena, Norfleet trailed Spencer north to the border town of Nelson, and then onward to the swindler's hometown of Kingston, Ontario.

If Norfleet's peripatetic searching charged him with purpose, it was proving to be a liability in Denver. In the days since Red Gallagher posted bond for them, Blonger and Duff had retained both Horace Hawkins, a lawyer who'd earned a reputation as a champion of the underdog after winning the freedom of the union leaders in the bloody Ludlow mine massacre, and S. H. Crump, noted for his belligerent cross-examinations, and they commenced to file every conceivable motion to delay, obfuscate, and attack the state's case against the bunco men in advance of the trial. Crump petitioned the district attorney for a reduction in thirty of the defendants' bonds, a tactic designed to force Van Cise to tip his hand, because he'd be required to divulge any evidence he possessed that justified such high bonds. But the proceedings before Judge Charles C. Butler could not begin on time. "Bunko 'Sucker' Disappears as Hearing Opens," cried the *Rocky Mountain*

News. The defendants had issued a subpoena for the prosecution's star witness, but the sheriff had been unable to find him in the entire city of Denver. Norfleet had vanished, which made Van Cise look very bad. Attorney Crump seized the upper hand: "I have strong intimations that as soon as this hearing came up he was advised to leave." Judge Butler requested that Van Cise do everything possible to rope his wayward witness, and the next day Norfleet was back in Denver, denying that he'd been kidnapped and held hostage by an evasive district attorney.

In mid-September 1922, Norfleet testified in the West Side Court before Judge Butler, as well as a special detail of police detectives hired to augment the sheriff's guard. As the bunco men glared at him, Norfleet related the story that everyone now knew from the newspapers. Yet his testimony actually dented Van Cise's conspiracy case, because he was able to provide direct evidence against only three of the men, Cooper, Davis, and Reamey. Van Cise was reduced to taking the witness stand himself to say that he would continue investigating, and "in all probability we will have other witnesses." Judge Butler ruled that nine of the bonds be reduced to $7,000, eight bonds to $5,000, one to $12,500, and one to $15,000. Van Cise had been forced to retreat from the defense's first sally. Yet even with the discounts, no one came forward to post bail for the other swindlers, and they smoldered in jail.

Norfleet, too, retreated. Ever since his presence in Denver had been publicly coerced, the rumors had flown that an attempt would be made on his life. The district attorney assigned two armed officers to shadow Norfleet around town throughout the day and night. Norfleet carried his own weapons, of course, and the *Post* helpfully listed their placement: "He carries two of the pistols on his belt. The third, a small automatic, is worn under his arm." When he left town the day after the hearing, Norfleet was accompanied by two different bodyguards, one of them his son Pete, the other a private detective who sat across the aisle of the Pullman car, ever vigilant. How the self-reliant hero must have chafed under the need for such supervision.

On his own again, Norfleet continued to charge around the country, pulled along by the very wispiest of clues to the whereabouts of Spencer. While he was in Canada, he wrote to the authorities in Montreal and learned that he'd just missed his prey. Spencer had been arrested and fingerprinted under the name William Percy Hurd, but he'd been let go. Fortunately, he'd also been photographed, so Norfleet ordered dozens of copies of the updated likeness and began sending it around in advance of his own travels. On a whim, he sent a copy to Lucille Carson, the teenage sleuth he'd deputized in San Francisco to capture Furey, and once again she proved her moxie. She telegrammed Norfleet to say that Spencer had, indeed, appeared in San Francisco for a few days, and when he left, he was headed to Salt Lake City. Norfleet sped to Cheyenne, hoping to head him off on the Lincoln Highway, but had no luck. He then tried his luck in Arvarda, Colorado, where Spencer's wife's family lived, and finding nothing there, he popped in on Van Cise in Denver, posting photographs of Spencer wherever he went. Then to Colorado Springs, south to Raton Pass, New Mexico, and farther south to Roswell.

All that train travel began to wear on Norfleet, and he longed for the flexibility of motor travel, so next he stopped at his ranch to pick up his car and his fifteen-year-old daughter, Ruth. For no reason at all, their first stop was Mineral Wells, a health resort sixty miles west of Fort Worth. Norfleet parked the car in a garage, and, as had become his routine, he showed the photograph of Spencer to the garage mechanic and asked if he'd seen him in the past few weeks. The mechanic called another man over, and they both peered at the photo. "Looks like the car belonging to that fellow is in the garage here now!" said the first man. "It sure does look like him all right," agreed the second, and they told Norfleet that the car's owner would be returning shortly. His blood quickening, Norfleet found an unobtrusive place to wait, and in just a few minutes a man walked past him. It was Spencer. Norfleet darted out of his hiding place, tapped Spencer on the shoulder, and, like the absolute ham that he was, cried out, "Howdy!"

When Spencer turned around, Norfleet saw that it was not he. He was face-to-face with a man who looked exactly like Spencer but without the bunco man's broken, crooked nose. "I beg your pardon," Norfleet murmured. "I thought you were a friend of mine."

"That's all right, Mr. Norfleet," replied the man with a laugh. "I know you and I'll bet I know who you thought I was. You thought I was your man Spencer! I have been told by several men who have seen his picture that we might be twin brothers."

It must have cleaved Norfleet in two to hear those words. On the one hand, his campaign to decoupage the nation with photographs of his quarry seemed to be working. On the other, his own personal notoriety was becoming so great it might be impeding his quest, since surely Spencer was as well-informed of Norfleet's plans as everyone else. But then the look-alike said something that sparked Norfleet's ever-ready hope. "Only a few minutes ago when I was getting some mineral water at the bar, the bartender remarked that he had seen my brother a few days before and thought it was I." Norfleet strode down the street to the bar and flashed his photograph to the bartender. "Yes, I seen that feller," the man replied. "He's been here 'bout a week. I ain't seen him for a day or two, but his woman was sittin' round the lobby of the hotel night before last. They got a cottage up on that hill there an' I been sending mineral water up to them regular." Now Norfleet was dead certain he was close.

In Denver, Philip Van Cise was meeting with far less success. The bunco men were safely behind bars, but his chances of winning a trial against them seemed increasingly remote, despite the spies and the Dictaphone and the crates of evidence they'd seized in the raid. In the weeks after the raid at the end of August 1922, Van Cise found himself waging two distinct campaigns, one against the Blonger gang in a fevered scramble to bolster the state's case, and one against the city machine that stood to lose in direct proportion to Van Cise's gain.

As the bunco spielers and ropers grew beards to disguise themselves from potential witnesses, Denver citizens grew suspicious that all was not as it seemed in their town. The first intimations that certain city officials had colluded with Blonger came a week after the raid. "Why did members of the police advisory board contribute funds for the Van Cise raids," wondered the *Rocky Mountain News.* "Did members of the board believe that the police department was not competent to participate in the raid? Is there a powerful influence brought to bear on the city administration that would frustrate such a raid?" Readers had only to glance at adjacent articles in the same newspaper editions to ascertain who might be on the swindlers' side. While Governor Oliver Shoup praised Van Cise and the Rangers "for their splendid work and the results obtained," Mayor Dewey C. Bailey let out a plume of vitriol against the district attorney. Naturally, he could not be seen to defend the debased bunco men, so his support took the form of an attack on Van Cise's use of money and personnel. He flatly denied Van Cise's request for $15,000 in city funds to reimburse the private donors who had bankrolled the sting, calling Van Cise extravagant in his use of the money and claiming that the city "does object to paying for the establishment of a national detective headquarters to work in competition with the police department and to do the work that should properly be done by the federal department of justice."

Mayor Bailey then took aim at the private citizens whom Van Cise conscripted as drivers on the day of the raid. He couldn't help wondering, he said, why so many of them were stockbrokers. Could it be that they had a vested interest in showily jailing the swindlers so that their own business practices might pass unscrutinized? "The questions that arise in my mind are: What is a 'con' man, what is a 'sucker,' and when do we get 'conned'?" This line of attack would recur in the trial itself, when defense attorneys would use the contemporary discourse about speculation and swindling to muddy the ethical waters in which their clients swam. But in the immediate aftermath of the raid, the mayor became increasingly isolated in his fight against the district attorney. Denver was awakening to the fact that it had been conned; there was little question of that in the people's minds. Their suspicions were confirmed by a widely publicized interview with Herbert N. Graham, a national expert on fraud with the U.S. postal inspectors, on the Denver situation. Why had strikingly few con men been arrested in Denver in the decades before the raid? "Where bunko men operate," he said, "they corrupt the police and officials as surely as a rotten apple pollutes the rest of the box. Once a police department is corrupt, anything goes. The underworld uses one crooked frame-up as a lever for prying loose the next, and crime of all descriptions goes unpunished. That's the real danger of the confidence game, and the hardest to remedy." A grand jury was charged with investigating police corruption, and witnesses were called before that jury as Van Cise continued building his case to present to a future trial jury.

Van Cise tried mightily to focus on the task at hand, which was to add more and stronger struts to his case than simply the pillar of J. Frank Norfleet, but distractions repeatedly punctured his concentration. "I never saw this man Norfleet in my life," declared Blonger righteously. "I intend to take legal action against those who so summarily arrested me at my office." Indeed Van Cise and his staff, as well as the citizens he deputized, soon found themselves on the other end of a

$200,000 civil suit for unlawful arrest, a cynical but effective tactic to bleed them of time and money in the days before the trial. An intense and public animosity had sprung up between the prosecution and the defense counsels, and Van Cise had already earned the rebuke of a judge after pounding his fist into Attorney William A. Bryans in one of the pretrial hearings, blackening his eye for daring to dispute a minor claim. The con men's lawyers seemed to delight in heckling and baiting him to set off his well-known meter for injustice. So it came as almost a relief when Van Cise was thrown off the case. The bunco counsel filed a motion to disqualify the district attorney on the basis of a technicality: he was mistakenly named as counsel for a plaintiff in a civil suit against some of the con men and was therefore a party of interest in the criminal case. Judge Butler appointed S. Harrison White, former chief justice of the Colorado Supreme Court, and Harry C. Riddle, former judge of the district court, as special prosecutors, leaving Van Cise free to work behind the scenes—and depriving the defense of their favorite target.

Van Cise wrote to every sucker he could unearth to invite him to Denver, and one Monday afternoon he staged a "revue" in the county jail. The outer door to the east wing shot back, and the bunco artists shuffled in single file before a table with an abandoned deck of cards and thirteen pennies. They stood there in their white undershirts and unshaven cheeks while men in suits leaned in and peered at their faces. Jackie French distinguished himself, as usual, by his air of ease and his shirt of cream brocaded Canton crepe. A fellow named Freeman, his anger manifest in his set jaw and the white-knuckled fingers grasping his hat, pointed out Leon Felix, the man Norfleet had known as Davis, while Adolph Wishropp of Kansas City convivially greeted two of his fleecers with a "How do you do?" The reporter for *The Denver Post* noted that even in their humiliating dishabille, the con men could not help but transmit their natural magnetism, "a certain 'I've waited all these years to meet YOU' manner." Blonger and Duff were notably absent from the lineup.

In the first two weeks after the raid, nearly a hundred men from around the country had journeyed to Denver in the hope of identifying the con men who had bilked them. At the same time, Van Cise and his staff mailed out hundreds of photographs, descriptions, aliases, and criminal records to other law enforcement officers to gather data on the careers of those in custody. Now his deputies worked with a stenographer each day and well into the night on the piles of evidence they had confiscated in the raid. They were confined in a windowless, locked basement room in the West Side courthouse, and only the deputies were allowed in the nearby vault of steel and concrete where the evidence was kept. Three deputies slept inside the vault on army cots each night, preventing janitors and even the sheriff's deputies from gaining access to the valuable cache of papers. Two months after the raid, Van Cise published a report detailing every touch that Blonger's gang had taken off its marks since late 1918. He did not explain how he'd managed to draw up a comprehensive list, and he wouldn't divulge his secret source until late in the trial, but he did publish the names of thirty-three marks and six almost-marks, and he listed the total amount of the conglomerate's profits at $506,270.

Coincidentally, that happened to be precisely the amount the swindlers were said to be raising for their defense. Also without disclosing his source, a reporter for the *Post* wrote, "Confidence men thruout the United States are being assessed 5 per cent of their 'earnings' to provide a $500,000 defense fund for members of the Denver swindle ring." He quoted an unnamed Denver official as saying that the Bertsche gang in Chicago had already forwarded $200,000 to a Denver bank for bonds and lawyers' fees and that the Gondorf syndicate in New York and the Rumer organization in Cleveland were also pitching in. Even the "reorganized remnants of the Furey gang" were said to be taking up a collection from their new headquarters in Tijuana. Yet Blonger and Duff paid only enough bond to allow Jackie French out of jail, leaving the others to stew in animosity, and the larger arc of events seemed to be bending toward the prosecution's efforts to build its conspiracy case.

Denver citizens began the year of 1923 with an unequivocal indictment of machine politics when the grand jury made its report on the corruption of the police department after its thirty-four-day investigation. "Confidence men have been operating openly under the eyes of the detective department," the report found. Still, even though it had examined more than three hundred witnesses, the jury was "unable to obtain sufficient evidence to warrant the indictment of any particular member of the department." It was as clear an announcement as possible: the city bureaucracy was not going to clean up the muck that Van Cise had stirred from the Denver bottoms. The day after the grand jury report, Van Cise sent a signal of his own. He took the witness stand at a pretrial hearing and was asked by the defense counsel Horace Hawkins to identify the exhibit numbers attached to various items seized on the day of the raid. Pointing to a bankbook, Van Cise said it was "a joint account of Duff and Blonger showing payments to Rinker—" "That's enough," roared Hawkins. "I don't care to hear any more about that." But everyone knew Van Cise meant Washington A. Rinker, captain of the detective bureau of the Denver Police Department. The following week, Lou Blonger's memorandum book surfaced with a notation for a $600 payment to another Denver police officer. The book was part of Special Prosecutor S. Harrison White's defense against Blonger's suit that his effects had been illegally seized in the raid. A few days later, Blonger and Duff dropped their civil suits against Van Cise and his staff when it became clear that they themselves would need to testify, potentially producing evidence that could be used against them in the upcoming criminal trial—the trial for which the entire city was now holding its breath.

The bunco trial began on Monday, February 5, 1923. The courtroom was bursting with people, and the lines of alliance and animosity were so thick as to be almost visible. To the right of Judge George F. Dunklee sat the defense, five attorneys at a long table with twenty defendants surrounding them in an L shape. Adolph Duff occupied the center of the group and reigned over the rank and file. Lou Blonger sat on the edge, hunched into himself, occasionally standing to get himself a drink of water but acknowledging no one. It was plain from their body language that Blonger and Duff had fallen out with each other. Van Cise was privy to Blonger's side of his dispute with Duff because the Dictaphone was still steadfastly transmitting every word from room 309 in the American Bank Building. "He talks too much," Blonger said to Garland "Pretty Kelley" Kelley. "He always wants his own way, and he wants everybody else to do as he says. If they don't, he is sore. He is chow-chowing all over the town. He don't do anything but raise hell." And then again to Walter Byland: "He was drunk last night and hollered his head off and cussed me out." Byland replied, "You know you'd get off a whole lot easier if you killed a son of a bitch like that." In the courtroom, only the debonair Jackie French dared approach Blonger during recesses.

The two special prosecutors spoke from a lectern in the center of the room, the jury to their right and their mortal enemies, the defense attorneys, to their left. Since Van Cise's dismissal from the case, White and Riddle had taken up his feud with Hawkins, Crump, and their colleagues. White and Hawkins had traded insults in court the previous December. A hot remark from White about needing someone from the state insane asylum to evaluate the defense counsel had prompted Hawkins to shout, "I come from a family that goes to battle over such statements and insinuations!" White challenged him to a duel, Hawkins agreed, and the two were halfway out of the courtroom before the judge put a stop to their theatrics. When the jury was sworn in on February 3, another lawyer on the defense team raised his fists and started after one of the district attorney's special investigators, only to be held back by a sheriff. As the trial began, bailiffs and deputy sheriffs punctuated the room. Whenever the prosecution and the defense engaged in verbal swordplay, Deputy Sheriff Doc Dawson would leave his corner and stand just behind one of them, ready to forestall a fistfight.

The tensions extended across the wooden balustrade to the spectators' side of the courtroom, where every seat was taken and territory was indelibly marked. The defendants' wives and girlfriends showed up each day and silently testified to the respectability of their menfolk by their elegant dress and impeccable demeanor. There were only two exceptions: Cora Blonger never once appeared at the trial, and neither did Blonger's mistress, Iola Readon, though she did drive Lou to and from her mansion on Williams Street each day. In daily attendance was the wife of Grove Sullivan, in her fur coat and trim little brown hat, who interestedly stood up and leaned toward the suckers as they testified so as to hear them better. There was Mrs. William Dougherty, with her enormous bone-rimmed spectacles and richly adorned coat. And there was the wife of J. H. Foster, the very picture of sweetness until the prosecution scored a point and her lips would arch downward into cruel slits. A Denverite named E. H. Miles, who came to the trial each day, approached the district attorney's staff and begged them to investigate the wives. He said that he'd attempted to sit down one day and had been prevented by a haughty woman who said the seat was reserved for her. "Not on your tintype," Miles said he replied, "I'll stay right here for the music." Their confrontation escalated, others were drawn into it, and finally the bailiff rapped for order, at which point the lady reached into her coat, held her hand inside it, and ordered Miles to "make himself scarce."

The wives weren't the only ones said to be armed. Opposite this steadfast trio sat a mysterious pair of men in the front row. They were always the first to arrive and the last to leave, and they were said to be gunmen hired by the prosecution, though Van Cise would only smile when asked about it. *The Denver Post,* for one, believed the rumor: "One is said to be an old-time Cripple Creek gunman—a sure shot with innumerable notices on the butt of his six-gun. The other used to hang out at Cheyenne and is reputed to be a wizard with a 'gat.'" In fact, the entire courtroom was linked to one another with invisible webs of surveillance. The prosecution hired undercover guards to protect its witnesses, and the defense hired detectives to shadow them and find ways to pierce their testimony. In a jury trial for conspiracy in a confidence game, information was the most valuable asset of all.

Also seated in the courtroom, despite the defense's attempt to bar him, was District Attorney Van Cise, the silent mechanism regulating the flow of information while remaining apart from the melodrama. And presumably Norfleet was hidden among the crowd. The newspapers had reported his arrival at the beginning of the year, disguised in colored glasses, a long mustache, and two pistols. "Every effort is being made to keep his presence in Denver a secret," deadpanned one reporter.

From almost the very first words of the opening statements, it was a spectacularly lopsided trial. Special Prosecutor White started off the festivities with a two-day-long aerial view of the Blonger syndicate. He began at the highest altitude with King Blonger, ruling in solitude and opulence from his office in the American Bank Building. Blonger allowed himself a small smile when he heard himself described as the mastermind of the ring, but was otherwise impassive. White then slowly zoomed down through the ranks of the organization to the street level, where he described the methods by which the ropers and spielers hooked their marks. He ended with several choice anecdotes showing how Blonger and Duff fixed city officials to keep their corps out of danger. To back up their case, White promised, the prosecution would call nearly two hundred witnesses, spending at least six weeks and $100,000 to minutely, incontrovertibly depict the criminality that had undergirded the city of Denver for the last few years. It was a risky strategy. White was essentially notifying the men of the jury, working-class men who received only $1.50 per day for their civic duty, that they'd be out of work for weeks as he drummed into them story after story of suckers and stock exchanges—a tactic of sheer repetition. But Van Cise's burden of proof was enormously heavy, because he hoped to win a blanket verdict against all twenty defendants, each of them linked to the others by overlapping testimonies.

Hawkins and Crump's strategy, by contrast, was less to defend the defendants than to prosecute the prosecuting witnesses. Crump began his opening statement by lambasting Norfleet as a publicity seeker and, curiously, a wiretapper. He asserted that Norfleet sent his wife to Blonger in an attempt to settle with the kingpin for $30,000. And when the prosecution called its first witness, a Michigan bank president named Paul G. Schaible, Sr., who'd been taken for $25,000, the tenor of the entire trial was set. Schaible told his story in great detail, relating whole swaths of dialogue from his scenes in the swindlers' play. Then Attorney Hawkins stepped up to cross-examine him, and the first words out of his mouth were "So you're a sucker?" He proceeded to grate Schaible on the blades of his own scruples, asking him, "Do you mean to tell this jury that you, as a banker, did not know he [the insideman] was going to make some money on the side and keep it a secret from his house?" When Schaible protested that he was just trying to help his new friend, Hawkins dug in further: "Mr. Banker, how much could you take without hurting your conscience? Just how elastic is your conscience?" After four hours of this, as the limp Mr. Schaible stepped down from the witness box, he was served with a summons to appear as a witness for the defense, a move calculated to scare away other witnesses who could not afford to stay in town for the weeks or even months of the ensuing trial, simply waiting at the pleasure of the defense to be called—or not. Sure enough, four witnesses suddenly bowed out of the trial. Rumors spread that "a vampire squad of women," the wives and girlfriends who were not in daily attendance at the trial, was traveling around the country to visit marks and deliver threats in person to keep them from testifying.

The defense's tactics were unapologetically squalid, and they spurred *The Denver Post* into its purplest prose. "Cruel claws of intimidation oozed thru the velvet glove of the bunco defense in the west side court Thursday," read its front-page account of the trial's third day. Yet there was a brand of sound if outdated legal logic behind their attacks on the prosecution's witnesses. Until just a few years before the Blonger trial, case law in several of the states held that the plaintiff in a suit for larceny by false pretenses must come into court "with clean hands," a doctrine which says that a plaintiff can only expect an equitable outcome if he or she has not acted unethically or in bad faith toward the defendant. A plaintiff who intended to violate the law together with the defendant put himself outside the scope of the law and could not then seek protection from the defendant's misrepresentations. As the New York Supreme Court stated in *McCord v. People,* an infamous decision from 1871, "Neither the law or public policy designs the protection of rogues in their dealings with each other." Such an interpretation was tantamount to a free pass for any criminal activity that implicated its victim, but the New York Supreme Court upheld the *McCord* decision in 1900 in *People v. Livingstone.* In a broader sense, American law did not recognize the category of fraud until well into the twentieth century. Nineteenth-century market culture privileged individual autonomy and judgment; the consumer had no legal recourse if his initial evaluation of the authenticity of the goods for sale proved incorrect.

Not until 1906 did the New York state legislature amend its Penal Code so that larceny by false pretenses might be prosecuted in the same way as common-law theft, in which stealing property from a thief is the same as stealing it from its rightful owner. Yet even when states sought specifically to outlaw confidence games, they further harmed the marks who brought their cases to court. Statutes in states such as Montana and Illinois held that a confidence game was distinguished by the fact that the criminal could operate only by gaining the victim's confidence. This instantly turned each trial into an inquiry into the victim's state of mind during the course of the crime. The prosecutor had to prove not only that the defendant had taken the plaintiff's money but that he had fully and consistently held the victim in his thrall with felonious intent. One swindler, who'd taken an elderly woman's diamond ring in exchange for a promise of monthly profit from his fabled oil properties, went free after the woman confessed that she'd entertained doubts about his honesty before she gave him the jewel, thus revealing that he hadn't held her complete confidence. Slowly, states began to wrench the law around so that it pointed at the defendants. They learned to fight a crime of information by requiring transparency. Yet the taint on the plaintiff remained, and the swindler's easiest defense was to attack the mark's cupidity, ignorance, and dishonesty.

Nonetheless, the Blonger ring's defense counsel seemed to succeed only in alienating the spectators, the press, and the judge with its age-old tactics. Hawkins and Crump objected to the state's every word and introduced frivolous motions to exhaust time, money, and patience; then they grew fiery with righteousness whenever the prosecution made a procedural move, arguing passionately for the defendants' right to a speedy trial. When Judge Dunklee finally broke his impassivity to rebuke the defense counsel for its unprofessional conduct, the spectators in the courtroom exploded with cheers, whistles, applause, and foot stomping. The uproar lasted for several minutes, until finally the judge ordered the courtroom cleared for the rest of the day. The bailiffs pulled out their billy clubs, but the crowd obediently shuffled out on its own, content to have expressed its pent-up feelings.

The bunco trial was turning out to be a good show after all, despite its repetitiveness. Sucker after sucker climbed onto the witness chair and spun out his story, at once improbable and increasingly commonplace. The spectators enjoyed the contrast between the different men on the stand: Simon Oppenheimer, a New York city resident who almost lost $50,000 to the swindlers, but who lost not a particle of dignity in his battle of wits with the defense counsel; Alfred Schedin, a Minnesota carpenter whose simplicity and honesty contrasted with Oppenheimer's shrewdness and who seemed especially to touch the audience with his pathos; C. E. Henson, a dentist from Oklahoma who lost $25,000 and then gave his last $200 to one of his swindlers to pay his expenses back home. Several moving picture house proprietors began to complain that they were losing too much business to the bunco trial.

Two weeks into the trial, J. Frank Norfleet, "nemesis of the speakeasy gentry," took the stand, sans glasses and mustache. While the special prosecutors spent a few minutes organizing the exhibits they planned to have him identify, Norfleet leaned forward from the witness stand with calm intensity to peer at the defendants. The bunco men averted their faces and squirmed away as he scrutinized their faces and filed them in his mental database. Finally, Special Prosecutor White began direct examination. "Thrill followed thrill," reported *The Denver Post*, "as he related the crucial moves in his vendetta against the facile-tongued parasites of society," his disguise, the letter written in the bath, the fake toothache, and the self-inflicted vomiting. The defense counsel objected to every exhibit and every other word, but the judge overruled them. Their only success came when they prevented Norfleet from testifying as to why he held such an overlarge hatred of confidence men in general, thus blocking his story of the Furey gang and limiting his answers to his time in Denver.

It wasn't until his second and final day of testimony, when Horace Hawkins cross-examined him, that Norfleet had occasion to reach for his gun—and Hawkins followed suit. The two men stood up, each with his right hand in his pocket, and edged toward each other. But it was only a bit of stage play. Hawkins asked Norfleet to reenact his arrest of Arthur B. Cooper, the inaugural act of the raid, and if there was a touch of real menace under the campy gesture, it was purely one-sided, as Norfleet remained perfectly jovial in the headwind of Hawkins's invective. The defense counsel's strategy toward Norfleet was to impugn, deride, and besmear the deceit he had practiced upon the unsuspecting swindlers in an attempt to discredit the arrests. Norfleet deflected the defense's most forceful arrows simply by agreeing that he'd lied his way into the swindlers' confidence. All that the defense had accomplished in their cross-examination, his amiable replies seemed to say, was to prove that deception was odious.

And then Norfleet left Denver and returned to zooming across the continent in search of Spencer, while the bunco trial wheeled slowly into its third week, and then its fourth. Norfleet was one of the last suckers to testify, and each of the ropers and spielers had been enmeshed in the web created by the overlapping testimony of so many victims. Only now did the prosecution begin to enfold Blonger and Duff—whom the *Post* had taken to calling "Blue" Blonger and Adolph "Bluff"—by calling upon hotel proprietors, Western Union officials, and letter carriers to link the co-conspirators to the everyday activities of their crew. The trial entered its fifth week, then its sixth. On the day that Van Cise's deputy Fred Sanborn testified to finding a check in Lou Blonger's desk for $39.77 made out to W. W. Arnett, a local agent of the federal department of justice, the jury shrugged and sent one of its members to the judge to ask him to speed up the trial. The next day, another jury man approached the bench with an even stronger version of the same plea. The trial entered its seventh week, a state record.

Every last person in Denver sat up a little straighter at noon on

March 8th. The prisoner dock, a row of benches behind the witness stand that had been used as additional seating for spectators in the crowded courtroom, was suddenly cleared. Sheriff Doc Dawson escorted a slight man with narrow shoulders and a long face onto the stand, past twenty pairs of glaring eyes behind the defense counsel's table. As the audience stood up to get a better view of him, Sheriff Dawson took up a post behind the witness and stared hard back at the audience. So the rumor that had been circulating for weeks was true: Van Cise had flipped one of the bunco men. Special Prosecutor Riddle stepped up and asked the witness to identify himself. "George L. Reamey," he answered, and that was all he managed to say for the rest of the day. The defense attorneys instantly objected to his presence on the witness stand, and for the next three hours and forty minutes lawyers for both sides presented intricate arguments for and against his testimony.

George L. Reamey was known to his friends as Len, and to his marks as Mr. Ross, Sprague, Bracken, Brown, Turner, or Rogers. Norfleet knew him as Zachary, the extravagantly mustachioed exchange secretary who had worked with Felix and Cooper. The rumor was that Reamey was sore at Blonger for refusing to post his bail; after five years of faithful service, he felt he deserved more. And so he instructed his wife, a tall, good-looking brunette from an honest background, to phone Van Cise and offer up his testimony in exchange for immunity.

The district attorney had received many such overtures in the months after the arrests, what he called "an interesting but highly secret game developed on the part of the wives to see which one could first obtain the ear of the District Attorney." Some of the wives carried genuine propositions from their husbands; others tried to entice Van Cise into a compromising romantic situation. He declined all such proposals, until the phone call from Mrs. Reamey. She said her husband was one of the senior members of the conglomerate, and she was so demure and so exact in her statements on the phone that Van Cise brought her to his home. He interrogated her for two hours, then sent her away with a list of questions for her husband, hoping the answers would tally with what he already knew from the Dictaphone. For two weeks, Mrs. Reamey visited her husband in jail and clandestinely procured information for the district attorney. At last, Van Cise was able to accept Reamey's offer to turn state's evidence. He sent Mrs. Reamey out of town, waited twenty-four hours to ensure her safety, and then

brought Len Reamey to his office for his first official interview, returning him that night to a special guarded cell. As a bookmaker, Reamey
was just beneath Jackie French in the hierarchy, and he was privy to
almost every swindle that threaded through the fake betting parlors
and stockbrokerages at the heart of the big con. He was present in the
Lookout every time a mark's touch was divvied up. He could supply the
inside story on nearly every tale that the parade of marks had already
told on the witness stand.

The defense counsel argued that Reamey could not testify as a prosecution witness until the charges against him had been dismissed and
he had been freed. The special prosecutors countered that they could
not risk turning him loose. The reason they maintained the charges
against him and kept him in jail was for his own safety; the very second he left their protection, he'd be subject to threats, intimidation,
or worse. At the end of the afternoon, Judge Dunklee agreed with the
prosecution and cleared Reamey to testify the next day.

The courtroom was, if possible, even more crowded on March 9th,
with spectators standing against the walls and in the aisles, riveted to
the sound of Reamey's thin but unwavering voice. The audience's rapt
attention struck some in the crowd as an opportunity, and hats and
watches vanished that day. Duff leaned forward and hooked his chin on
Attorney Hawkins's shoulder from behind, staring at Reamey with his
jaw relentlessly chewing something, while Reamey proceeded to hand
him over to the jury. He said that Duff had put him to work as a steerer
when he had first arrived in Denver in 1918. In 1921, Duff opened his
own store in Kansas City and Jackie French ran it, coaching Reamey
to be a bookmaker. That season, he booked three marks for free to
prove his mettle, then he took the touch off fourteen more marks, and
soon he was promoted up the hierarchy in Denver. Whenever Reamey
related part of his bookmaker's script, his voice would speed up and
flatten to a monotone, and the special prosecutors would have to ask
him to slow down; the defense counsel complained that he sounded
like a phonograph. He gave the big con a new name. It was a tripar-
tite drama of three acts: steerers "bringem," spielers "bunkem," and
bookmakers "bouncem." The "tricky twenty" glared at him minute by
minute, and they swore at him as he entered and exited the courtroom
during recesses, always accompanied by at least two armed guards, but

he never lost his composure, and he never faltered in the relation of his story.

Throughout Reamey's testimony, Blonger leaned impassively against the railing of the prisoner dock, and for the first three days his name was mentioned but once. His turn came on Reamey's fourth day on the stand, and the bookmaker's testimony was the first that directly implicated Blonger in the state's case. He said it was Blonger who brought him back to Denver that year, after years of proving himself under Duff. He described running into Blonger in a hotel lobby in Hot Springs, Arkansas, early in 1922. He asked if the store would be open that season, and Blonger replied, "Sure, come on out," offering Reamey 5 percent of every swindle he booked for them. He told how, at the opening of the store, Duff sent him over to Blonger's office and instructed him to park across the street and honk his horn twice; Blonger then emerged from the building and handed Reamey the boodle, $500 in $1 bills.

Reamey then methodically ran down through the calendar, cataloging each swindle that occurred, year by year, and mapping out how the Blonger organization had split the money in each case. At last, Reamey was revealed as the source for the list that Van Cise had published the previous October which totaled Blonger's profits at half a million dollars. He also revealed the backstory of another list, the running tally of Denver swindlers that Van Cise and his crew had drawn up the night before the raid, only to discover it on Duff's person the next morning. Reamey said Duff got it from Blonger, who obtained it from a Denver detective named George Sanders, who'd received it from a police officer in Colorado Springs, where Van Cise had sent an earlier draft to his good friend Captain Bruce. The existence of the list had not troubled Duff and Blonger, Reamey asserted. They had assumed the police would alert them as soon as Van Cise was ready to make a move, and they could simply go undercover.

Reamey gave the flip side of the swindles that the jury had heard about from the marks. The defense could do little to stop the flow of damaging testimony. "The phonograph is revolving again," complained Horace Hawkins when Reamey launched into yet another version of his spiel, but Judge Dunklee snapped back, "It is improper to refer to the testimony of the witness as a phonograph. If it is a fact that they did use the same language and make the same talk every time, then it would sound like playing the same record on a phonograph." Hawkins's objection was overruled.

Reamey testified for six devastating days, and he was a paragon of calmness—until the cross-examination. As if admitting defeat, the defense counsel did not challenge a single one of Reamey's statements, but instead aimed their fire at his character with a long string of invented claims. Wasn't it true that he was known at the racetracks as Reamey the Rat? Hadn't he at one time spied for the Pinkerton Detective Agency? Wasn't he drug addled when he was arrested the previous August? Wasn't it true that he fought a man over a woman, stabbed him with a knife, and had to leave town? Reamey denied all but the last of those claims, allowing a small smile to ornament his reply that he did, indeed, lightly scratch a man in a fight. But when Attorney Crump characterized Reamey's wife as a prostitute, Reamey jumped out of his chair with his fists clenched, causing Crump to run behind his lectern and change the subject. Crump's mention of drugs allowed Special Prosecutor White to reexamine Reamey on the subject, and Reamey claimed that Duff and French had given him their opium to store in a safety-deposit box. As Reamey left the stand for the last time, he tried in vain to catch French's eye.

Reamey's stories had been so effective that they prompted the prosecution to alter their strategy. Andrew Koehn and Robert Maiden, two of Van Cise's private detectives, were next on the stand, but in a move that would have been unthinkable just a few weeks earlier, Van Cise elected to withhold the evidence he'd so painstakingly gathered from the Dictaphone. The defense had vigorously objected to Dictaphone conversation as "of doubtful competency," pointing out that the detectives had never met or spoken with the persons whom they claimed to overhear on the Dictaphone. The special prosecutors shocked the courtroom by agreeing to forgo such testimony. They were leery of introducing "reversible error" into the long and costly trial and potentially handing the defendants a lever with which to overturn the jury's decision in the event of a conviction. And then, after only a few more routine days of testimony, livened only by the drunken appearance of Lou Blonger's brother Joe, who was promptly asked to leave ("I object, if the court please," cried Joe. "Objection overruled," muttered the bailiff as he dragged the man out), the prosecution rested its case on March 23, 1923.

Seven minutes after the state rested, Attorney Crump rose to announce that the defense also rested. Just like that, the landmark case—the longest criminal trial in Colorado history, longer than the Chicago trial of a hundred Wobblies for espionage, longer than the glamorous murder trial of Harry K. Thaw, sixty-two days long, in which eighty-three witnesses testified, 524 exhibits were submitted, and the stenographer logged 1.4 million words totaling four thousand pages, a stack nineteen and a half inches high—ended without the defense calling a single witness and without either side making a closing argument. The city was stunned, and speculation bloomed, grew, and fed upon itself. Some watchers noticed that twenty new beds had just been installed in the lower west wing of the county jail, and they assumed the jury would return a verdict of guilty within hours. The theory was that the defense was banking on the state supreme court to reverse the decision and prompt a lengthy retrial, for which the prosecution would lose most of its witnesses by attrition. Others looked outside the courtroom for evidence. They observed that Denver gamblers were offering two-to-one odds *against* conviction. Why such good money on such a long shot? People assumed that the "sure thing lads" knew that the jury had been rigged. Within the first two hours of the jury's deliberation, as the defendants paced between the courtroom and an anteroom, reports filtered out that the jurors had taken two ballots on blanket verdicts for all twenty men, and that both ballots had stood at 9–3 for conviction. By the end of that day, they'd cast twenty-five ballots—all of them at 9–3 for conviction.

Despite the defection of their number-four man, the top three leaders of the conglomerate were feeling confident that night, as Van Cise discovered the next morning when four empty whiskey bottles were brought to his desk. They'd been discovered in the grand jury room of the West Side courthouse, where Deputy Sheriff Tom Clarke had watched over the three defendants free on bail: Blonger, Duff, and French. Four more empties were found in janitors' closets, and a full bottle of whiskey still sat in silent testimony on the table in the room, as did a mess in the lavatory where one of the partygoers—perhaps one of the six women who'd been seen to enter the room—had gotten sick. The rumor on the street was that the party was to celebrate the successful fix. The next day, the ballot stood at 11–1, with no news to break the monotony of the wait except the forced resignation of Sheriff Clarke for his complicity with the accused. A third day of deliberation, a Sunday, during which a pastor warned in his sermon that if the jury failed to convict the bunco men, citizens would lose faith in the ability of the municipal institutions to provide law and order, and the Ku Klux Klan would see a rise in its membership. Then a fourth, during which the judge called the jurors back to the jury box to give them the "third degree instruction" for how to resolve the deadlock of a lone dissenting juror. As the twelve men filed into the courtroom, their faces appeared drawn and tense, and rumors flew that they'd been arguing to the point of fistfights. A fifth day, during which a grand jury indicted Blonger, Duff, French, and Clarke for "violation of the intoxicating liquor law," and the incredulity of the Denver populace grew. One juror received a letter threatening his death if any of the swindlers were acquitted. Van Cise spoke up to say that that particular juror's integrity was beyond reproach, and then he dashed back into the courthouse for a secret conference, supposedly to prepare a handful of arrests for bribery if the jury was hung.

At 4:45 on the afternoon of the sixth day, after 102 hours of deliberation, a bailiff announced to Judge Dunklee that a verdict had been reached. The judge summoned the lawyers back to the courtroom. The twenty defendants took their seats, palpably nervous for the first time. Lou Blonger's impassivity was smeared with a weak smile. Adolph Duff's tremble was visible to the thronged spectators. After all the exits were locked and deputy sheriffs had taken up their positions, the judge convened the court, scanned the verdict, and then handed it back to the clerk to read: "We, the jury, find the defendants guilty as charged in the information." Thirty seconds after the clerk uttered the word "guilty," before he'd even finished listing all of the defendants' names, the *Post*'s extra edition, which it had prepared in advance, was out on the streets.

Several of the wives in the audience burst into noisy tears, but the twenty men on trial were silent. Jackie French raised an eyebrow but did not pause in the cleaning of his fingernails. And the prosecution refrained from a single cry of triumph. At defense counsel's request, Judge Dunklee polled the jurors: "Was this and is this your verdict?" The answer of juror number three, George E. Sharp, caused considerable commotion: "It is—under the conditions. I was sick and had to get out of there." Attorney Hawkins leaped to his feet and demanded that the juror explain his statement, crying out that his verdict had been coerced. The judge questioned him repeatedly, and eventually Sharp simplified his answer to "It is," which the judge let stand. He formally dismissed the jury after thanking them for their extraordinary service, and as they gathered their overcoats and left the courtroom, they were enveloped by reporters. Juror Sharp was photographed leaving the courthouse on the arm of one of Lou Blonger's personal attorneys. Only then did the courtroom break out into a rising hum of conversation.

A deputy sheriff then called the twenty convicted criminals to order, and they rose from their seats. Every last spectator noticed Lou Blonger's weak step, his hands grasping the railing, and his ashen countenance. Under heavy guard, the men were guided over "the bridge of sighs" from the West Side courthouse to the county jail, where they too were assaulted by reporters. "Perjured evidence," said Lou Blonger heavily. "That's what convicted me. I'm speaking for myself and not for the others. Reamey never saw me in his life. When he testified that I had handed out a bundle of money he lied. Not a single one of the alleged victims ever testified that he saw me, or identified me in any way." Meanwhile, District Attorney Van Cise was held up in the courtroom by the congratulations of the spectators who rushed to his side. As soon as he had the chance, Van Cise wired to Norfleet in Hale Center, "All con men convicted. My thanks to you for your good citizenship."

Over the next two months, as the convicted bunco men waited in the county jail for their sentences, Blonger made all the gestures of a warrior only temporarily defeated and preparing his glorious comeback. The very day after his conviction, miners in his Forest Queen silver mine found a four-foot-wide vein of gold, said to be worth many thousands of dollars, enough to fund several years of legal delays and appeals. As the entire city of Denver implored Van Cise to run for mayor, Blonger sat in his jail cell and made his own political appointments, naming the men he thought should be the next mayor and governor. He also loudly indicted his lawyers for botching the trial; he wanted to testify in his defense, Blonger claimed, but his attorney prevented him. The seventy-three-year-old's power was draining away from him, though, most noticeably in terms of his health as he suffered from asthma, heart trouble, and swollen legs and ankles.

On June 1, 1923, Judge Dunklee called the twenty prisoners back into court to hand them their sentences. Though they were each eligible for up to thirty years in the state penitentiary, Judge Dunklee was comparatively lenient, giving Blonger, Duff, French, and eight others seven to ten years, and three to ten years to another eight men. One man, Grove Sullivan, escaped sentencing on the grounds of insanity. Attorney Hawkins immediately prepared an appeal to the supreme court, but in early October, Blonger and his crew learned that they'd been denied a writ of supersedeas, which would have allowed them to remain free until the higher court had heard their appeal, and which also meant that a reversal was unlikely. "It's all over—we've got to go," Blonger was overheard sobbing to his wife on the phone. As he turned away from the phone, he stumbled forward and had to be carried to his cell. On October 18, 1923, after meeting with two Catholic nuns, phoning his wife to instruct her not to accompany him, and shaking hands with all of the guards, Blonger departed for the Cañon City penitentiary. As he was helped into the car by his physician and a friend, Blonger was too overcome with tears to speak and could only curtly wave his hand to those who had gathered to watch his departure.

In Cañon City, Blonger changed dramatically. He grew pale, palsied, and weak, but he also grew garrulous. When the news of his double life with the young Iola Readon broke in the newspapers, he uncharacteristically granted an interview, though he denied everything. "Say, what would a girl want with an old man like me," he said, laughing. For better or worse, he did finally get his opportunity to testify under oath. One of his marks, John S. Peck of Flemingsburg, Kentucky, named Blonger, Duff, French, and others in his suit to recover the $17,000 they'd taken from him in Denver. Blonger admitted that he'd once been involved in the Denver gambling scene but said he had given it up when gambling became illegal. He stated his occupation as farmer. And he claimed Adolph Duff was the true ringleader and that any paperwork found in his desk relating to the management of the bunco crew must have been put there by Duff. The courts would eventually find against Blonger in the Peck suit.

Blonger even effected a reconciliation with his wife, Cora. Though she never once appeared in the courtroom, she began visiting him regularly in jail when no one else would, bringing him clothes and news of his legal appeals. "Toward Lou Blonger I have the same kindly feeling as I would for a brother who had always been kind to me," she told the *Rocky Mountain News*. It was rumored that at one of her visits, the couple signed papers giving over his property to the "motherly, gray-haired" Mrs. Blonger. Perhaps she had learned a little something about disguising her cunning while she lived with Lou Blonger.

Blonger declined rapidly, and soon Cora was the only visitor his doctors allowed him. He began to lose his eyesight. He was ordered to stay off his feet and cease playing the card games that had been his only solace. He was restricted to a milk diet, supplemented by the digitalis that kept his heart going.

Six months after arriving at the penitentiary, he would be dead. In the last two weeks of his life, he would try desperately to obtain a transfer to a private hospital, so much did he dread dying in the prison, but to no avail. His body would be transferred to a Denver funeral home, where for several days he would be visited by a line of mourners, from Civil War veterans to beggars to businessmen. Mrs. Blonger would be the executrix and sole heiress of his estate, but there wouldn't be much left after the state and federal government had collected back taxes, the cost of his prosecution in the state courts, and the judgment against him in the Peck case.

Adolph Duff would also die "stony," as the gamblers say, or penniless and estranged from his family and friends. In 1929, after serving four years in the penitentiary and then returning to Denver to try to gamble back his fortune, Duff would be found dead on the seat of his coupe, a suicide by carbon monoxide poisoning.

In October 1923, as the Blonger organization prepared to move from the county jail to the state penitentiary, Norfleet and his daughter, Ruth, circled around W. B. Spencer's haunt in Mineral Wells, Texas. They enlisted the help of the local police chief, but after a day of no results they headed east to Fort Worth, then to Dallas, dealing out Spencer's photograph to every police station along the way. In Dallas, Norfleet met with the detective chief and the Bertillon expert, and both men promised to tap their networks for any information. Norfleet took his daughter back home, then returned to Dallas, where he received a wire from George Chase, a Bertillon expert in the Salt Lake City Police Department: a man answering Spencer's description was there. Arrest him, Norfleet telegraphed back, and he hitched a ride with a honeymooning couple down to New Mexico and then over to Utah. He didn't allow his hopes to soar. Well, maybe he did a little.

And when he walked into the jail, there was his man—for real this time, and most definitely behind bars. "How are you, Spencer?" Norfleet asked solicitously. "Don't you call me Spencer! I am Mr. A. P. Hunt," answered the prisoner, and he was indeed booked as Hunt, a salesman arrested for violating the narcotics law. But his story fractured when a petite woman on the other side of the bars ran up to Norfleet and cried, "Spencer isn't our name. Our name is Harris! That's Charlie and I'm Mildred." In only a few minutes, Spencer had broken character and confessed to everything. "That man," he complained, pointing to Norfleet, "can be in the way more than any damned man in the world. He always comes along at the right minute for himself and the wrong minute for me." As his wife began to cry in contemplation of their grim future, Spencer comforted her by saying, "I'd rather die and go to hell tonight than live as I have since I met Norfleet. Every knock on the door, every telephone bell, every stranger in the night has raised hell with my nerves." Or at least that's how Norfleet remembered Spencer's words.

That night, Norfleet telegraphed his triumph to his friends in district attorney offices and police departments across the Southwest, and newspapers from Los Angeles to Dallas carried the news of his final triumph. In March 1924, after he served time for his infractions in Salt Lake City, Spencer was found guilty on two counts of theft against J. Frank Norfleet and sentenced to eight years in the Texas penitentiary. Spencer appealed and was freed and was jailed again in a roller-coaster ride of legal complexities. And then, in 1927, Governor Miriam "Ma" Ferguson granted Spencer a full pardon, on the grounds that he suffered from chronic rheumatism and his family was "destitute and dependent on his wife's father for sustenance." In fact, Spencer was one of thirty-seven hundred pardons that Governor Ferguson issued during her two years in office, reportedly in exchange for bribes priced in accordance with the severity of the crime. Spencer became the only swindler on Norfleet's long list of prey to squirm out of his net. But by then, Norfleet's autobiography had been serialized, published, and serialized again, and his reputation had been hardened in the kiln of public adoration. He was the Boomerang Sucker who kept arcing back until he had snagged every last one of the men who dared to make him look foolish.

CHAPTER THIRTEEN

The Mark Inside

In the summer of 1957, Philip Van Cise received a letter penned in a sprawling hand. It was from Norfleet, then ninety-two years old, and it comfortably complained about the latest version of their long-ago adventures to appear in the media. The Norfleet story had been told many, many times in the intervening thirty years, and each of the writers invariably got something wrong. This writer, one John Gregor of *True* magazine, as Norfleet wrote to Van Cise, "told at Least 3 lies About me in his story he says I Smoked Cigars Drank Whiskey And Swore or Cussed. I have never yet Done Either." Gregor portrayed Norfleet complacently sipping drinks in his Fort Worth hotel room while Furey and his gang skipped town. Then Gregor invented a phone call to disturb Norfleet's boozy calm; when he picked it up, Norfleet heard Furey say, "Hello sucker!" Norfleet was glad to know that he wasn't the only one to be outraged by Gregor's literary license. "I was just Ready to write True Magazine," he wrote to Van Cise, "*No use* You have told it to them *mildly.*" Apparently, both men had been grooming their reputations in their twilight years, but *True* declined to publish either letter.

After the climax of events in 1923, Norfleet returned to his ranch a changed man. Even if he had wanted to recapture the lifestyle he'd enjoyed before his collision with the Furey gang, he wouldn't have had an easy time of it. His four-year absence from the ranch meant that its income had plummeted. He had funneled all available profits from cattle raising to manhunting, and he'd even taken $40,000 from his son Pete's burgeoning sheep and cow farm. In 1924, the Norfleets found themselves unable to make their mortgage payments. The bank was about to foreclose when a rancher named Berryman stepped up with a better offer. He bought the 4,989-acre parcel for $153,000 and then rented it back to the Norfleets. They soon moved to a smaller ranch, where they pared down their livelihood to gamecocks and racing horses.

For the rest of his life, Norfleet sought every possible opportunity to capitalize on his story. He told his saga so many times that he soon sounded like the phonograph that characterized his enemies' spiels. Truly, for Norfleet, the con would never die. The tale of his manhunt became his urtext, his explanatory narrative, the organizing logic of his very identity. He cultivated his legacy for the next forty years, feeding, fertilizing, and harvesting it like the world's most miraculous cash crop. By packaging and selling his thrilling melodrama in as many different media as he could, Norfleet took part in a distinctly modern trend that the confidence artists themselves had initiated: the commodification of personality.

First there was his autobiography. *Norfleet: The Actual Experiences of a Texas Rancher's 30,000-Mile Transcontinental Chase After Five Confidence Men* came out the same year he rescued his ranch from fore- closure, and the local reviews were adulatory. The *Lubbock Morning Avalanche* declared, "English literature has been enriched by a most gripping, startling compilation of thrills, laughter and pathos, held together by a thread of stupendous human endeavor, tempered by tol- erance and compassion." The paper meant it as a compliment when it wrote, "The plot of this true account is as perfectly constructed as any work of a master fiction writer." *The Dallas Morning News* was a speck more temperate in its evaluation. It heartily approved of the book as "our own indigenous detective story—of, by and for Texas"—none of the tweedy armchair cogitation of a Sherlock Holmes for Norfleet, no sir. But the *News* did find the book to be "cheap and crudely sensa- tional." The reviewer saw all its flaws and its singular virtue. "The book, in many ways, seems to be modeled on the dime novel of a generation ago. But one must admit in all honesty that Norfleet himself stands out to the reader of the book in a vital and memorable clearness and it seems entirely possible that he contains the germ of a legendary hero that may someday develop to the proportions of a Jesse James or even a Robin Hood."

Norfleet certainly thought so. The next year, he accepted a contract to tour on the vaudeville circuit "at a liberal weekly stipend." The year after that, he embarked on his own lecture tour of the United States, following the same scribbled trail over the map that he'd marked on his original chase. And the year after that, he helped to found the Imperial Press of Sugar Land, Texas. One of his partners in the venture was W. T. Eldridge, a man who had reason to be expansive toward the enterprising rancher. Back in the days of his manhunt, when Norfleet's identity was discovered in the Daytona Beach clubhouse high over the cliff and he'd made his armed escape, Steel and the other swindlers fled the house right after him. Unbeknownst to Norfleet, there had been a con in progress on the second floor, and as buy sheets and telephone receivers clattered to the floor in the wake of the exodus, one man stared around him, puzzled. W. T. Eldridge had been about to hand over $75,000 in the stock market swindle. When he later read the rest of the story in Norfleet's first autobiography, he thought the adventure should be better told. Imperial Press hired a Texas newspaper columnist named Gordon Hines to interview Norfleet and completely rewrite his autobiography, which was then sold for $2 a copy. The second edition is largely identical to the first, only peppier; Hines never wrote "gun" when he could write "gat" or "blunderbuss" or "persuader." And unlike the first edition, the second acknowledges the fantastic nature of the story. "For the benefit of doubters," wrote Hines in a foreword, "considerable substantiating material has been added to this work," including photostats of the front pages of Denver newspapers from Norfleet's testimony in the Blonger trial. Hines and Norfleet tried to trim the humbug from the edges of the adventure tale.

In 1929, Norfleet began filming himself for a motion picture version of the swindle and the revenge, but Black Tuesday brought the scene to a halt, and a dancer named Jackie Dola sued Norfleet for neglecting to pay the $125 weekly salary he'd promised for her acting services. He also regularly traveled to New York City to appear in radio broadcasts.

None of these enterprises ever amounted to anything, but to Norfleet they must have felt like movement, progress, feats of savvy and cunning. And in between telling his story to anyone who would pay him, Norfleet just kept apprehending criminals. He couldn't help it. People would approach him with their stories, and before he knew it, he'd find himself on a train, pursuing a slight lead with a heavy pistol in his pocket. In 1927, he tracked down a murderer in Arkansas and

Stills from Frank Norfleet's
never-released silent film,
starring himself

brought him home to Texas, his seventy-seventh criminal. The newspapers adored him, and his every step brought headlines. In 1928, he declared that he'd set himself a new goal of arresting one swindler for each $1,000 of the $45,000 he'd lost to the Furey gang. How many notches were there on his gun? reporters wanted to know. None, Norfleet told them, because "I only put notches on when I miss a shot." In 1940, when he was seventy-five years old, he arrested his ninety-third man; surely forty-five of them were swindlers.

His name regularly cropped up in newspaper articles having nothing to do with him. Any time the victim of a crime helped to arrest his or her perpetrators, he or she was referred to as "another Norfleet." A swindler named J. R. Bing was arrested for taking $16,000 off a Reno man, and Bing proudly identified himself as a member of the "J. Frank Norfleet gang," claiming to have been arrested and convicted by the famed manhunter in 1924 along with Joe Furey. As late as 1939, marks were still succumbing to what was now referred to as the "old Norfleet swindle"—the phonograph of the big con revolved around and around long after the Roaring Twenties had stopped winding it. Indeed, Norfleet himself was not immune to deception. In 1958, when he was ninety-three, a man named Dallas contracted to buy seven Thoroughbred horses from him, payable by installment, then vanished with the valuable mounts. This event, alone among the many deeds of Norfleet's lengthening life, was not publicized in the newspapers; it was not discovered until the next century when someone in New Mexico unearthed a cache of letters to the county sheriff, one of which was Norfleet's appeal for help in the matter. But it was that first, spectacular deception that captivated Norfleet, and as long as he was physically able, he made the rounds of all the cattle sales, rodeos, and county fairs in the Southwest, selling copies of his autobiography by hand from the side of the cow pens. He boosted the price to $3, then $4, and was shameless about signing a copy of his book over to someone and then asking him or her for payment.

Norfleet excelled at selling himself, and in this quality he was the quintessential American. In the span of Norfleet's lifetime—indeed, within his own life story—a gigantic transformation had occurred in the American cultural imagination. In the antebellum era, the confidence man was the manifestation of the very devil himself. As one writer warned in 1850, just one year after the appearance of the watch swindler Samuel Williams-Thomas-Thompson, the confidence man may be "gifted in intellect, eloquent in speech, beautiful in person, commanding in attainments, captivating and shining in all that he does," but in truth his talents were like "the beautiful hues on the back of the serpent, the more hideous in proportion to their power to charm the victim." Those venturing into the city were never to forget, as another advice writer cautioned, that the confidence man "had a pleasant address, was mild and courteous in his manner,—but within him was the spirit of a fiend."

Yet by the second decade of the twentieth century, what had been the confidence man's most odious quality, his chameleonlike ability to change himself to meet the moment, was becoming the modern era's hallmark. The sociological trends that gave rise to the big con—such as the growth of the cities, the distension of local networks of trust, the creation of the professional-managerial class that relied on expertise and confidence for its authority, and explosive middle-class participation in the consumer marketplace and the financial markets—also rendered the swindling arts a necessary part of success in the business world. To succeed in this exuberantly redrawn landscape, the ambitious American needed, above all else, to compel others to like him.

Self-help writers, like the wildly popular Orison Swett Marden, exhorted traveling salesmen, store clerks, insurance agents, stockbrokers, and the ambitious new cohort of advertising men to develop "impelling personalities," yet to be "all things to all men," turning the kaleidoscope of their being in accordance with their audiences' needs. Marden asked the readers of his 1921 book, *Masterful Personality*, "Did you ever feel yourself reinforced, your ability doubled, your power to do things increased tremendously in the presence of some powerful personality whom you admired?" In books like *How to Get What You Want, Selling Things*, and *Making Yourself*, Marden offered ways to magnetize your customers or audience and align them so that your interests would come to seem their interests, and you could move them in any direction.

By the 1920s, the same middle-class monthly magazines that serialized Norfleet's story and published articles exposing the tricks of the swindlers also ran essays that frankly acknowledged that confidence artists had perfected what the rest of the middle class must now hurry to emulate: salesmanship as a science, with codified principles and measurably successful techniques. As a 1925 *Collier's* article, "Take a Tip from the Con Man," explained, swindlers had been successful "for nearly two centuries" because "they have what is virtually a standardized presentation of each confidence game," handed down from generation to generation. It further explained that "their proficiency is due to the fact that they adopt a definite method of procedure and painstakingly perfect themselves in the details of its practice. Nothing is overlooked." The modern businessman, it seemed, should make himself over into a phonograph of dynamism and charisma. He should work on his self-presentation as arduously as an actor in a play or a swindler in a con, yet with a vast enough repertoire to turn any situation to his advantage.

This rehabilitation of the confidence man's social status, from a villain to a near-Napoleonic hero, signaled a larger revolution in American values that began around the time of Norfleet's birth and was nearly complete by the era of his swindling. The nineteenth century valued above all else the notion of character. An individual with character was someone who integrated moral law deep into his or her being, yet also interlocked with the larger societal prerogatives of hard work and self-control. In a survey of over two hundred nineteenth-century works of literature and popular culture, the words that repeatedly accompanied the idea of character were "citizenship, duty, democracy, work, building, golden deeds, outdoor life, conquest, honor, reputation, morals, manners, integrity, and above all, manhood."

The industrial age invented a host of metrics by which to weigh the American individual's character, and soon, quite noticeably, the thing being measured itself began to change. Life insurance agencies, with their accounting methods and actuary tables, expressed in dollar signs a man's productive capacity. Credit-rating bureaus, with their spies in every city and their ledgers tallying each man's reputation, calculated just how risky it was to invest confidence and money in each new endeavor. Contract theory—which expresses the doctrine of possessive individualism, in which the individual is the proprietor of his or her own capacities and the law exists to preserve his freedom to exchange them—became solidified in the American legal system in the 1850s under the direction of the Massachusetts chief justice, Lemuel Shaw, Herman Melville's father-in-law. In the age of Samuel Williams and Melville's *Confidence-Man,* the law enshrined the individual as an entrepreneur of himself, personhood as something fungible, the self as capital. As Henry David Thoreau wrote, the American man's highest calling was "to invent something, to be somebody,—*i.e.,* to invent and get a patent for himself,—so that all may see his originality."

The self-made mythology, which in the nineteenth century was expressed in highly loaded terms like "the go-ahead spirit" and "the wide awake man," began to take root at such an intimate level of the American psyche that identity itself became precisely commensurate with financial circumstance. The word "failure" initially meant "breaking in business" or going broke, and it described a singular, fairly rare event in an adult's life. The expansion of the word to describe an individual himself, his substance and core, marked the breach in the stone wall that had fortified the idea of character: the penetration of the marketplace into the heart of American identity. Norfleet, who used to define himself by the firm grip his cowboy boots had on the prairie of the Texas Panhandle, came dangerously close to such failure. His subsequent actions, the manhunt, all those trial testimonies, and the autobiographical story told and retold, speak to the American response in the face of any failure of selfhood: reinvention.

By the time Norfleet encountered Joseph Furey and Lou Blonger, "character" had begun to give way to the entirely different idea of "personality." Sincerity was replaced with appearance, morality with efficacy. The vocabulary of personality included words like "fascinating, stunning, attractive, magnetic, glowing, masterful, creative, dominant, forceful." Gone was the notion that tending to one's own moral core with industry and sobriety would be enough to earn God's favor and a steady income. Now the material rewards of the Roaring Twenties economy went to the one who aggressively pursued the main chance and who mastered the dual art of managing his own impression and managing others so that they contributed to his own destiny.

And with the advent of the mass market, the entrepreneurial self had a wealth of media outlets in which to grow his capital, as Norfleet so restlessly demonstrated. This archetype was necessarily a speculator, living in the moment to come, anticipating future gains, ever confident that continuous risk would bring an expanded asset base. Capitalism had shaped the American soul in its own image, from P. T. Barnum, who taught people how to enjoy being duped, to J. Frank Norfleet, who learned how to enjoy being inauthentic, a self-invented imposture of himself, forever spieling his tale of deception reversed.

Norfleet's life is the story of triumphing over his susceptibility by embracing it. Perhaps one of the reasons why he captivated so many listeners and readers with his tale is that he gave expression to an aspect of his identity that few would otherwise be able to admit they shared. Norfleet never possessed that hard carapace of skepticism that the experts of his day tried to instill in the American populace. Instead, he let out his inner mark, that fragile bubble of hope and optimism. It's what led him into Furey's trap, but it's also what led him to believe he had a chance at succeeding on his quixotic quest—two stories that would never have happened without a large measure of gullibility. Certainly this credulity is as essential to American mythology as the self-made man, but Norfleet's adventures go further to suggest that the mark inside is the first requirement for narrative itself. What he did was cultivate this characteristic until it became knowing, self aware, perennially game for a kind of wide-awake deception. Norfleet came to represent the personality type that best fits American modernity: the sophisticated sucker.

Norfleet and Van Cise kept in touch all their long lives. In his early nineties, Norfleet sent Van Cise a postcard to ask him for the address of Len Reamey, and Van Cise supplied it to him. After turning state's evidence, Reamey had reverted to a life of honest enterprise; he and Van Cise exchanged Christmas cards each year. When he was ninety-five, Norfleet wrote to Van Cise again, this time to complain about his treatment in the hands of *Argosy* magazine, which also portrayed him as an alcoholic gentleman rancher. Norfleet wondered if he shouldn't write the editor and "ask The writer of the Story if he dont think he Should Give me a Quart of Old Scotch. So I can taste it. I Never Have." Norfleet's letters to Van Cise are touching in their garrulous sameness. In one, he wrote, "I am not too Frisky. I have been Shot Down 6 times Stabbed Down Twice. Been in 4 accidents When I was the only Survivor in Each Accident. The Last one June 20th 54 I got my Left Hip and Knee Badly Crushed. Have been in Doctor Shops nearly ever since can walk some by using 2 canes but cannot Dance a Step. But wife says I still make a Full Hand at the Dining Table only." Three years later, he wrote, "I am still here and My Wife Says I Still Make a Full hand At the Dining Table Only. We both have Good Health. Our Wheat Looks Fine Prospects Looks good for a Bumper Fruit Crop. Cattle and Race Horses Fat. I hope to see you in Denver this Fall At the Fair."

All too soon afterward, Norfleet's good health deteriorated. He began to lose his hearing and his patience. In 1960, when someone asked him if he had hated Joseph Furey, those many years ago, Norfleet shouted, "I had to do it, don't you understand? Why I had to do it man." He was turning ninety-five that year, and his family threw him a big party at his home with hundreds of guests from the Texas Panhandle and New Mexico, but Norfleet was certain about one thing. "I'm 100 years of age, never mind what the papers say," he bellowed. "You're 95," his wife shouted back at him, then, turning to the assembled guests, she explained in a softer voice, "He's always wanted to live to be 100, so he says he's 100. He's 95. I'm 89." But Norfleet heard her. "I'm 10 years older than you by three days," he hollered. In other respects, though, Norfleet didn't want to admit that he was getting older. His grandniece, Sandi Clark, remembers that when the family was gathered together for Easter the year that Norfleet was ninety-eight, someone dared him to do a headstand on the front lawn. He stood up from his chair, grabbed his cane, and started out toward the center of the lawn. Sandi's mother ran into the house, calling for her father and uncles to come save Uncle Frank from a broken hip. Sandi's father came running out, but he was holding a camera, and he took pictures as Norfleet did his headstand. He always did love an audience.

Sure enough, Norfleet lived to be 100, and a reception was held at the Hale Center City Hall for the "living legend of the old West." On his 102nd birthday, President Lyndon Johnson sent his personal congratulations to him, a man who'd been born at the end of the Civil War. Eight months later, on October 15, 1967, Norfleet died peacefully in bed. Even *The Washington Post* carried the news. Norfleet's account at the great brokerage of American culture had been closed out, his speculation in the field of deception and con artistry finally brought to a halt for lack of funds, but it had been a grand run.

Acknowledgments

My first thanks go to my husband, Jay Farmer, who had unwavering confidence in this speculative enterprise. I cannot put a value on the easy grace with which he supported me, his unconditional endorsement of my uncertain career after those financially unproductive graduate student years. Every writer should have such a backstop.

Thank you to my daughter, Lucy, for writing circles around me and humbling me with her artistic freedom. One day when she was three, I told her part of Norfleet's story, and then she asked me to transcribe *her* book. It went like this: "Chapter 1. Norfleet. He used to put saddles on horses so the horses could be ridden at races. Then when they were tired he would take the saddle blankets off and he would untie the gwumph and that is because he wasn't a helper on a farm. He was the owner of the farm so he could decide what to do on the farm." She petered out after that first chapter, but I think it's pretty clear that a writing career is hers if she wants it.

My son, Jasper, deserves credit for being present at the creation. I worked on the proposal the whole time he grew in my belly. Then he was born, and I worked on the proposal some more while he napped in a sling on my belly. He was in the background trying to get my attention during every phone call with agents and editors. And for the next few years, he perfected his uncanny skill at slapping my keyboard and causing my screen to do alarming things.

I cannot thank my writing group enough for treating me *as if* I was a writer and thus making me believe it. I am especially indebted to Aaron Sachs, my first reader, whose fingerprints are all over this book. I am so grateful to have had the wit and wisdom of Andrea K. Summers, Lizabeth Cain, Michael Sharp, Geno Tournour, Jennifer Wilder, and Rachel Dickinson, not to mention the spouses who peered over their shoulders, including Christine Evans, Alison Shonkwiler, Eric Geissinger, and Erik Hoover.

Erik Hoover deserves a special mention for countless research leads, and for the title. Thank you to everyone who participated in the Name That Book contest.

This project was incubated in the American studies program at Yale University, where I had the honor to work with Jean-Christophe Agnew, Wai Chee Dimock, Amy Hungerford, and Lara Cohen. When it came time to turn an academic idea into a trade book, Nancy Bereano and Joan Jacobs Brumberg saw the possibilities and helped me get started.

Along the way, I had many readers, commiserators, and cheerleaders, including Rebecca Peabody; Angela Macey-Cushman; Lucia Silva; Sandy Zipp; Karen, Ann, and Bob Shepherd; and Anisa, Linda, and Bob Mendizabal. I appreciated the coffeeshop companionship of Robert Danberg, Roger Kimmel Smith, and Melanie Bush. A special thanks to Davina Morgan-Witts for feeding the flame with books.

The Historians Are Writers graduate student group at Cornell University is also a world-class group of readers, and their comments helped catapult the manuscript from a draft to a book: Sarah Ensor, Heather Furnas, Melissa Gniadek, Amy Kohout, Rebecca Macmillan, Laura Martin, Daegan Miller, Katie Proctor, and Josi Ward.

For help procuring primary source materials from all over the country, I am indebted to a whole host of research librarians and archivists, including June Gilligan at the Finger Lakes Library System; Nancy Stoehr at the Tompkins County Public Library; Bruce Hanson and the staff of the Western History and Genealogy Department at the Denver Public Library; John Sigwald at the Unger Memorial Library in Plainview, Texas; Patricia Clark at the Southwest Collection at Texas Tech University in Lubbock, Texas; Elva Hipolito at the Llano Estacado Museum at Wayland Baptist University in Plainview, Texas; Thomas A. Wilder, the Tarrant County District Clerk in Fort Worth, Texas; Deborah Bales at Brown, Dean, Wiseman, Proctor, Hart & Howell, LLP, in Fort Worth, Texas; Ellen Belcher at the Lloyd George Sealy Library at John Jay College of Criminal Justice in New York; Sylvia Rowan at the San Francisco Public Library; Ryan Roenfeld, president of the Historical Society of Pottawattamie County in Council Bluffs, Iowa, for sharing his research on Ben Marks; Barry Cohen of Northwestern University, Evanston, Illinois, for sharing his research on credit reporting agencies; and Khanh Hoang at the Archives and Regional History Collections at Western Michigan University in Kalamazoo, Michigan.

I benefited from the research assistance of Noah Wheeler in New Haven, Connecticut; Lou-Jean Holland Rehn in Denver, Colorado; and Curtis Peoples in Lubbock, Texas.

Phil Goodstein, the people's historian of Denver, happened to sit down next to me while I was reading one of his books at the Denver Public Library and was gracious when I accosted him and beyond generous with information and research leads.

A heartfelt thank-you to Jen, Chris, Roan, and Conall O'Brien for their hospitality and good humor on my research trips to Colorado, and to Fred and Sally Lippert for providing such a gorgeous place to write a few pages.

My huge appreciation goes to Mary Biggs, Marcia TenWolde, Heather Peluso, Anya Small, Ben Cayea, Bronwyn Losey, Katie Trojnor-Riley, Jude Keith Rose, Sandy Allen, and Sharon Champion, because I couldn't do what I do if you didn't do your jobs so well.

I cannot believe my good fortune to have landed at Writers House, where I thank Simon Lipskar, Josh Getzler, and Katie Zanecchia for unparalleled support. At Knopf, Edward Kastenmeier performed the difficult trick of suggesting revisions in a way that fostered more rather than less confidence in my writing. I am grateful to Emily Giglierano for undaunted professionalism and Ingrid Sterner for her exactitude.

Though I have mentioned them elsewhere, I cannot resist another opportunity to thank the descendants of the historical figures I write about. All of them were gracious, enthusiastic, and generous with their knowledge and time. Thank you to Sandi Clark, Susannah Touzel, Scott and Craig Johnson, Cindy Van Cise, Simon Peter O'Hanlon, and Rod Drake.

My final thanks go to my larger family, whose perennial interest in the manuscript as it grew was so vital to my energy for and pleasure in writing it: David, Lydia, Jeff, Timothy, Stephanie, Niki, Josephine, Ed and Pam Reading, Hallie MacDonald, Betty Rodgers, Jim and Sally Farmer, and Jamie and Ed Schiefen.

A Note on Sources

This is a work of nonfiction. Nothing has been invented; every line of dialogue and atmospheric detail has come from a published source. But, of course, just because something is published doesn't mean it's true. Moreover, what counts as historical evidence when the players in the drama are all professional liars?

My main source for this book is J. Frank Norfleet's 1924 autobiography, *Norfleet*. I first read it in graduate school, as I wrote a dissertation on strategies of deception in American autobiography. I loved his story, but I wasn't consumed by it. I thought I knew exactly what I was dealing with: a false autobiography in which the author passes as someone else, like Forrest Carter's *Education of Little Tree*, Clifford Irving's *Autobiography of Howard Hughes*, or, more recently, James Frey's *A Million Little Pieces*. I thought Norfleet was pretty clever, and I thought I'd made a nice little discovery of a writer who pretended to have been a mark who went on to masquerade as a mark. Very postmodern, I thought to myself, very knowing about the literary codes of autobiographical self-presentation. And then I did a little research and found out that the whole story was true. I felt abundantly foolish, duped by my own sophisticated skepticism. *That feeling* is what I wanted to probe, re-create, historicize.

Philip Van Cise's 1936 autobiography, *Fighting the Underworld*, was my second major source for the second half of the book. I discuss the credibility of both memoirs within the main body. As I alternated between the two books, they came to sound like the straight man and the joker in an old comedy routine, which was at once reassuring and disconcerting. Norfleet and Van Cise were clearly talking to and working with each other in their books, and my task became to identify what kind of project they had undertaken.

My first strategy was, of course, to back up their autobiographies with primary documents, but this was more frustrating than it should have been. Like Norfleet on the trail of a hot tip, I headed straight to Denver to locate the district court documents from the Blonger trial. All the trials from 1923 have been microfilmed, and they are all there in orderly sequence—except for the Blonger case, which has been pilfered right out of the historical record, a single note photographed within the microfilm to testify to its disappearance. Newspaper accounts of the trial and Norfleet's exploits were the best source, and luckily the principal actors in the drama attained such notoriety that the public coverage of their actions became reasonably complete, but the details were perennially wrong. Norfleet's name was Jasper, he'd been swindled by six men, his total loss was a mere $50,000. These errors, unimportant in themselves, shook my confidence in the tellability of the whole chronicle. After all, when it came to telling the history of the big con, newspapers were all I had. Criminals don't tend to leave traces of their moves; there are no university archives stuffed with con man correspondence, no brittle newspapers with breaking news from the underworld. I could only narrate them when they'd slipped up and entered the mainstream record of the newspapers, and those newspapers were disquietingly fallible. Even so, whenever in the research of this book I felt as if I'd fallen into the rabbit hole of noir fiction, the newspapers would tell me, "It happened. Put your cynicism aside and believe it."

The archival research was not all frustration and perceptual confusion; it also proved to be full of serendipity and fortuitous connections. I had the benefit of several valuable archives, as well as the memories of many descendants of the story's main characters. The biggest treasure trove was the Robert R. Maiden archive at the Denver Public Library. Maiden, one of the private detectives that Van Cise hired as part of his sting against Blonger, saved many of the documents they used to prepare the case against the bunco ring, including some of the transcripts of their interviews with Len Reamey. Cindy Van Cise, the granddaughter of the district attorney, hosted me in her home on the day that she cut the ribbon on the Van Cise–Simonet Detention Center, and she spread out on her dining room table an enormous two-volume scrapbook of Philip's life and career. Susannah Touzel, the granddaughter of the Fort Worth district attorney Jesse Brown, sent me a copy of Brown's limited-edition autobiography, *A Judge Looks at Life*. Sandi Clark, Norfleet's grandniece, shared with me her photographs and memories. Craig and Scott Johnson, descendants of Lou Blonger, have put their archive up on the Web for everyone to enjoy. Their Web site, www.blongerbros.com, is a bottomless cache of primary sources on Blonger's life, trial, and death, not to mention confidence artistry and the outlaw West in general.

My second strategy was to read the sources skeptically, to report what they say but also to register my bemusement. Perhaps this is the closest that a twenty-first-century reader can come to being engrossed and subsumed within an adventure tale from a simpler age. I became less interested in precisely what happened and more intrigued with how Norfleet chose to represent his tale. Even his distortions are telling, though we have to step into the realm of speculation in order to draw meaning from them. He wrote from within a set of literary codes learned by reading dime novels, detective fiction, and true-life stories serialized in the monthly magazines. Norfleet worked with several ghostwriters in the course of his long attempt to capitalize on his story, and those writers were surely more versed than he in such literary conventions. Ultimately, for me, the most generative question is not how historically accurate Norfleet was but how influential he was. Could his book have been found on the shelves of Dashiell Hammett, Raymond Chandler, and Damon Runyon (who, before he moved to New York, was a *Denver Post* writer in the era of Blonger's ascendance)?

Anyone interested in reading more on the subject should not consider the works of Norfleet and Van Cise exhausted by this retelling, because I have had to omit many thinner, shorter narrative strands in order to follow the twisting main thread. In Norfleet's book you will find, for instance, the menacing character of one Mrs. Street, who turns up every so often to bedevil and endanger the wily sleuth. I've pared away the many, repetitious instances when Norfleet came close to catching Spencer. I've similarly concentrated on only the most colorful details of the unbelievably convoluted Blonger trial, and have skipped right over the story of the anonymous letters that Van Cise received when he first took office, which turned out to be from a disgruntled bunc snitching on the swindling gang. These stories are fantastic and almost—almost—too good to be true. The classics of the far-too-small con man literary genre are David Maurer's *Big Con: The Story of the Confidence Man* and Joseph "Yellow Kid" Weil's *Con Man: A Master Swindler's Own Story*. More recent entries include Frank Abagnale's *Catch Me If You Can* and Luc Sante's *Low Life*.

The only exception to the rule of footnoted narrative history is the prologue, which I took the liberty of writing from Mulligan's perspective. It's a kind of literary impersonation along the lines of what I originally thought Norfleet was doing—me writing within the perspective of a mark impersonating a mark. Actually, let's just call it what it is: a con. Do forgive me.

Notes

Unless otherwise indicated, all dialogue comes from J. Frank Norfleet's first autobiography, *Norfleet: The Actual Experiences of a Texas Rancher's 30,000-Mile Transcontinental Chase After Five Confidence Men.* Because of the similarity of their titles, this first autobiography will be referred to in the notes as *Norfleet* (1924), and his second autobiography, which he revised with Gordon Hines, will be referred to as *Norfleet* (1927).

CHAPTER ONE
Confidence

5 "I don't drink": Jamar, "Norfleet Pioneers of the Plains," p. 14.
6 "I saw the best carload": U.S. Congress, *Hearing on the Relief of J. Frank Norfleet*, p. 2.
7 When Norfleet stepped into: The nine stages come from Maurer, *Big Con*, p. 4. See also Edward H. Smith, *Confessions of a Confidence Man*, p. 35; and Conwell, *Professional Thief*, p. 57.
8 In fact the swindlers had framed: Goffman, *Frame Analysis.*
8 The big con works: Bell and Whaley, *Cheating and Deception*, pp. 124, 134–35.
8 Hamlin had sifted the crowd: Swann, "Wiles of the Confidence Man."
10 "the cleverest bunco man": *Oakland Tribune*, August 6, 1922.
10 "Gentlemen, without this wallet": U.S. Congress, *Hearing on the Relief of J. Frank Norfleet*, p. 4.
12 "started in as": *Dallas Morning News*, December 10, 1919.
13 "the men I swindled": Weil and Brannon, *Con Man*, pp. 322–23.
13 "I have often wondered": Edward H. Smith, *Confessions of a Confidence Man*, p. 134.
14 And so the swindler claims: Leff, *Swindling and Selling*, pp. 12, 45.
15 Furey was passing off: Bentley, "Norfleet—Man-Hunter," p. 35.
16 Furey would most likely have claimed: Van Cise, *Fighting the Underworld*, pp. 277–79.
16 Norfleet's share of the profits: Measuring Worth, "Purchasing Power of Money in the United States from 1774 to Present."
19 "This is our last day": U.S. Congress, *Hearing on the Relief of J. Frank Norfleet*, p. 6.
21 The swindlers design the endgame: Goffman, "On Cooling the Mark Out."
22 In one, Furey gave in: Bentley "Norfleet—Man-Hunter," p. 37.
22 In the second version: Norfleet, *Norfleet* (1924), p. 16, and *Norfleet* (1927), p. 33.

CHAPTER TWO
Benjamin Franklin's Disciples

24 "Have you confidence": *New York Herald*, July 8, 1849.
24 In the span of just a few days: *New York Herald*, July 10, 1849.

24 A few weeks later: *New York Herald,* July 9, 1849.

24 "a graduate of the college": *New York Herald,* July 8, 1849.

25 One visitor from Philadelphia: *National Police Gazette,* September 22, 1849.

25 "The prisoner, yesterday": *New York Herald,* July 10, 1849.

25 "putting them to sleep": *New York Herald,* July 14, 1849.

25 a second confidence man: *New York Herald,* August 5 and October 9 and 10, 1849.

25 "We trust this word": *National Police Gazette,* October 20, 1849.

25 Two weeks after Williams's arrest: Bergmann, "Original Confidence Man," p. 568. For a similar account of the activities and legacy of the first confidence man, see Reynolds, "Prototype for Melville's Confidence-Man."

26 "What are you?": Melville, *Confidence-Man,* p. 227.

26 "CONFIDENCE MAN": Quoted in Bergmann, "Original Confidence Man," p. 574.

26 As early as 1860: Halttunen, *Confidence Men and Painted Women,* p. 7.

27 Con men differ: Hyde, *Gift,* p. 89.

27 In 1739, Benjamin Franklin: Bullock, "Mumper Among the Gentle."

28 "In order to secure": Franklin, *Autobiography,* p. 73.

28 It is passages like this: Zuckerman, "Selling of the Self"; Gary Lindberg, *Confidence Man in American Literature,* pp. 73–89; and Hauck, *Cheerful Nihilism,* pp. 32–39.

28 "an inveterate impersonator": Updike, "Many Bens," p. 106.

29 The trouble was, Bell's pretenses: Bullock, "Mumper Among the Gentle," pp. 246–50.

29 In January 1792: Matson, "Public Vices, Private Benefit."

30 "From ill-placed Confidence": Quoted in Mann, *Republic of Debtors,* p. 145.

31 "gains of money or estate": Quoted in Fraser, *Every Man a Speculator,* p. 13.

31 "He that goes a borrowing": Quoted in Mann, *Republic of Debtors,* p. 56.

31 "that all the capital employed": Randall, *Life of Thomas Jefferson,* p. 62.

32 Duer went much further: Matson, "Public Vices, Private Benefit," pp. 77–91.

32 In the 1780s: Mann, *Republic of Debtors,* pp. 175–76.

32 "Every thing that has value": Hamilton, *Papers of Alexander Hamilton,* pp. 246–47.

33 Duer, of course, was one of those elites: Matson, "Public Vices, Private Benefit," p. 101.

33 The unraveling came quickly: Gordon, "Great Crash (of 1792)."

34 He owed an astonishing: Matson, "Public Vices, Private Benefit," pp. 104–7.

34 One contemporary calculated: Measuring Worth, "Purchasing Power of Money in the United States from 1774 to Present."

34 Thomas Jefferson, for one: Jefferson and Madison quoted in Chernow, *Alexander Hamilton,* p. 383.

35 "it must have, thickened here and there": Melville, *Confidence-Man,* p. 294.

36 One commentator in 1839: Quoted in Mihm, *Nation of Counterfeiters,* p. 9.

36 Paper money, for all its glaring flaws: Baker, *Securing the Commonwealth,* p. 20.

37 In 1729, just twenty-three years old: Franklin, *Modest Enquiry into the Nature and Necessity of a Paper Currency.*

37 "My Friends there": Franklin, *Autobiography,* p. 72.

37 Yet there were precisely as many ways: Mihm, *Nation of Counterfeiters,* pp. 255, 257.

38 "Proves what I've always thought": Melville, *Confidence-Man,* p. 294.

38 "Money, of itself": Burroughs, *Memoirs of Stephen Burroughs,* p. 83.

39 Stealing a page from Bell's playbook: There is another eighteenth-century impostor whose career matches Bell's and Burroughs's. See Tufts, *Autobiography of a Criminal;* and Higginson, "New England Vagabond."

39 After his release: Mihm, *Nation of Counterfeiters,* pp. 20–62.

39 For Burroughs, the turn from imposture: Williams, "In Defense of Self," pp. 100, 114. See also Gross, "Confidence Man and the Preacher."

39 At the very close: Franklin, *Autobiography*, pp. 189–91; and Baker, *Securing the Commonwealth*, p. 91.

40 "counterfeiting and issuing worthless": Quoted in Mihm, *Nation of Counterfeiters*, p. 159.

40 "plodding, methodical, gradual": Ibid., p. 15.

CHAPTER THREE
Cowboy Justice

41 One of Reno Hamlin's marks: *Dallas Morning News*, November 27, 1919.

46 The Norfleet families: U.S. Census Bureau, 1850 and 1860.

46 Jasper came of age: Jamar, "From Virginia to Texas"; U.S. Census Bureau, 1900 and 1910.

46 Frank would often tell: Norfleet, *Norfleet* (1927), pp. 3–6.

47 When tanners learned: Lott, *American Bison*, p. 176.

47 In just three years: Hornaday, *Extermination of the American Bison*, pp. 419, 444–45, 465–69.

47 While Norfleet was on the buffalo hunt: *San Antonio Light*, January 14, 1945.

49 Norfleet's main task: Hamner, *Short Grass and Longhorns*, pp. 208–9.

49 Ellwood's company expanded: Handbook of Texas Online, "Ellwood, Isaac L."

49 "The drouth is at last broken": Norfleet to Arnett, June 18, 1892, Arnett Papers.

50 Several summers later: Norfleet to Arnett, July 13, 1907, Arnett Papers.

50 "I took a notion": Cox, *History of Hale County, Texas*, pp. 212–13.

50 There's the version steeped: *San Antonio Light*, January 14, 1945.

50 There's the melodramatic version: *Danville Bee*, April 10, 1925.

51 And then there is the likely version: *Plainview Daily Herald*, June 10, 1990.

51 In all three versions: *Lubbock Avalanche*, June 13, 1952.

51 "I was the *only* woman": *Hale Center American*, January 19, 1972. Emphasis mine.

51 "I got her cut off": Jamar, "Norfleet Women," p. 49.

51 Over 4.8 million Texas acres: Rathjen, *Texas Panhandle Frontier*, pp. 189–90.

51 This was a dugout: Hamner, *Short Grass and Longhorns*, p. 6; and Cox, *History of Hale County, Texas*, p. 186.

51 The Norfleets' second child: Norfleet, *Norfleet* (1927), p. 9.

52 "From this time on": Ibid., p. 3.

52 One day, the family: *Plainview Daily Herald*, May 10, 1968.

52 In 1907, the Panhandle Short Line Railroad: Cox, *History of Hale County, Texas*, pp. 20–21; and Wofford, *Hale County Facts and Folklore*, p. 383.

53 "Quite frank": Norfleet, *Norfleet* (1927), p. 3.

54 "It's the degree of confidence": Gober, *Cowboy Justice*, p. 315.

54 "I tell you every[one]": American Life Histories, "Mrs. Cicero Russell."

54 "Bones, do you know": American Life Histories, "Bones Hooks."

55 He wrote it in conjunction: *Plainview Reporter News*, November 24, 1974.

55 Cowboy stories from Bret Harte: Slotkin, *Gunfighter Nation*, pp. 125–55.

CHAPTER FOUR
Humbug

65 "organ of acquisitiveness": Barnum, *Life of P. T. Barnum*, p. 20.

65 "Sharp trades, especially dishonest tricks": Ibid., p. 39.

66 "The public appears disposed": Ibid., p. 171.

66 One Sunday morning in July: *New York Mercury, New York Atlas,* and *New York Herald,* July 17, 1842.

66 "eminent Professor of Natural History": Reprinted in Cook, *Colossal P. T. Barnum Reader,* pp. 110–11.

66 "Humbug—the Mermaid—and no mistake": *New York Herald,* August 11, 1842.

67 When the *Herald* announced: *New York Herald,* August 14, 1842.

68 "If the whole world": Melville, "View of the Barnum Property," p. 448.

68 "spurious relics": James, *Autobiography,* pp. 94, 95. Emphasis mine.

68 "an ugly, dried-up": Barnum, *Life of P. T. Barnum,* p. 212.

68 "continually finds himself": Weschler, *Mr. Wilson's Cabinet of Wonder,* p. 60.

69 "a peculiar and masterly way": Harris, *Humbug,* p. 56.

70 "like a revolving Drummond light": Melville, *Confidence-Man,* p. 282.

70 "putting on glittering appearances": Barnum, *Humbugs of the World,* pp. 8–9.

70 "Is this advertised commodity": Cook, *Arts of Deception,* p. 103.

70 "vernacular philosophy": Lears, "Birth of Irony," p. 50.

71 There is no attempt to conceal: Staiti, "Illusionism, Trompe l'Oeil, and the Perils of Viewership," p. 35.

71 "Your name was sent to me": *New York Times,* November 25, 1887.

71 "I am dealing in articles": Quoted in Gilfoyle, *Pickpocket's Tale,* p. 212.

71 One steerer: Ibid., p. 204.

72 "I will trust you": *New York Times,* November 25, 1887.

72 Another version was the "gold brick" swindle: *New York Times,* May 4, 1881.

73 Gerber suggested they return: *State of Texas v. John Gerber,* May 10, 1920.

73 Certainly it happened before: *Fort Worth Star-Telegram,* December 23, 1919.

74 The proceedings were routine: *Fort Worth Star-Telegram,* January 10, 1920.

74 Norfleet was standing: *Fort Worth Star-Telegram,* January 13, 1920.

74 "Some of the facts recited": Brown, *Judge Looks at Life,* p. 46.

74 "a sombrero and a corduroy suit": *Mexia Evening News,* January 25, 1921.

75 And yet, just a few days later: *Lubbock Avalanche,* May 20, 1920.

75 Within eleven days: *Lubbock Avalanche,* May 13 and 20, 1920.

75 "Ten years—the limit": *Fort Worth Star-Telegram,* May 9, 1920.

75 The day he was to stand trial: *Dallas Morning News,* November 12, 1920.

76 The Associated Press article: The article does not appear in any of the Panhandle newspapers, including the *Plainview Daily Herald,* the *Lubbock Avalanche, The Dallas Morning News,* and the *Fort Worth Star-Telegram,* nor can it be found in any of the minor and major newspapers around the nation whose holdings have been digitally archived.

76 Mrs. J. F. Norfleet joined her husband: *Plainview Evening Herald,* December 12 and 29, 1919.

77 "He thinks himself philosophic": Barnum, *Humbugs of the World,* pp. 16–17.

77 "It is a good thing": Quoted in Bergmann, "Original Confidence Man," p. 566.

CHAPTER FIVE

Double-Crossings

89 He sold the cattle at $23.75: Norfleet, *Norfleet* (1927), pp. 150–51.

97 Only a few weeks earlier: *Los Angeles Times,* February 1, 1921.

98 Anderson was an officer: *Oakland Tribune,* March 3, 1921.

98 "Chief Lips entered the department": *Los Angeles Express,* April 7, 1906.

98 Anderson appeared puzzled: *Modesto Evening News,* March 3, 1921.

98 As Norfleet would later learn: *Los Angeles Times,* March 4, 1921; and Norfleet, *Norfleet* (1924), pp. 199–201.

99 After their indictment: *San Francisco Chronicle,* March 4, 1921.

99 "We were tempted and we fell": *Modesto Evening News,* April 6, 1921.

99 "It seems this statement": *Los Angeles Times,* April 7, 1921.

99 "a small, compact, quiet-looking": *Los Angeles Times,* June 17, 1921.

99 "Her recital of the sacrifice": *Oxnard Daily Courier,* June 17, 1921.

99 The defense rested: *Los Angeles Times,* June 23, 1921.

100 The decision was appealed: *People v. Walter Lips; People v. W. J. Anderson; Modesto Evening News,* April 19, 1922.

CHAPTER SIX

A Small History of the Big Con

101 "internationally known": *Fort Worth Star-Telegram,* March 14, 1921.

101 "one of the smartest": *Oakland Tribune,* March 2, 1928.

101 "one of the most dangerous": *San Francisco Chronicle,* February 14, 1913.

101 as soon as he was able: Ibid.

101 In the first decade: *Trenton Sunday Advertiser,* July 19, 1908.

101 "well known to the police": *San Francisco Chronicle,* December 10, 1904.

101 One son, John: *Portland Morning Oregonian,* August 25, 1909.

102 One of them would befriend: *San Francisco Call,* September 15, 1903.

102 He "died" by gunshot: *San Francisco Chronicle,* December 10, 1904.

102 He kept getting arrested: *Los Angeles Times,* March 16, 1912; *San Francisco Chronicle,* April 24, 1914; and *Fort Worth Star-Telegram,* January 22, 1921.

103 Over the objections: Ruby and Brown, *Spokane Indians,* pp. 238–43.

103 Joseph Furey was the first: *Portland Morning Oregonian,* August 14, 1909.

103 Seattle area newspapers: *Portland Morning Oregonian,* August 24 and 26, 1909.

103 Edward Clifford left: *San Francisco Chronicle,* February 14, 1913.

103 And yet just ten days: *Los Angeles Times,* February 14, 1913; *Nevada State Journal,* February 20, 1913; and *San Jose Mercury News,* February 23, 1913.

103 The following year, Joseph: *Davenport Democrat and Leader,* August 11, 1922.

105 "the greatest gambling place": Dodge, *How We Built the Union Pacific Railway,* pp. 53, 116.

105 "a carefully set up": Maurer, *Big Con,* pp. 5–11.

105 He set up some tables: Roenfield, "Benjamin Marks and the Hog Ranch."

106 In 1898, he built: Smetana, *History of Lake Manawa,* pp. 120–21.

107 Mary's refinement: Ibid., pp. 136–47.

107 Marks joined forces: Raymond A. Smith, Jr., "John C. Mabray," pp. 123–39.

109 "Owing to a change": Hawkins, *Mabray and the Mikes,* pp. 37–38.

109 "Play of 49": Ibid., pp. 54–55.

110 Once the detectives: Makris, *Silent Investigators,* pp. 120–23.

110 Ben Marks was also tried: *New York Times,* December 19, 1911.

110 But the long trial: *Daily Nonpareil,* April 26, 1919.

110 One of them was Joseph: Hawkins, *Mabray and the Mikes,* p. 113.

111 "department store of gambling": Richard C. Lindberg, *Gambler King of Clark Street,* pp. 34–53.

111 At a young age, McDonald : Ibid., pp. 11–13, 32, 39.

111 Most important, the Store: Ibid., pp. 29–30.

112 McDonald never held office: Asbury, *Gem of the Prairie*, pp. 142–51.

112 Coughlin and Kenna ran: Abbott, *Sin in the Second City*, pp. 161–74.

112 "one of Chicago's landmarks": *Chicago Daily Tribune*, October 31, 1917.

112 "Mr. Weil wore blue": *Chicago Daily Tribune*, November 21, 1917.

112 When Mrs. Anna J. Weil sailed: *Chicago Daily Tribune*, October 27, 1918.

113 "Why they say he lost": *Chicago Daily Tribune*, January 6, 1918.

113 In that instance, Weil's: Richard C. Lindberg, *Gambler King of Clark Street*, p. 227.

114 "Mr. Furey's chances": *Chicago Daily Tribune*, November 15, 1918.

114 According to his self-mythologizing: Weil and Brannon, *Con Man*, pp. 20–40.

114 "the glass of fashion": *New York Times*, September 10, 1907.

114 Jay Robert Nash: Nash, *Hustlers and Con Men*, pp. 256–57; and *New York Times*, July 21, 1907. See also "Passing of the Wireless Wire-Tappers," pp. 363–64.

114 An obscure con man: *Chicago Daily Tribune*, August 23, 1905.

114 But the real inventor: *Washington Post*, January 15, 1905.

114 Bookmakers all across the country: *New York Times*, December 21, 1885.

115 In 1896, a well-coordinated: *Chicago Daily Tribune*, March 15, 1896.

115 "perhaps not a half dozen": *New-York Tribune*, March 17, 1896.

115 "When the workmen": *Washington Post*, April 5, 1896.

115 Similar exposés: See, for instance, *National Police Gazette*, March 29, 1902; and *Los Angeles Times*, September 14, 1902.

116 "valuable telegraphic equipment": *Chicago Daily Tribune*, September 29, 1896.

116 As late as 1902: *Los Angeles Times*, September 14, 1902.

116 In 1905, a consortium: *New-York Tribune*, February 8, 1905.

116 "well known about the Tenderloin": *New York Times*, April 20, 1907.

116 Like Weil, Fred and Charley: Asbury, *Gem of the Prairie*, p. 150.

116 Even after Walker: *Hartford Courant*, July 29, 1908.

117 "one of the shrewdest": Hoover, "Man with the Magic Wallet," p. 44.

117 Joseph Furey learned it: Nash, *Great Pictorial History of World Crime*, p. 411.

117 He contacted a plastic surgeon: Collins, *FBI in Peace and War*, p. 18.

117 "The trick by which he": Hoover, "Man with the Magic Wallet," p. 73.

118 In the mid-1930s: Nash, *Great Pictorial History of World Crime*, pp. 416–17.

118 publicly forswore con artistry: Bellow, "Talk with the Yellow Kid," p. 41.

118 "I see how despicable": "Yellow Kid Returns," p. 20.

118 One time Nash came: Nash, *Great Pictorial History of World Crime*, p. 418.

118 "Crooked money disappears": Sharpe, *Chicago May*, p. 1.

CHAPTER SEVEN
The Con Never Dies

119 But Norfleet couldn't help notice: Norfleet, *Norfleet* (1927), pp. 188–91.

125 "Have Joe Furey": *Fort Worth Star-Telegram*, January 22, 1921.

126 "Furey jumped through": Ibid.

127 On January 24, 1921: *Fort Worth Star-Telegram*, January 25, 1921.

127 It was discovered: *Fort Worth Star-Telegram*, January 22 and 29, 1921.

127 "I can go back now": *Fort Worth Star-Telegram*, February 6, 1921.

127 He made a full confession: *Fort Worth Star-Telegram*, March 3, 1921.

127 Furey hobbled into court: *Fort Worth Star-Telegram*, March 14, 1921.

128 he hobbled from the county jail: *Fort Worth Star-Telegram*, March, 20, 1921.

128 As if resigned: *Fort Worth Star-Telegram,* December 18, 1921.

128 In May, just a few weeks: *Fort Worth Star-Telegram,* May 9, 1921.

128 Three days later, Governor: *Los Angeles Times,* May 9, 1921.

129 "Prison authorities said": *Fort Worth Star-Telegram,* May 12, 1921.

129 According to legend: *Wichita Daily Times,* July 31, 1922.

129 On July 29, 1922: *Fort Worth Star-Telegram,* July 29, 1922.

129 Because his wife had long: *Wichita Daily Times,* July 31, 1922.

129 It was a deputy: *Los Angeles Times,* August 5, 1922.

130 "Some day you will read": *Fort Worth Star-Telegram,* August 5, 1922.

130 Woolwine telegrammed District Attorney Brown: Brown, *Judge Looks at Life,* p. 46.

130 "I doubt it": *Fort Worth Star-Telegram,* August 5, 1922.

130 "I'd hate to be as dead": *Reno Evening Gazette,* August 5, 1922.

130 No, make that stomach: *Ogden Standard-Examiner,* August 6, 1922.

130 *The New York Times* mentioned: *Oakland Tribune,* August 5, 1922; and *New York Times,* August 6, 1922.

130 The undertaking firm: *San Francisco Chronicle,* August 6, 1922.

130 It was soon revealed: *Los Angeles Times,* August 7, 1922.

130 She was named administratrix: *Los Angeles Times,* August 10, 1922.

131 "Joe Furey is dead": *Fort Worth Star-Telegram,* August 11, 1922.

131 "The king of bunco men": *Waterloo Evening Courier and Reporter,* August 11, 1922.

131 "Tell this committee": *Dallas Morning News,* February 10, 1925.

131 Six years after his death: *Reno Evening Gazette,* March 1, 1928.

132 "Furey is dead and buried": *Oakland Tribune,* March 2, 1928.

132 "Joe Furey had been 'dead' ": *San Antonio Light,* March 4, 1928.

132 Days later, in October 1921: *Lubbock Avalanche,* October 27, 1921.

133 Norfleet found himself in a race: *Atlanta Constitution,* October 21 and 22, 1921.

133 Norfleet and Flynn personally: *Lubbock Avalanche,* October 27, 1921.

133 His obituary remembered him: *Jefferson City Post-Tribune,* July 10, 1933.

CHAPTER EIGHT

The Making of a Confidence Kingpin

135 The ranch was in dire straits: Norfleet, *Norfleet* (1927), pp. 298–99.

136 "short, rotund, affable": Parkhill, *Wildest of the West,* p. 98.

136 "always a big-hearted": *Denver Post,* April 21, 1924.

136 "generous and kind": *Denver Times,* April 22, 1924.

136 "He would peel off": *Denver Post,* April 21, 1924.

136 The mine had quickly proved: *Colorado Springs Gazette,* January 30, 1909, and November 5, 1911.

136 Each Saturday morning: *Rocky Mountain News,* April 21, 1923.

136 In the evenings: Parkhill, *Wildest of the West,* p. 98.

137 The ropers, spielers, and bookmakers: File folder 4, p. 35, Maiden Papers.

137 As early as 1895: *Rocky Mountain News,* October 17, 1895.

137 "the recognized leader": *Denver Times,* July 1, 1901.

137 By the 1920s: Van Cise, *Fighting the Underworld,* p. 261; and Goodstein, *Seamy Side of Denver,* p. 124.

137 They'd work in Florida: File folder 20, p. 5, Maiden Papers.

137 In the 1920s, the newspapers called him: See, for instance, *Denver Post,* March 29, 1923.

137 He had come a long way: Blonger Bros., "True History of the Famous Blonger Bros."

138 Between 1860 and 1870: Barth, *Instant Cities,* pp. viii, 135.

138 "crowding a century": Quoted in ibid., p. 128.

138 The first thing a miner: Goodstein, *Seamy Side of Denver,* p. 23.

139 "a fleet of old shoes": *Rocky Mountain News,* July 15, 1890.

139 "Ladies and gentlemen": Roy D. White oral history. Mr. White was trained by Soapy Smith as a young man.

140 Afterward, they'd further sweeten: Dorset, *New Eldorado,* p. 394.

140 "non-ordained preacher": Quoted in Goodstein, *Seamy Side of Denver,* p. 116.

140 "Winnings: $4,087": Jeff Smith, *Alias Soapy Smith,* p. 128.

140 "After a man once comes": *Rocky Mountain News,* September 8, 1893.

140 The Palace Theatre: Noel, *City and the Saloon,* pp. 37–38.

141 Chase hired a string: Joseph Emerson Smith, "Personal Recollections of Early Denver," p. 14.

141 "a thoroughly tough, hard place": Quoted in Secrest, *Hell's Belles,* p. 136.

141 The two men coexisted: Jeff Smith, *Alias Soapy Smith,* p. 79.

141 From his tenure: Noel, *City and the Saloon,* p. 39; and Secrest, *Hell's Belles,* p. 60.

141 By 1886, the fix: Secrest, *Hell's Belles,* p. 149.

141 Police regularly staged raids: *Rocky Mountain News,* January 4, 1896.

141 He quickly went to work: *Rocky Mountain News,* March 20, 1890.

142 They owned it jointly: *Rocky Mountain News,* October 11, 1892.

142 "17th Streeters": Whitacre, *Denver Club,* pp. 1–7.

142 One visitor to Denver: King, *A Mine to Make a Mine,* p. 28.

143 Even the 17th Streeters: Barth, *Instant Cities,* p. 147.

143 But the ore specimens: King, *A Mine to Make a Mine,* pp. 33–34, 60–61.

144 Colonists had used lotteries: Findlay, *People of Chance,* pp. 31–32. See also Fabian, *Card Sharps, Dream Books, and Bucket Shops,* pp. 113–28; and Lears, *Something for Nothing,* p. 70.

144 At the end of the eighteenth century: Chafetz, *Play the Devil,* p. 41.

144 By 1815, every town: Fabian, *Card Sharps, Dream Books, and Bucket Shops,* p. 114.

145 In 1830, there were only: Gordon, *Empire of Wealth,* p. 150.

145 In 1835, only three railroads: Ibid., pp. 148–50.

145 A full third of the tracks: Fraser, *Every Man a Speculator,* pp. 112, 120.

145 If, at the beginning: Zelizer, *Morals and Markets,* p. 88; and Lears, *Something for Nothing,* pp. 97–146.

146 At the beginning of the war: Gordon, *Empire of Wealth,* p. 193.

146 "What do you think": Sobel, *Panic on Wall Street,* p. 136.

146 Norvin Green, the president: Chandler, *Nation Transformed by Information,* p. 79; and U.S. Congress, *Postal Telegraphs,* p. 30.

146 In his private correspondence: King, *A Mine to Make a Mine,* pp. 61, 73, 77–78.

148 A customer would enter: Hochfelder, " 'Where the Common People Could Speculate,' " pp. 342–43.

148 While he waited: Teague, "Bucket-Shop Sharks," p. 35.

148 What happened next: Fabian, *Card Sharps, Dream Books, and Bucket Shops,* p. 192; and Hochfelder, " 'Where the Common People Could Speculate,' " p. 344.

148 In the event: Lefèvre, "Bucket Shop Education," p. 77.

148 And rival bucket shops: Geisst, *Wheels of Fortune,* p. 56.

149 "so infected with illegality": Hochfelder, " 'Where the Common People Could Speculate,' " p. 351.

149 In just a few pithy phrases: *Board of Trade of the City of Chicago v. Christie Grain and Stock Company.*

149 As Christie pointed out: Christie, "Bucket-Shop vs. Board of Trade," pp. 707–13.

150 The first official to win: *Los Angeles Times*, July 9, 1925.

150 Woolwine and his counterparts: Hochfelder, " 'Where the Common People Could Speculate,' " pp. 354–55.

150 In 1913, New York: *New York Times*, May 16, 1913; and Hochfelder, " 'Where the Common People Could Speculate,' " p. 355.

150 In Denver, they would not: *Rocky Mountain News*, May 13, 1919.

150 "sporty municipality": *Rocky Mountain News*, August 6, 1895.

151 The Blongers were squeezed: *Boulder Daily Camera*, September 26, 1891; and *Denver Times*, April 7, 1892.

151 "You put that money": *Denver Times*, January 11, 1921.

151 True to his word: *Aspen Weekly Times*, April 26, 1894.

151 Next, he arrested Ed Chase: *Rocky Mountain News*, May 8, 1894.

151 The following month: *Denver Republican*, May 11, 1894.

151 "moral, social, and legal": *New York Times*, November 28, 1894.

151 "many buildings and parts of buildings": Quoted in Knapp, "Making an Orderly Society," p. 134.

151 Rumor had it: See Jeff Smith, *Alias Soapy Smith*, pp. 356–58, for a discussion of Soapy Smith's attribution of the petition to Lou Blonger.

152 When the newspapers reported: *Rocky Mountain News*, October 17, 1895.

152 "Nowadays men drink". *Rocky Mountain News*, October 25, 1896.

152 In 1897, Lou and Sam: *Mercantile Agency Reference Book and Key*, "Blonger Bros."

152 One ambitious young lawyer: Lindsey, *Beast*, pp. 60–63, 324.

153 As Chase advanced: Noel, *City and the Saloon*, p. 110; and Bretz, *Mansions of Denver*, p. 18.

153 "He Buncoed Blonger": *Denver Times*, October 10, 1898.

153 "All the detectives": Quoted in Van Cise, *Fighting the Underworld*, p. 5.

153 "The funniest part of the joke": *Denver Times*, February 24, 1902.

153 nor did they dwell: *Emporia Gazette*, August 6, 1906.

153 The newspapers largely confined: *Denver Republican*, October 28, 1902.

153 Lou racked up two more: "Colorado State Penitentiary Record of Lou Blonger #12258," file folder 29, Maiden Papers.

154 "I must say that if I were": *New York Times*, February 16, 1904.

154 In the suit that Bonynge had filed: U.S. Congress, *Contested Election Case of Robert W. Bonynge vs. John F. Shafroth*, pp. 240, 423.

154 "What's the use of staying": *Denver Republican*, February 4, 1904.

CHAPTER NINE

The Machine and the Sting

155 Hermann H. Heiser: *Rocky Mountain News* and *Denver Times*, June 30, 1915.

156 who would one day serve: Goodstein, *Robert Speer's Denver*, p. 299.

156 jailed along with the Mabray gang: Hawkins, *Mabray and the Mikes*, p. 113.

156 Duffield readied himself: *Denver Times*, July 1, 1915.

156 Sure enough, two weeks later: *Denver Times*, July 6 and 13, 1915.

156 For the next decade: Blonger Bros., "Blonger Bros. Timeline."

157 Other evidence suggests: Parkhill, *Wildest of the West*, p. 99.

158 If the answers were satisfactory: File folder 20, n.p., Maiden Papers.

159 On any given day: File folder 25, pp. 2–3, Maiden Papers.

159 A week or ten days later: File folder 26, pp. 10–12, Maiden Papers.

159 And then they'd all go: File folder 4, p. 10, and file folder 25, n.p., Maiden Papers.

160 A bunco man could be fired: File folder 25, p. 59, and file folder 29, pp. 34–35, Maiden Papers.

160 "Don't look around": File folder 26, p. 40, Maiden Papers.

160 Another time: File folder 25, p. 9, Maiden Papers.

160 "Well, Doc, you are a pretty": Van Cise, *Fighting the Underworld*, p. 100.

161 "I offered a $1,000.00 reward": File folder 1, n.p., Maiden Papers.

161 The men who accepted his money: Parkhill, *Wildest of the West*, p. 98.

162 "abrupt, incisive": *Rocky Mountain News*, May 28, 1943.

162 His family remembers: Rod Drake and Cindy Van Cise, conversation with author.

162 He'd distinguished himself: *Denver Post*, December 10, 1969; and *Rocky Mountain News*, December 9, 1969.

163 "I wear the same G.A.R.": Van Cise, *Fighting the Underworld*, p. 15.

163 "I like your style": Ibid., p. 16.

163 "This is the first time": Ibid., p. 17.

163 On election night: *Denver Post*, November 2, 1920.

164 "His victory is chiefly due": *Denver Post*, November 3, 1920.

164 Once, he stormed into: Secrest, *Hell's Belles*, p. 293.

164 If he caught: Keating, *Gentleman from Colorado*, p. 71.

164 "What do you mean, Chief": Van Cise, *Fighting the Underworld*, p. 20.

165 "But, son," said Chief: Ibid., p. 24.

165 "I am being jobbed": *Denver Times*, January 10, 1921.

165 "general lawlessness": *Denver Post*, January 11, 1921.

165 "We are laying off": *Denver Times*, January 11, 1921.

166 "Who were the men": Van Cise, *Fighting the Underworld*, pp. 49–50.

166 "We can't do much more": Ibid., p. 52.

167 "Keep that date open": Ibid., p. 94.

167 Van Cise wrote: File folder 8, n.p., Maiden Papers.

168 "#1 and another stranger": File folder 11, n.p., Maiden Papers.

169 "I saw the bunc that limps": File folder 16, n.p., Maiden Papers.

169 "See that room": Van Cise, *Fighting the Underworld*, p. 118.

170 "Colonel, is there anything": Ibid., p. 64.

171 "as our friend Van Cise": Ibid., p. 71.

171 "What do you think": Ibid., p. 146.

172 One of the detectives on the force: File folder 25, p. 3, Maiden Papers.

172 That spring, a spieler: File folder 25, pp. 4–5, Maiden Papers.

172 "There is nothing doing": Van Cise, *Fighting the Underworld*, p. 158.

172 "Hell, the District Attorney": Ibid., pp. 154–55.

173 "Why, these seem to be": Ibid., p. 156.

CHAPTER TEN
The Raid

176 "Norfleet did not look": Van Cise, *Fighting the Underworld*, p. 183.

176 "For God's sake": Ibid., p. 184.

177 "the greatest kind of luck": Ibid., pp. 182–83.

178 Or perhaps Norfleet: *Lubbock Avalanche*, June 17, 1920.

181 He says that he gave: *Denver Post*, August 26, 1922.

183 In one version of his story: Bentley, "Norfleet—Man-Hunter," p. 39.

183 Robert Maiden was on duty: File folder 16, n.p., Maiden Papers.

186 Beginning at seven o'clock: *Denver Post*, August 31, 1922.

187 In Norfleet's account: Norfleet, *Norfleet* (1924), p. 322.

187 Van Cise's version: Van Cise, *Fighting the Underworld*, p. 196.

187 Much later, a fellow swindler: File folder 4, p. 17, Maiden Papers.

187 "There is no need": Van Cise, *Fighting the Underworld*, p. 197.

187 In Felix's bags: File folder 4, pp. 26–27, Maiden Papers.

188 "By God," Duff exclaimed: Van Cise, *Fighting the Underworld*, p. 202.

188 Sanborn recalled that: *Denver Post*, August 31, 1922.

188 "Shoot the works": Van Cise, *Fighting the Underworld*, p. 204.

189 "Randle York 3201": Ibid., pp. 204–5.

189 Roy Samson, for his part: Ibid., pp. 205–8.

189 Two men stood: *Denver Post*, August 25, 1922.

190 Then the prisoners: *Denver Times* and *Denver Post*, August 25, 1922.

190 The prisoners were photographed: File folder 29, n.p., Maiden Papers.

190 Only when he reached: Van Cise, *Fighting the Underworld*, p. 205.

191 "like a great, gray spider": *Denver Post*, August 27, 1922.

192 Prisoners outnumbered guards: *Denver Times*, August 25, 1922.

192 Others tried to buy: *Denver Times*, August 26, 1922.

192 The transcript of Norfleet's statement: *Denver Times* and *Denver Post*, August 25, 1922.

193 But Van Cise forestalled: Van Cise, *Fighting the Underworld*, p. 213; and Parkhill, *Wildest of the West*, pp. 103–5.

193 Many years later, Parkhill: Van Cise, *Fighting the Underworld*, p. 213.

194 That morning, as Norfleet: Parkhill, *Wildest of the West*, p. xxv.

194 The phone in the Lookout: Van Cise, *Fighting the Underworld*, pp. 208–9.

194 Robert Maiden, in his zeal: Ibid., pp. 210–11.

194 "desperate character": *Denver Post*, August 25, 1922.

194 He was forced to spend: *Denver Post*, August 27, 1922.

194 But on the positive side: File folder 4, n.p., Maiden Papers.

194 Jackie French, the Beau Brummell: Van Cise, *Fighting the Underworld*, p. 109.

194 After the last of the Denver: *Denver Post*, August 26, 1922.

195 He checked into the Columbia: *Rocky Mountain News*, August 26, 1922.

195 Duff's little memorandum: File folder 4, p. 44, Maiden Papers; and *Rocky Mountain News*, August 29, 1922.

195 "well-known in sporting circles": *Denver Post*, August 26, 1922.

196 "He's all right": Van Cise, *Fighting the Underworld*, p. 214.

196 But Mrs. Franklin had: Ibid., p. 230.

CHAPTER ELEVEN
Pure Speculation

197 "They picked the wrong bird": *Oakland Tribune*, August 25, 1922. See also *New York Times*, August 25, 1922.

197 "I know 24 men": *Syracuse Herald*, August 26, 1922.

198 "If there is one thing": Barnes, "Fighting the Fakirs in Finance," p. 618.

199 "A little knowledge": Rice, *My Adventures with Your Money*, p. 96.

199 "The average professional man": Edward H. Smith, *Confessions of a Confidence Man*, p. 105.

199 "While apparently written": Review of *The Professional Thief*, p. 625.

200 Charlie Chaplin was nervous: Chaplin, "Charlie Chaplin Learns to Sell Liberty Bonds," pp. 109–11.

201 "capitalize patriotism": Rockoff, "Until It's Over, Over There," p. 13.

201 McAdoo's troops created: Ibid., p. 31.

202 Before the war: Cowing, *Populists, Plungers, and Progressives*, p. 95.

202 The Liberty Loan program arguably: Cohen, *Making a New Deal*, p. 77.

202 Later, corporations would use: Ibid., p. 175.

202 "INTEGRITY . . . INTELLIGENCE": Quoted in Calder, *Financing the American Dream*, p. 87.

202 Gradually, it became common: Ibid., pp. 98–104.

203 The forced austerity: Olien and Olien, *Easy Money*, pp. 3–6.

203 The stock market began to rev: Cowing, *Populists, Plungers, and Progressives*, p. 75.

203 Jobs were created: Baritz, *Good Life*, p. 71.

203 Within the first few months: Guenther, "Wreckage," p. 509.

203 "The war and the activities": Bulger, "Psychology of the Sucker," p. 107.

204 "Send us your $100 Liberty Bond": Guenther, "Pirates of Promotion, Who Are After Your Liberty Bonds," p. 32.

205 Like the commodities: Keys, "Get-Rich-Quick Game," p. 14121.

205 The swindlers' term: Barnes, " 'Reloading' and 'Dynamiting' Financial Dupes," p. 322.

205 One mark estimated: Frasca, *Stock Swindlers and Their Methods*, p. 6.

205 In 1905, the *Chicago Tribune* tabulated: *Chicago Tribune*, June 25, 1905.

205 In 1926, the New York: "Gyp's Dirty Dozen," p. 61.

205 *The New York Evening Post*: Quoted in "War on the 'White Collar Bandits,' " p. 11.

206 "Every dollar so lost": Escher, "Finance," p. 30.

206 "The swindler steals money": Simmons, "What the Swindler Steals Besides Money," p. 25.

206 Small, traditional family firms: Chandler, *Visible Hand*, pp. 1–2.

207 In 1921, a share in Radio: Kyvig, *Daily Life in the United States*, p. 214.

207 He hoarded, manipulated: Cowing, "Market Speculation in the Muckraking Era," pp. 411–12.

208 In 1919, the NYSE: Ott, "The 'Free and Open' 'People's Market,' " p. 16.

208 "It is his business": "Merchants of Credit and the Pirates of Promotion," pp. 539–40.

208 "The man with money": *Denver Times*, August 30, 1922.

209 In 1918, the Federal Trade Commission: Cowing, *Populists, Plungers, and Progressives*, pp. 115–17.

209 "Perhaps you think": Woolwine, "Would You Walk into a Trap Like This?" p. 19.

209 "This ignorance and credulity": "Baffling Kinds of Ignorance," p. 499.

209 "It seems quite hopeless": Keys, "Get-Rich-Quick Game," p. 14121.

209 A Harvard study: Cowing, *Populists, Plungers, and Progressives*, p. 165.

209 "the fundamentals of sound": "Poison-Ivy Securities," p. 20.

CHAPTER TWELVE
The Showdown

211 "Bunko 'Sucker' Disappears": *Rocky Mountain News*, September 14, 1922.

212 "in all probability": *Rocky Mountain News*, September 15, 1922.

212 "He carries two": *Denver Post*, September 15, 1922.

214 "Why did members": *Rocky Mountain News*, August 31, 1922.

214 "for their splendid work": *Denver Times*, August 25, 1922.

215 "does object to paying": *Denver Times,* August 31, 1922.
215 "The questions that arise": *Denver Post,* September 2, 1922.
215 "Where bunko men operate": *Denver Times,* September 2, 1922.
215 "I never saw this man": *Denver Post,* August 26, 1922.
215 Indeed Van Cise: *Denver Post,* January 10, 1923.
216 An intense and public: *Denver Times,* August 29, 1922.
216 So it came as almost: *Rocky Mountain News,* October 1 and 6, 1922.
216 "a certain 'I've waited'": *Denver Post,* August 29, 1922.
217 Now his deputies worked: *Denver Post,* September 8, 1922.
217 Two months after the raid: *Rocky Mountain News,* October 26, 1922.
217 "reorganized remnants": *Denver Post,* September 21, 1922.
217 "Confidence men have been": *Denver Post,* January 3, 1923.
218 "a joint account": *Denver Post,* January 4, 1923.
218 The following week: *Denver Post,* January 12, 1923.
218 A few days later: *Denver Post,* January 17, 1923.
218 The courtroom was bursting: *Rocky Mountain News,* February 6, 1923.
218 "He talks too much": Van Cise, *Fighting the Underworld,* p. 313.
218 "He was drunk last night": Ibid., p. 315.
218 The two special prosecutors: *Denver Post,* February 8 and 18, 1923.
219 "I come from a family": *Denver Post,* December 10, 1922.
219 When the jury was sworn: *Denver Post,* February 3, 1923.
219 Whenever the prosecution: *Denver Post,* February 8, 1923.
219 There were only two: Van Cise, *Fighting the Underworld,* p. 255.
219 In daily attendance: *Denver Post,* February 13, 1923.
219 "Not on your tintype": *Denver Post,* February 18, 1923.
220 "One is said to be": *Denver Post,* February 11, 1923.
220 "Every effort is being made": "J. Frank Norfleet Arrives in Denver for 'Bunko' Trial," unpaginated scrapbook page, Maiden Papers.
220 From almost the very first: *Rocky Mountain News,* February 6, 1923.
220 To back up their case: *Denver Post,* February 5, 1923.
221 Crump began his opening: *Denver Post,* February 7, 1923.
221 "a vampire squad of women": *Denver Post,* February 8, 1923.
221 "Cruel claws of intimidation": Ibid.
222 "Neither the law": *McCord v. People.*
222 Such an interpretation: *People v. Livingstone.*
222 Nineteenth-century market culture: Gilfoyle, *Pickpocket's Tale,* pp. 220–21.
222 Not until 1906: *People v. Tompkins,* 186 N.Y. 413 (1906).
222 One swindler: Crowley, "New Weapon Against Confidence Games," pp. 233–36.
223 When Judge Dunklee finally: *Denver Post,* February 16, 1923.
223 The spectators enjoyed: *Denver Post,* February 9 and 13, and March 21, 1923.
223 Several moving picture: *Denver Post,* March 9, 1923.
223 "Thrill followed thrill": *Denver Post,* February 21, 1923.
224 It wasn't until his second: *Denver Post,* February 22, 1923.
224 On the day that Van Cise's: *Denver Post,* March 2, 1923.
224 The trial entered its seventh: *Denver Post,* March 4, 1923.
225 "an interesting but highly": Van Cise, *Fighting the Underworld,* p. 351.
225 He interrogated her: Ibid., pp. 252–54.
226 The defense counsel argued: *Denver Post,* March 8 and 9, 1923.
226 The courtroom was: *Denver Post,* March 12, 1923.

226 steerers "bringem": *Denver Post*, March 10, 1923.

227 His turn came on Reamey's: *Denver Post*, March 12, 1923.

227 He told how: *Denver Post*, March 13, 1923.

227 At last, Reamey was revealed: Ibid.

227 "The phonograph is revolving": *Denver Post*, March 10, 1923.

228 As if admitting defeat: *Denver Post*, March 14, 1923.

228 Reamey's stories had been: *Denver Post*, March 20, 1923.

228 "I object, if the court please": *Denver Post*, March 21, 1923.

229 the longest criminal trial: *Denver Post*, March 24 and 29, 1923; and "Supreme Court to Get Million Words to Read When Hearing Appeal in Denver 'Bunk' Case," unpaginated scrapbook page, Maiden Papers.

229 Some watchers noticed: *Denver Post*, March 23, 1923.

229 Others looked outside: *Denver Post*, March 11, 1923.

229 Within the first two hours: *Denver Post*, March 25, 1923.

229 The next day: *Denver Post*, March 26, 1923.

230 A third day of deliberation: Ibid.

230 Then a fourth: *Denver Post*, March 27, 1923.

230 A fifth day: *Denver Post*, March 28, 1923.

230 At 4:45 on the afternoon: *Denver Post*, March 29, 1923.

231 "Perjured evidence": Ibid.

231 The very day after: *Dallas Morning News*, March 31, 1923.

231 As the entire city: *Denver Post*, March 30, 1923.

231 He also loudly indicted: *Denver Post*, March 31, 1923.

231 On June 1, 1923: *Denver Post*, June 1, 1923.

232 Attorney Hawkins immediately: *Denver Post*, October 11, 1923.

232 "It's all over": *Denver Post*, October 12, 1923.

232 On October 18, 1923: *Denver Post*, October 18, 1923.

232 "Say, what would a girl": *Rocky Mountain News*, April 21, 1923.

232 Blonger admitted: "Blonger Swears Duff Led Million-Dollar Bunko Ring That Operated in Denver," unpaginated scrapbook page, Maiden Papers.

232 "Toward Lou Blonger": *Rocky Mountain News*, April 21, 1923.

232 "motherly, gray-haired": *Denver Post*, June 12, 1923.

233 Blonger declined rapidly: "Blindness and Death Steal upon Lou Blonger in Cell as He Pins Life Hope on Appeal," unpaginated scrapbook page, Maiden Papers.

233 In the last two weeks: *Rocky Mountain News*, April 21, 1924.

233 His body would be transferred: *Denver Times*, April 22, 1924.

233 Mrs. Blonger would be: *Rocky Mountain News*, April 23, 1924.

233 Adolph Duff would also die: *Denver Post*, November 25, 1929.

234 "How are you, Spencer": *Dallas Morning News* and *Oakland Tribune*, October 2, 1923.

234 In March 1924: *Dallas Morning News*, March 9, 1924.

234 "destitute and dependent": Texas, "Full Pardon."

234 In fact, Spencer was: *Galveston Daily News*, January 15, 1927; and Ferguson, *Executive Branch of State Government*, p. 51.

CHAPTER THIRTEEN
The Mark Inside

235 "told at Least 3 lies": Norfleet to Van Cise, July 4, 1957, Van Cise Scrapbook, vol. 2.

235 Gregor portrayed Norfleet: Gregor, "Sucker Who Turned Tiger," p. 88.

235 His four-year absence: *Dallas Morning News*, December 10, 1989.

236 The bank was about: *Dallas Morning News,* November 5, 1924.

236 "English literature has been": *Lubbock Morning Avalanche,* April 6, 1924.

236 "our own indigenous detective": *Dallas Morning News,* August 17, 1924.

237 "at a liberal weekly stipend": *Dallas Morning News,* July 11, 1925.

237 The year after that: *Los Angeles Times,* June 10, 1926.

237 And the year after that: *Dallas Morning News,* June 28, 1927.

237 One of his partners: *Dallas Morning News,* March 2, 1986.

237 "For the benefit of doubters": Norfleet, *Norfleet* (1927), p. vii.

237 In 1929, Norfleet began: *San Antonio Light,* November 2, 1929.

237 And in between telling: *Galveston Daily News,* April 22, 1927.

239 In 1928, he declared: *San Antonio Light,* May 16, 1928.

239 "I only put notches": *San Antonio Light,* July 30, 1929.

239 In 1940, when he was: *Brownsville Herald,* January 25, 1940.

239 His name regularly cropped: See *San Antonio Light,* December 25, 1932, and January 5, 1933.

239 A swindler named J. R. Bing: *Nevada State Journal,* June 12, 1936; and *Fresno Bee Republican,* June 18, 1936.

239 As late as 1939: *Dallas Morning News,* March 3, 1939.

239 In 1958, when he was ninety-three: *Hale Center American,* January 10, 2003.

239 He boosted the price: *Dallas Morning News,* June 21, 1955, and March 2, 1986.

240 "gifted in intellect": Quoted in Halttunen, *Confidence Men and Painted Women,* p. 42.

240 "had a pleasant address": Quoted in ibid., p. 5.

240 "impelling personalities": Marden, *Masterful Personality,* p. 11. See also Spears, " 'All Things to All Men.' "

241 "they have what is virtually": Maxwell, "Take a Tip from the Con Man," p. 20.

241 "citizenship, duty, democracy": Susman, *Culture as History,* pp. 273–74.

241 The industrial age invented: Sandage, *Born Losers,* p. 63.

241 Contract theory: Macpherson, *Political Theory of Possessive Individualism.*

242 "to invent something": Quoted in Sandage, *Born Losers,* p. 13.

242 The word "failure": Ibid., pp. 2, 5.

242 "fascinating, stunning, attractive": Susman, *Culture as History,* p. 277.

242 Now the material rewards: Halttunen, *Confidence Men and Painted Women,* pp. 198–210.

242 This archetype was necessarily: Sandage, *Born Losers,* p. 88.

243 After turning state's evidence: "Letter from Texas Is Voice from Past," n.p., Van Cise Scrapbook, vol. 2.

243 "ask The writer": Norfleet to Van Cise, February 21, 1960, Van Cise Scrapbook, vol. 2.

243 "I am not too Frisky": Norfleet to Van Cise, July 4, 1957, Van Cise Scrapbook, vol. 2.

244 "I am still here": Norfleet to Van Cise, April 8, 1960, Van Cise Scrapbook, vol. 2.

244 "I had to do it": *Big Spring Herald,* April 1, 1960; and *Dallas Morning News,* February 23, 1960.

244 His grandniece: Sandi Clark, interview with author.

244 Even *The Washington Post: Washington Post,* October 17, 1967.

Bibliography

ARCHIVES

Arnett, D. N. (David Nathan). Papers, 1866–1939. Southwest Collection/Special Collections Library, Texas Tech University, Lubbock.
Maiden, Robert R. Papers. Western History Collection, Denver Public Library.
Van Cise, Philip. Scrapbook, 2 vols. Private Collection, Denver.
White, Roy D. Oral History, February 10, 1968. Western History Collection, Denver Public Library.

NEWSPAPERS

Aspen Weekly Times
Atlanta Constitution
Big Spring Herald
Boulder Daily Camera
Brownsville Herald
Chicago Daily Tribune
Colorado Springs Gazette
Daily Nonpareil
Dallas Morning News
Danville Bee
Davenport Democrat and Leader
Denver Post
Denver Republican
Denver Times
Emporia Gazette
Fort Worth Star-Telegram
Fresno Bee Republican
Galveston Daily News
Hale Center American
Hartford Courant
Jefferson City Post-Tribune
Los Angeles Express
Los Angeles Times
Lubbock Avalanche
Lubbock Morning Avalanche
Mexia Evening News
Modesto Evening News
National Police Gazette

Nevada State Journal
New York Atlas
New York Herald
New York Mercury
New York Times
New-York Tribune
Oakland Tribune
Ogden Standard-Examiner
Oxnard Daily Courier
Plainview Daily Herald
Plainview Evening Herald
Plainveiw Reporter News
Portland Morning Oregonian
Reno Evening Gazette
Rocky Mountain News
San Antonio Light
San Francisco Call
San Francisco Chronicle
San Jose Mercury News
Syracuse Herald
Trenton Sunday Advertiser
Washington Post
Waterloo Evening Courier and Reporter
Wichita Daily Times

GOVERNMENT DOCUMENTS

Board of Trade of the City of Chicago v. Christie Grain and Stock Company, 198 U.S. 247, 249 (1905).

McCord v. People, 46 N.Y. 470 (1871).

People v. Livingstone, 47 App. Div. 283 (1900).

People v. Tompkins, 186 N.Y. 413 (1906).

People v. Walter Lips (Crim. No. 826), Cal. Ct. App., 2nd Dist., Div. 2, 59 Cal. App. 381; 211 P. 22; 1922 Cal. App. Lexis 218. Decided October 20, 1922.

People v. W. J. Anderson (Crim. No. 907), Cal. Ct. App., 2nd Dist., Div. 2, 62 Cal. App. 22; 216 P. 401; 1923 Cal. App. Lexis 475. Decided May 16, 1923.

State of Texas v. John Gerber, Crim. Dist. Ct. Tarrant County, Tex. Defendant's Bill of Exception No. 19. May 10, 1920.

Texas. Proclamation by the Governor of the State of Texas, No. 20496. "Full Pardon," January 13, 1927.

U.S. Census Bureau 1850.

U.S. Census Bureau 1860.

U.S. Census Bureau 1900.

U.S. Census Bureau 1910.

U.S. Congress. House. Committee on Claims. *Hearing on the Relief of J. Frank Norfleet.* 68th Cong., 1st sess., 1924.

U.S. Congress. House. Committee on Post Offices and Post Roads. *Postal Telegraphs: Statements of Norvin Green, President Western Union.* 51st Cong., 1890.

U.S. Congress. House. *Contested Election Case of Robert W. Bonynge v. John F. Shafroth from the First Congressional District of Colorado.* 58th Cong., 1903.

BOOKS AND ARTICLES

Abbott, Karen. *Sin in the Second City: Madams, Ministers, Playboys, and the Battle for America's Soul.* New York: Random House, 2008.

American Life Histories: Manuscripts from the Federal Writers' Project, 1936–1940. "Bones Hooks." http://memory.loc.gov/cgi-bin/query/D?wpa:1:./temp/~ammem_VnfT, accessed June 8, 2011.

———. "Mrs. Cicero Russell." http://memory.loc.gov/cgi-bin/query/D?wpa:1:./temp/ ~ammem_N3q9, accessed June 8, 2011.

Asbury, Herbert. *Gem of the Prairie: An Informal History of the Chicago Underworld.* New York: Knopf, 1940.

"Baffling Kinds of Ignorance." *World's Work,* March 1912.

Baker, Jennifer J. *Securing the Commonwealth: Debt, Speculation, and Writing in the Making of Early America.* Baltimore: Johns Hopkins University Press, 2007.

Baritz, Loren. *The Good Life: The Meaning of Success for the American Middle Class.* New York: Knopf, 1988.

Barnes, John K. "An Arabian Night's Tale of High Finance." *World's Work,* February 1923.

———. "Fighting the Fakers in Finance." *World's Work,* October 1925.

———. " 'Reloading' and 'Dynamiting' Financial Dupes." *World's Work,* January 1923.

Barnum, P. T. *The Humbugs of the World.* New York: G. W. Carleton, 1865.

———. *Life of P. T. Barnum, Written by Himself.* New York: Redfield, 1855.

Barth, Gunther. *Instant Cities: Urbanization and the Rise of San Francisco and Denver.* New York: Oxford University Press, 1975.

Bell, J. Bowyer, and Barton Whaley. *Cheating and Deception.* New Brunswick, N.J.: Transaction, 1991.

Bellow, Saul. "A Talk with the Yellow Kid." *Reporter,* September 6, 1956.

Bentley, Max. "Norfleet—Man-Hunter." *McClure's Magazine,* June 1924.

Bergmann, Johannes Dietrich. "The Original Confidence Man." *American Quarterly* 21, no. 3 (Autumn 1969), pp. 560–77.

Blonger Bros. "The True History of the Famous Blonger Bros." http://www.blongerbros .com/history/, accessed June 10, 2011.

Bretz, James. *The Mansions of Denver: The Vintage Years, 1870–1938.* Boulder, Colo.: Pruett, 2004.

Brown, Jesse M. *A Judge Looks at Life.* Fort Worth, Tex.: Branch-Smith, 1976.

Bulger, Bozeman. "The Psychology of the Sucker." *Saturday Evening Post,* April 15, 1922.

Bullock, Steven C. "A Mumper Among the Gentle: Tom Bell, Colonial Confidence Man." *William and Mary Quarterly* 55, no. 2 (April 1998), pp. 231–58.

Burroughs, Stephen. *Memoirs of Stephen Burroughs,* with a preface by Robert Frost. Boston: Northeastern University Press, 1988.

Calder, Lendol. *Financing the American Dream: A Cultural History of Consumer Credit.* Princeton, N.J.: Princeton University Press, 2001.

Chafetz, Henry. *Play the Devil: A History of Gambling in the United States from 1492 to 1955.* New York: C. N. Potter, 1960.

Chandler, Alfred Dupont. *The Visible Hand: The Managerial Revolution in American Business.* Cambridge, Mass.: Harvard University Press, 1977.

Chandler, Alfred Dupont, and James W. Cortada, eds. *A Nation Transformed by Information: How Information Shaped the United States from Colonial Times to the Present.* New York: Oxford University Press, 2000.

Chaplin, Charlie. "Charlie Chaplin Learns to Sell Liberty Bonds, 1918." In *Eyewitness to Wall Street,* edited by David Cobert, pp. 109–11. New York: Broadway Books, 2001.

Chernow, Ron. *Alexander Hamilton.* New York: Penguin, 2004.

Christie, C. C. "Bucket-Shop vs. Board of Trade." *Everybody's Magazine,* November 1906.

Clark, Sandi. Interview with author. April 13, 2008.

Cohen, Lizabeth. *Making a New Deal: Industrial Workers in Chicago, 1919–1939.* New York: Cambridge University Press, 1990.

Collins, Frederick L. *The FBI in Peace and War.* New York: G. P. Putnam's Sons, 1943.

Conwell, Chic. *The Professional Thief, by a Professional Thief.* Annotated by Edwin H. Sutherland. Chicago: University of Chicago Press, 1937.

Cook, James W. *Arts of Deception: Playing with Fraud in the Age of Barnum.* Cambridge, Mass.: Harvard University Press, 2001.

———, ed. *The Colossal P. T. Barnum Reader: Nothing Else Like It in the Universe.* Urbana: University of Illinois Press, 2005.

Cowing, Cedric B. "Market Speculation in the Muckraking Era: The Popular Reaction." *Business History Review* 31, no. 4 (Winter 1957), pp. 403–13.

———. *Populists, Plungers, and Progressives: A Social History of Stock and Commodity Speculation, 1890–1936.* Princeton, N.J.: Princeton University Press, 1965.

Cox, Mary L. *History of Hale County, Texas.* Plainview, Tex., 1937.

Crowley, William F. "A New Weapon Against Confidence Games." *Journal of Criminal Law, Criminology, and Police Science* 50, no. 3 (1959), pp. 233–36.

Dodge, Grenville Mellen. *How We Built the Union Pacific Railway and Other Railway Papers and Addresses.* N.p., 1909.

Dorset, Phyllis. *The New Eldorado: The Story of Colorado's Gold and Silver Rushes.* New York: Macmillan, 1970.

Drake, Rod. Interview with author. Denver, April 14, 2010.

Escher, Franklin. "Finance: The Government and the Get-Rich-Quick Industry," *Harper's Weekly,* December 10, 1919.

Fabian, Ann. *Card Sharps, Dream Books, and Bucket Shops: Gambling in 19th-Century America.* Ithaca, N.Y.: Cornell University Press, 1990.

Ferguson, Margaret Robertson, ed. *The Executive Branch of State Government: People, Process, and Politics.* Santa Barbara, Calif.: ABC-CLIO, 2006.

Findlay, John M. *People of Chance: Gambling in American Society from Jamestown to Las Vegas.* New York: Oxford University Press, 1986.

Franklin, Benjamin. *The Autobiography of Benjamin Franklin.* Edited by Kenneth Silverman. New York: Penguin, 1986.

———. *A Modest Enquiry into the Nature and Necessity of a Paper Currency.* School of Cooperative Individualism. http://www.cooperativeindividualism.org/franklin_money.html, accessed March 1, 2009.

Frasca, Charles B. *Stock Swindlers and Their Methods.* New York: C. B. Frasca, 1931.

Fraser, Steve. *Every Man a Speculator: A History of Wall Street in American Life.* New York: Harper Perennial, 2005.

Geisst, Charles. *Wheels of Fortune: The History of Speculation from Scandal to Respectability.* Hoboken, N.J.: John Wiley and Sons, 2002.

Gilfoyle, Timothy. *A Pickpocket's Tale: The Underworld of Nineteenth-Century New York.* New York: Norton, 2007.

Gober, Jim. *Cowboy Justice: Tale of a Texas Lawman.* Edited by James R. Gober and B. Byron Price. Lubbock: Texas Tech University Press, 1997.

Goffman, Erving. *Frame Analysis: An Essay on the Organization of Experience.* Cambridge, Mass.: Harvard University Press, 1974.

———. "On Cooling the Mark Out: Some Aspects of Adaptation to Failure." In *The Goffman Reader,* edited by Charles Lemert and Ann Branaman, pp. 3–20. Malden, Mass.: Blackwell, 1997.

Goodstein, Phil. *In the Shadow of the Klan: When the KKK Ruled Denver, 1920–1926.* Denver: New Social Publications, 2006.

———. *Robert Speer's Denver, 1904–1920: The Mile High City in the Progressive Era.* Denver: New Social Publications, 2004.

———. *The Seamy Side of Denver: Tall Tales of the Mile High City.* Denver: New Social Publications, 1993.

Gordon, John Steele. *An Empire of Wealth: The Epic History of American Economic Power.* New York: Harper Perennial, 2004.

———. "The Great Crash (of 1792)." *American Heritage,* May/June 1999.

Gregor, John. "The Sucker Who Turned Tiger." *True,* July 1957.

Gross, Robert A. "The Confidence Man and the Preacher: The Cultural Politics of Shays's Rebellion." In *In Debt to Shays: The Bicentennial of an Agrarian Rebellion,* edited by Robert A. Gross, pp. 297–320. Charlottesville: University Press of Virginia, 1993.

Guenther, Louis. "In the Partial Payment Plan." *World's Work,* November 1918.

———. "Market Manipulation and Its Part in the Promotion Game." *World's Work,* February 1919.

———. "Methods of the Industrial Promoters." *World's Work,* January 1919.

———. "The Oil Flotation Game." *World's Work,* December 1918.

———. "Pirates of Promotion . . . George Graham Rice." *World's Work,* November 1918.

——— "Pirates of Promotion, Who Are After Your Liberty Bonds with Their Get-Rich Quick Schemes." *World's Work,* October 1918.

———. "The Wreckage." *World's Work,* March 1919.

"The Gyp's Dirty Dozen." *Literary Digest,* January 30, 1926.

Halttunen, Karen. *Confidence Men and Painted Women: A Study of Middle-Class Culture in America, 1830–1870.* New Haven, Conn.: Yale University Press, 1982.

Hamilton, Alexander. *The Papers of Alexander Hamilton.* Vol. II. New York: Columbia University Press, 1967.

Hamner, Laura V. *Short Grass and Longhorns.* Norman: University of Oklahoma Press, 1943.

Handbook of Texas Online. "Ellwood, Isaac L." http://www.tshaonline.org/handbook/online/articles/fel17, accessed June 8, 2011.

———. "Norfleet, James Franklin." http://www.tshaonline.org/handbook/online/articles/fno16, accessed June 8, 2011.

Harris, Neil. *Humbug: The Art of P. T. Barnum.* Chicago: University of Chicago Press, 1973.

Hauck, Richard Boyd. *A Cheerful Nihilism: Confidence and "the Absurd" in American Humorous Fiction.* Bloomington: Indiana University Press, 1971.

Hawkins, J. J. *Mabray and the Mikes.* Little Rock, Ark.: Democrat Printing and Lithographing, n.d.

Higginson, Thomas Wentworth. "A New England Vagabond." *Harper's New Monthly Magazine,* March 1888.

Hochfelder, David. " 'Where the Common People Could Speculate': The Ticker, Bucket Shops, and the Origins of Popular Participation in Financial Markets, 1880–1920." *Journal of American History* 93, no. 2 (2006), pp. 335–58.

Hoover, J. Edgar. "The Man with the Magic Wallet." With Courtney Ryley Cooper. *American Magazine,* March 1937.

Hornaday, William T. *The Extermination of the American Bison, with a Sketch of Its Discovery and Life History.* Washington, D.C.: Government Printing Office, 1889.

Hyde, Lewis. *The Gift: Creativity and the Artist in the Modern World.* New York: Vintage, 2007.

Jamar, Dorothy Watters. "From Virginia to Texas." *Hale County History* 8, no. 4 (1978), pp. 5–10.

———. "The Norfleet Pioneers of the Plains." *Hale County History* 8, no. 4 (1978), pp. 11–36.

———. "The Norfleet Women." *Hale County History* 8, no. 4 (1978), pp. 47–62.

James, Henry. *Autobiography.* Edited by Frederick W. Dupee. New York: Criterion Books, 1956.

Keating, Edward. *The Gentleman from Colorado: A Memoir.* Denver: Sage Books, 1964.

Keys, C. M. "The Get-Rich-Quick Game." *World's Work,* March 1911.

King, Joseph E. *A Mine to Make a Mine: Financing the Colorado Mining Industry, 1859–1902.* College Station: Texas A&M University Press, 1977.

Knapp, Anne Curtis. "Making an Orderly Society: Criminal Justice in Denver, Colorado, 1858–1900." Ph.D. diss., University of California, San Diego, 1983.

Kyvig, David E. *Daily Life in the United States, 1920–1940: How Americans Lived Through the "Roaring Twenties" and the Great Depression.* Chicago: Ivan R. Dee, 2004.

Lears, Jackson. "The Birth of Irony." *New Republic,* December 20, 2001.

———. *Something for Nothing: Luck in America.* New York: Viking, 2003.

Lefèvre, Edwin. "A Bucket Shop Education." In *Eyewitness to Wall Street,* edited by David Cobert, pp. 75–79. New York: Broadway Books, 2001.

Leff, Arthur Allen. *Swindling and Selling.* New York: Free Press, 1976.

Lindberg, Gary. *The Confidence Man in American Literature.* New York: Oxford University Press, 1982.

Lindberg, Richard C. *The Gambler King of Clark Street: Michael C. McDonald and the Rise of Chicago's Democratic Machine.* Carbondale: Southern Illinois University Press, 2009.

Lindsey, Benjamin. *The Beast.* New York: Doubleday, Page, 1910.

Lott, Dale F. *American Bison: A Natural History.* Berkeley: University of California Press, 2002.

Macpherson, C. B. *The Political Theory of Possessive Individualism: Hobbes to Locke.* Oxford: Clarendon Press, 1962.

Makris, John N. *The Silent Investigators: The Great Untold Story of the United States Postal Inspection Service.* New York: E. P. Dutton, 1959.

Mann, Bruce H. *Republic of Debtors: Bankruptcy in the Age of American Independence.* Cambridge, Mass.: Harvard University Press, 2002.

Marden, Orison Swett. *Masterful Personality.* New York: Thomas Y. Crowell, 1921.

Matson, Cathy. "Public Vices, Private Benefit: William Duer and His Circle, 1776–1792." In *New York and the Rise of American Capitalism: Economic Development and the Social and Political History of an American State, 1780–1870,* edited by William Pencak and Conrad Edick Wright, pp. 72–123. New York: New-York Historical Society, 1989.

Maurer, David W. *The Big Con: The Story of the Confidence Man.* New York: Anchor Books, 1999.

Maxwell, William. "Take a Tip from the Con Man." *Collier's,* January 10, 1925.

Measuring Worth. "Purchasing Power of Money in the United States from 1774 to Present." http://www.measuringworth.com/ppowerus/, accessed June 8, 2011.

Melville, Herman. *The Confidence-Man: His Masquerade.* Edited by Stephen Matterson. New York: Penguin Books, 1990.

———. "View of the Barnum Property." In *The Piazza Tales, and Other Prose Pieces, 1839–1860,* edited by Harrison Hayford, Alma A. MacDougall, Hershel Parker, George Thomas Tanselle, and Merton M. Sealts, pp. 447–48. Chicago: Northwestern University Press, 1987.

Mercantile Agency Reference Book (and Key). New York: R. G. Dun, 1897.

"Merchants of Credit and the Pirates of Promotion." *World's Work,* September 1918.

Mihm, Stephen. *A Nation of Counterfeiters: Capitalists, Con Men, and the Making of the United States.* Cambridge, Mass.: Harvard University Press, 2007.

Nash, Jay Robert. *The Great Pictorial History of World Crime.* Vol. 1. Wilmette, Ill.: History, 2004.

———. *Hustlers and Con Men: An Anecdotal History of the Confidence Man and His Games.* New York: M. Evans, 1976.

Noel, Thomas J. *The City and the Saloon: Denver, 1858–1916.* Lincoln: University of Nebraska Press, 1982.

Norfleet, J. Frank. *Norfleet: The Actual Experiences of a Texas Rancher's 30,000-Mile Transcontinental Chase After Five Confidence Men.* Fort Worth, Tex.: White, 1924.

———, as told to Gordon Hines. *Norfleet: The Amazing Experiences of an Intrepid Texas Rancher with an International Swindling Ring.* Sugar Land, Tex.: Imperial Press, 1927.

Olien, Roger M., and Diana Davids Olien. *Easy Money: Oil Promoters and Investors in the Jazz Age.* Chapel Hill: University of North Carolina Press, 1990.

Ott, Julia. "The 'Free and Open' 'People's Market': Public Relations at the New York Stock Exchange, 1913–1929." *Business and Economic History Online* 2 (2004), pp. 1–43.

Parkhill, Forbes. *The Wildest of the West.* New York: Holt, 1951.

"The Passing of the Wireless Wire-Tappers." *Outlook,* February 16, 1912.

Patterson, Schuyler. " 'Petering' and 'Electing' Financial Babes." *World's Work,* March 1923.

"Poison-Ivy Securities." *Saturday Evening Post,* July 26, 1930.

Randall, Henry S. *The Life of Thomas Jefferson.* Vol. 11. Philadelphia: J. B. Lippincott, 1871.

Rathjen, Frederick W. *The Texas Panhandle Frontier.* Austin: University of Texas Press, 1973.

Review of *The Professional Thief,* by Chic Conwell. *Journal of Criminal Law and Criminology* 28, no. 4 (1937), p. 625.

Reynolds, Michael S. "Prototype for Melville's Confidence-Man." *PMLA* 86, no. 5 (1971), pp. 1009–13.

Rice, George Graham. *My Adventures with Your Money.* Boston: Gorham Press, 1913.

Rockoff, Hugh. "Until It's Over, Over There. The U.S. Economy in World War I." National Bureau of Economic Research Working Paper No. 10580 (June 2004). http://www.nber.org/papers/w10580.

Roenfield, Ryan. "Benjamin Marks and the Hog Ranch." Paper presented at the Pottawattamie County Historical Society, Council Bluffs, Iowa, September 2000.

Ruby, Robert H., and John A. Brown. *The Spokane Indians: Children of the Sun.* Norman: University of Oklahoma Press, 1970.

Sandage, Scott. *Born Losers: A History of Failure in America.* Cambridge, Mass.: Harvard University Press, 2005.

Secrest, Clark. *Hell's Belles: Prostitution, Vice, and Crime in Early Denver.* Boulder: University Press of Colorado, 2001.

Sharpe, May Churchill. *Chicago May: Her Story.* London: Sampson Low, Marston, 1930.

Simmons, E. H. H. "What the Swindler Steals Besides Money." *Collier's,* May 16, 1925.

Sinise, Jerry. *Pink Higgins, the Reluctant Gunfighter, and Other Tales of the Panhandle.* Quanah, Texas: Nortex Press, 1973.

Slotkin, Richard. *Gunfighter Nation: The Myth of the Frontier in Twentieth-Century America.* New York: Atheneum, 1992.

Smetana, Frank W. *A History of Lake Manawa, 1880–1981.* Council Bluffs, Iowa: Lake Manawa Centennial Committee, 1981.

Smith, Edward H. *Confessions of a Confidence Man: A Handbook for Suckers.* New York: Scientific American, 1923.

Smith, Jeff. *Alias Soapy Smith: The Life and Death of a Scoundrel.* Juneau, Alaska: Klondike Research, 2009.

Smith, Joseph Emerson. "Personal Recollections of Early Denver." *Colorado Magazine,* January 1943, pp. 5–16.

———. "Personal Recollections of Early Denver." *Colorado Magazine,* March 1943, pp. 56–71.

Smith, Raymond A., Jr. "John C. Mabray: A Con Artist in the Corn Belt." *Palimpsest* 64, no. 4 (1983), pp. 123–39.

Sobel, Robert. *Panic on Wall Street: A History of America's Financial Disasters.* Washington, D.C.: Beard Books, 1999.

Spears, Timothy B. " 'All Things to All Men': The Commercial Traveler and the Rise of Modern Salesmanship." *American Quarterly* 45, no. 4 (1993), pp. 524–57.

Staiti, Paul. "Illusionism, Trompe l'Oeil, and the Perils of Viewership." In *William M. Harnett,* edited by Doreen Bolger, Marc Simpson, and John Wilmerding, pp. 30–47. New York: Metropolitan Museum of Art, 1992.

Susman, Warren I. *Culture as History: The Transformation of American Society in the Twentieth Century.* New York: Pantheon, 1984.

Swann, Edward. "The Wiles of the Confidence Man," *Munsey's Magazine,* pp. 702–9.

Teague, Merrill A. "Bucket-Shop Sharks." *Everybody's Magazine,* July 1906.

Tufts, Henry. *The Autobiography of a Criminal.* Edited by Edmund Pearson. New York: Duffield, 1930.

Updike, John. "Many Bens." *New Yorker,* February 22, 1988.

Van Cise, Cindy. Interview with author. Denver, April 14, 2010.

Van Cise, Philip S. *Fighting the Underworld.* Cambridge, Mass.: Riverside Press, 1936.

"War on the 'White Collar Bandits.' " *Literary Digest,* March 6, 1926.

Weil, J. R. "Yellow Kid," and W. T. Brannon. *Con Man: A Master Swindler's Own Story.* New York: Broadway Books, 2004.

Weschler, Lawrence. *Mr. Wilson's Cabinet of Wonder: Pronged Ants, Horned Humans, Mice on Toast, and Other Marvels of Jurassic Technology.* New York: Vintage, 1996.

Whitacre, Christine. *The Denver Club, 1880–1995.* Denver: Historic Denver, 1998.

Williams, Daniel E. "In Defense of Self: Author and Authority in the *Memoirs of Stephen Burroughs.*" *Early American Literature* 25, no. 2 (1990), pp. 96–122.

Wofford, Vera Dean. *Hale County Facts and Folklore.* Lubbock, Tex.: Pica, 1978.

Woolwine, Thomas Lee. "Would You Walk into a Trap Like This?" *American Magazine,* March 1921.

"The Yellow Kid Returns." *Newsweek,* December 24, 1956.

Zelizer, Viviana. *Morals and Markets: The Development of Life Insurance in the United States.* New York: Columbia University Press, 1979.

Zuckerman, Michael. "The Selling of the Self." In *Benjamin Franklin, Jonathan Edwards, and the Representation of American Culture,* edited by Barbara B. Oberg and Harry S. Stout, pp. 152–67. New York: Oxford University Press, 1993.

Index

Page numbers in *italics* refer to illustrations.

PHOTO CREDITS

A NOTE ABOUT THE AUTHOR

Amy Reading holds a Ph.D. in American Studies from Yale University. She lives in upstate New York with her husband and two children.

A NOTE ON THE TYPE

This book was set in a modern adaptation of a type designed by the first William Caslon (1692–1766). The Caslon face, an artistic, easily read type, has enjoyed over two centuries of popularity in the United States. It is of interest to note that the first copies of the Declaration of Independence and the first paper currency distributed to the citizens of the newborn nation were printed in this typeface.

Composed by North Market Street Graphics
Lancaster, Pennsylvania

Printed and bound by Berryville Graphics
Berryville, Virginia

Designed by Soonyoung Kwon